# Clinical Social Work Practice with the Elderly

Primary, Secondary, and Tertiary Intervention

**The Dorsey Series in Social Welfare**

# Clinical Social Work Practice with the Elderly

Primary, Secondary, and
Tertiary Intervention

**Marion L. Beaver, D.S.W.**
**Don Miller, Ph.D.**
Both of the School of Social Work
University of Pittsburgh

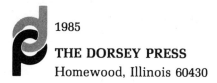

1985

**THE DORSEY PRESS**
Homewood, Illinois 60430

ISBN 0-256-03052-9

Library of Congress Catalog Card No. 84–72287

*Printed in the United States of America*

1 2 3 4 5 6 7 8 9 0 ML 2 1 0 9 8 7 6 5

# Preface

The most important goal for social workers and other helping professionals is to improve the quality of life for older people through effective interventions in their behalf. For many reasons, this task is more difficult said than done. Aging is a complex and multifaceted phenomena, as it inevitably brings with it decline and changes that have negative consequences for the elderly. In the face of an imposing array of age-linked changes and the consequent vulnerability of the elderly to hazards that would be trivial for a younger person, preventive measures must be stressed.

How do we keep older people functioning at optimal levels for as long as possible? How do we instruct the aging and the aged on how to stay well? What kinds of educational measures requiring individual action in matters of health and social welfare are useful for working with the elderly? What preventive interventions are useful to forestall the development of less desirable states or to modify the effects of a problem, so the elderly can regain as much of their usual or customary functioning as possible? Preventive social work, with its emphasis on the promotion of positive outcomes, attempts to strengthen or build strengths into people through interventions directly with them or on their behalf.

This textbook is about clinical social work practice with the elderly—those who are well, those who have acute problems, and those who are functionally impaired. Clinical social work practice with the elderly involves knowledge and understanding of older peoples' behavior, as well as skill development in preventive intervention at the primary, secondary, and tertiary levels of prevention. Clear knowledge and understanding of clinical social work roles at the three levels of intervention is also desirable.

The public health approach to prevention is the basic frame of reference used in this text. This framework is supplemented with interventive activities that are useful in working with the elderly at the primary, secondary, and/ or tertiary levels of intervention. Thus the preventive focus is viewed as significant in bringing about desirable outcomes.

The aging and the aged are, in a sense, populations "at-risk" and although many are currently functioning at high levels, there is no guarantee that they will continue to do so. Therefore, preventive interventions at the primary, secondary, and tertiary levels are essential.

It has become apparent that not only has the number of older people in the total population increased, but the numbers of older people in need of agency services has also expanded. Thus social caseworkers now include more older people among their clientele than in earlier years. Many practitioners currently providing services to the elderly have never had any formal training in gerontology and have had to rely on their insights, practice wisdom, and day-to-day experience in providing services to this population.

The fact that the elderly are an extremely heterogeneous group, and that growing old is the result of a number of variables means that helping professionals engaged in clinical social work practice with older people must be informed with respect to both theory and practice. Social work practice can be strengthened by knowledge of primary preventive strategies, as well as by an awareness of a variety of practitioner roles available to the clinical social worker.

The authors have tried to arm the reader with a wide range of knowledge about aging, especially that related to loss and change, social-environmental change, supportive networks in the client's environment that may be instrumental in effectuating changes in a client's functioning, and strategies useful for working with a variety of older people at the three levels of preventive intervention.

## Organization

This book contains eight chapters. Each chapter begins with an introduction and ends with a summary. Chapter 1 describes the nature and scope of the field of aging. Three major components including the biophysiological, the psychological, and the social are examined in relation to the several changes and losses associated with each. Eriksonian developmental theory is discussed to enable the reader to grasp more easily the uniqueness of each stage of life—especially the aging stage. The chapter closes with a general discussion of the variety of roles and methods of intervention available to social workers for intervening with the elderly.

Chapter 2 focuses on the three major levels of intervention—primary, secondary, and tertiary—and uses the public health approach to preventive intervention as its conceptual model. A distinction is made among the various levels of prevention, particularly with respect to each of their specified purpose(s). Case examples are included throughout the chapter to illustrate preventive strategies at each of the three levels of intervention. Finally, specific social worker roles and activities germane to primary, secondary, and tertiary intervention are identified and discussed.

Chapter 3 provides a definition of eclectic clinical social work practice and identifies relevant treatment procedures from five approaches: psychoso-cial systems, client-centered, crisis intervention, behavioral, and cognitive.

The preventive measures discussed in Chapter 4 focus primarily on inter-personal practice with the well-elderly. Preventive measures for health pro-motion that aim at furthering health and well-being through such general measures as education, nutrition, and the provision of social services are emphasized. Such measures are singled out for their value in fostering the well-being of successful agers. A number of definitions of successful aging are given.

Chapter 5 defines and discusses the secondary level of clinical social work practice with elderly people who experience acute problems in func-tioning. Attention is given to problems of stress associated with relocation, social isolation, sexual functioning, marriage-family relationships, widow-hood, and retirement. Also discussed are the mental health problems of aging neurosis, abnormal grief reaction, depression, and alcoholism.

Chapter 6 discusses clinical social work practice with the community-based, functionally impaired elderly and their informal caretakers. The focus of this chapter is on interventions with those elderly who have impaired functioning associated with chronic mental illness, organic brain disorders, and chronic physical illness. The clinical social work function of service case management is defined and illustrated. This function is important be-cause it encompasses a variety of roles.

Chapter 7 addresses clinical practice with the institutionalized elderly—specifically, those older people who are in mental hospitals and in nursing homes. Individual and group treatment procedures are discussed as they relate to promoting the best possible level of physical, psychological, and social functioning for the elderly patient.

Chapter 8 identifies and discusses a number of issues and barriers that interfere with clinical practice with older people at the primary, secondary, and tertiary levels of intervention. Barriers associated with knowledge, gov-ernment policy, agency procedures, and clinical practitioners are discussed and their implications for practice are considered.

## For Whom this Book Is Intended

This textbook is intended for those who are engaged in formal educational programs designed to prepare professional clinical practitioners for the field of aging, as well as for those who are currently working directly with or in behalf of the elderly. The book should also be useful for agency personnel such as those serving in administrative, planning, and supervisory capacities who wish to upgrade their knowledge and skills about preventive interven-tion with the elderly. The authors are of the opinion that those helping professionals in such disciplines as nursing, medicine, and psychiatry who are providing services to the elderly should also find this text useful.

We believe the reader will find this an informative and practical textbook.

The writing style is clear and the information easy to grasp. The reader is challenged throughout the text by the issues that are raised and the preventive strategies that are shared. Implications for practice are provided where they are relevant and appropriate.

The idea for this text originated with Marion L. Beaver. Dr. Beaver felt the need to develop a textbook that was more clinically oriented and specialized in its approach to the elderly than the one she had completed. At that point Dr. Miller was asked to join in the enterprise, primarily for his clinical experience in social work practice. Thus the substantive content and organization of the text were jointly arrived at by both authors. More specifically, Dr. Beaver wrote Chapters 1, 2, and 4, and Dr. Miller wrote Chapters 3, 5, 6, and 7. Chapter 8 represents the thinking and writing of both authors.

No textbook would be complete without the invaluable assistance and painstaking efforts of the supportive staff who generously gave of their time and expertise. We wish to thank Jean Quam of the School of Social Work at the University of Minnesota, Sheldon Gelman of Pennsylvania State University, and Lucinda Lee Roff of the University of Alabama, all of whom carefully read, reviewed, and commented on the manuscript. Their useful comments helped to modify and clarify the materials.

We wish to thank Virginia Rhodes and Mary Pat Campbell for the efficient manner in which they approached their work, including the many hours they spent typing, editing, and providing useful comments on the materials.

We also wish to thank our families for their support, patience, and understanding throughout this project.

Marion L. Beaver
Don Miller

# Contents

# Clinical Social Work Practice with the Elderly

Primary, Secondary, and Tertiary Intervention

# Chapter 1

CHAPTER OUTLINE

# Chapter 1

# The experience of aging

## INTRODUCTION

The need for more information on the aging experience and on coping with life's changes and losses has stimulated a great deal of scientific research in the last several years. In social work as in other fields, there is an increasing demand for the kind of content that will address the application of social work practice theory to work with older persons.

In this chapter the authors describe the nature and scope of the field of aging. The major components of the aging process—the biophysiological, the psychological, and the social—are examined in light of the changes and losses associated with each.

Since aging is inevitably accompanied by numerous stresses and losses, loss is discussed in terms of the central role it plays in the aging phase of life. In addition, the diverse characteristics and dimensions of loss in old age are considered in terms of their consequences for the biophysiological and psychosocial functioning of older individuals.

Erik H. Erikson's eight stages of life are discussed briefly to provide a framework for viewing and understanding personality development and to enable the reader to more easily grasp the uniqueness of each stage of life. Each of Erikson's stages involves an age-appropriate conflict that—if resolved—leads to growth.

Chapter 1 identifies a variety of issues and themes commonly associated with the advancing years. Rather than presenting a comprehensive discussion of this material, the authors have selected those themes and issues that frequently pose problems, concerns, or challenges for those older people with whom social workers work. Insights gleaned from these materials should help readers to increase their awareness and understanding of older life, and to utilize more preventive strategies when dealing with older people.

## THE STUDY OF AGING

Gerontology is the scientific study of the aging process and of the problems of older people (see *Webster's,* 1970). It is especially concerned with differences in aging; that is, how some people age successfully, how others experience increasing problems and difficulties along the way, how one person continues to learn and grow, while another gets stuck and is seemingly halted in growth (see Zarit, 1977). Gerontology deals with all of these differences: It is the study of the "whole person" and the aging process as reflected in all aspects of life functioning (see Zarit, 1977).

The field of gerontology has three major components: the biophysiological, the psychological, and the social. The biophysiological component consists of two parts: the biological and the physiological. The biological part is concerned with changes in physical appearance and declines in physical ability, the progressive loss of vigor and loss of ability to resist disease that every individual must eventually face. Biologists refer to this process as senescence (normal biological aging). Senescence is the period of late life when people become more susceptible to disease and death and less able to withstand stress (see Rakowski & Hickey, 1976). The causes of senescence are still unknown. Although senescence occurs gradually, the results of this process are known to have a deleterious effect on the individual (see Crandall, 1980).

The physiological part is concerned with the impact of aging on the organs and organ systems, tissues, cells, subcellular particles, and molecules. Such physiological aging is apparent after individuals reach the age of 30 (see Beaver, 1983).

The psychology of aging is a wide area that encompasses the sensory processes (such as vision and hearing), perception, psychomotor performance, mental functioning (such as memory, learning, and intelligence), drives, motives, and emotions (see Atchley, 1977). As the individual grows psychologically older, a number of age-related changes are known to take place.

The social component of gerontology focuses on what happens to people in our society as they grow old. Here social gerontologists explain how society treats older people and how older people adjust to their own aging. Old age is thus a multiply determined experience dependent upon an intricate balance of physical, emotional, and social forces.

### The Nature of Aging

Aging is a heterogeneous and highly individual process; that is, each person ages at different rates and in different ways. The aging process will vary for each individual depending on a number of factors including health, income, family circumstances, and personality; in short, on all the circumstances that shape each person's life (see Saul, 1974).

The very nature of the aging process makes it difficult to define or measure when a person is old. Old age does not begin on some predetermined birthday. Actually, each of us constantly and continuously ages from the moment of birth. Changes from one day to the next may be ever so slight; nonetheless, physical, social, and psychological changes accumulate with the passage of time. Often only the outward manifestations of these changes are postponed until old age.

The aging process is complicated and involves each system of the body including the central nervous system, the cardiovascular system, and the sensory system. There are no specific indicators that point to when this process begins. According to Brody "they vary among each individual's organs, parts, and body systems and from one individual to another" (1977, p. 55).

By the time most individuals reach the age of 65, they have experienced numerous stresses, some of which have taken a considerable toll on their lives. Life stresses are cumulative, as one stress builds upon another. In this connection Lowenthal and her colleagues (1967) contend that the cumulative effects of loss experienced as stress may lead to breakdown.

Generally, when these stresses occur they have a tremendous impact upon the aging process (see Beaver, 1983). Schwartz points out that "left untouched and unmodified, cumulative stress signals an increasing loss of control over one's environment and with it an increasing subjective sense of loss of impact upon and effectiveness within the environment" (1974, p. 10). Consider the case of Mrs. Trent.

Mrs. Trent, a 76-year-old retired legal secretary, has experienced a number of significant losses over the past eight years. Eight years ago her husband of 47 years died of a heart attack. The death was sudden and occurred shortly after her husband returned home from work. Mr. Trent had been an attorney and had spent most of his last few years as a consultant for various industrial corporations.

Mrs. Trent took her husband's death hard, but managed to adjust to the loss with the help of her daughter (an only child) and a few close friends and relatives. Mrs. Trent had a part-time job and found going to work therapeutic.

Three years after Mr. Trent's death, Mrs. Trent's home was burglarized. Fortunately for Mrs. Trent, her jewelry, valuable family pictures, legal documents, and a variety of mementos had been placed in a safety deposit box. However, even though Mrs. Trent increased the security measures around the house, she was fearful that her home would be broken into again. She was unable to sleep at night and was very nervous and "jumpy" around the house. Once she left for work she was afraid to return home for fear of what she might find. She was aware that her fears were threatening her physical and mental health.

Six months after the break-in Mrs. Trent sold her home and moved in with her daughter. It was difficult for Mrs. Trent to give up the home in which she had spent so many happy years with her husband and daughter. Besides, she had come to know the people and the neighborhood quite well.

A year after having moved in with her daughter, Mrs. Trent gave up her part-time job. The 22-mile, round-trip commute combined with the vision problems she was having were too much for her. Once Mrs. Trent moved in with her daughter much of her time was spent in the house. Even so she managed to maintain phone contact with her family (two younger sisters and a brother) and friends, whom she visited occasionally or who visited her at her daughter's home. Mrs. Trent appeared to be adjusting relatively well to these major social stresses. Her appetite was good, she maintained contact with her family and friends, and she found time to take short trips with her daughter.

Then nine months ago her daughter died unexpectedly of a cerebral hemorrhage. Mrs. Trent was devastated but managed to make arrangements for the funeral and to attend to all legal documents. However, since that time she has lost interest in everything. Her family and friends are extremely concerned, especially since she has lost quite a bit of weight, sits around the house all day, doesn't answer the telephone, sleeps sporadically, has no interest in her appearance, and is totally withdrawn.

It is obvious that Mrs. Trent experienced a number of significant losses (stressful events), each of which undoubtedly affected her health. Crandall asserts that "the literature indicates that the more stress individuals suffer, the poorer their health" (1980, p. 167). But stressful events are a common occurrence among the elderly. In fact, because of their age, older people are more likely to be subject to stressful situations (see Crandall, 1980). The nature of the stresses to which the elderly must adjust exacts a heavy toll on them, especially if losses or changes occur one after the other. Thus it is not unusual for some older people, in a weakened physical and/or mental condition, to give up and die.

**Discussion Questions.**   In reviewing the circumstances of Mrs. Trent's situation, at what point(s) in her life, that is, young adulthood, middle age, and so on, would an emphasis on primary prevention have been useful? What kinds of preventive efforts would have been most appropriate? Prompt intervention by caseworkers and other helping professionals when personal catastrophes appear imminent or have already occurred is regarded as beneficial and essential to the well-being of the client. What kind of casework knowledge and skill would you bring to this situation, especially now that Mrs. Trent has lost her daughter and appears to be extremely depressed? Do you believe that Mrs. Trent will be amenable to casework services? Explain your answer.

### Change Experienced as Loss: A Predominant Theme

Change experienced as loss is inevitable for everyone and everything that lives. Even though individuals may protest the inevitability of certain losses—such as the death of a loved one—those persons must begin to accept loss as the law of life—indeed, the law of the universe.

Loss has been characterized as the one phenomenon that is synonymous with aging. Some losses most common to aging are the loss of loved ones, productivity, accustomed roles, income, mobility, health and physical capacities, home and other possessions, usefulness, relationships, and purpose in life. According to Ebersole and Hess "losses occur throughout life, but their cumulative effects may be felt acutely in old age; old feelings resurge with new losses which occur with increasing frequency" (1981, p. 384).

To the older person each loss represents a setback. It means that the thing missing is no longer available—it cannot be seen, heard, touched, or experienced. Whatever the nature of the loss or how it is perceived, the older individual is required to deal realistically with it and with the new set of circumstances it mandates.

Such realism may be particularly difficult for older individuals, especially if they have experienced other, concurrent losses. However, the necessity of coping with the demands of life, no matter how difficult, characterizes maturation at each stage of development. The older individual is therefore challenged to adjust, perhaps by finding replacements for that which they have lost. Some older people may replace changes or losses with new relationships such as new friends, remarriage, new roles (such as second and third careers), and volunteer activities (see Beaver, 1983).

Others may find different ways of dealing with stressful situations, which may involve the exertion of a tremendous amount of psychic energy. But if older people are to go on living they will almost inevitably have to cope with a number of losses. Butler and Lewis contend that "losses in every aspect of late life compel the elderly to expend enormous amounts of physical and emotional energy in grieving and resolving grief, adapting to the changes that result from loss, and recovering from the stresses inherent in these processes" (1977, p. 34).

Unquestionably, many losses experienced by the older person are difficult to adjust to, especially if that person is in poor physical and/or mental health. And research has proven that poor health is not uncommon among the elderly.

## Change or Loss: A Challenge to the Elderly

While aging is characterized by a number of changes and losses, adjusting to those changes and losses can be challenging and eventually rewarding. Older people frequently perceive the adjustment process as a challenge to their internal strength, motivation, and resilience.

If the elderly are to transcend their losses they must remain invested in life and living. The older person who becomes a bystander invites personal disaster, disappointment, and untold grief. Therefore, older people must retain a continuing and vibrant connection with other people and become engaged in meaningful activities and pursuits. Such an approach enables them to remain emotionally attached to the ongoingness of life. When loss does occur, the elderly are challenged to regroup (often with the help of significant others) and draw upon the kind of internal strength that enabled them to overcome painful and problematic situations in the earlier years of their lives.

How one builds internal strength, develops more self-awareness, learns new ways of coping with oftentimes cumulative losses, and seeks richness from living has a lot to do with one's attitudes, belief systems, and previous ways of adjusting to loss. Experience teaches us, and subsequent studies and new findings support the view that we can continue to develop and grow—often through painful and trying experiences. Many examples can be cited of people who regardless of age found new meanings in their lives after the most trying and devastating circumstances.

The authors in no way wish to overemphasize or even to minimize the impact of change experienced as loss and aging. In the context of this discussion, we view loss as somewhat synonymous with change. When change occurs older people are challenged to adjust or adapt. There are many styles and patterns of adaptation or adjustment to change or loss: no single approach can be cited as the most effective. As Brody points out, "Each has potential for success and must be evaluated in the framework of the individual's previous life history" (1977, p. 60).

The authors contend that the majority of older people are essentially healthy, vigorous, capable, and quite productive. Many may have long years of relatively good physical and mental health before they experience a major setback. But the reader must keep in mind that change and loss are inevitable, unavoidable, and often very stressful. No doubt good mental attitudes and continuing socialization, spontaneity, and ability and desire to cope with new situations are key factors in assisting older people to cope with unduly taxing life situations. Emphasis is on progressive rather than on regressive forces, on health rather than on sickness, and on the older person's potential for growth (Germain, 1979).

Social worker action directed toward the older person entails the kinds of procedures that will increase self-confidence and self-esteem, "reduce psychic discomfort, strengthen adaptive patterns, teach coping skills, provide information," and so on (Germain, 1979, p. 18). Each of these activities at the person-system level is designed to increase competence, autonomy, and relatedness, and strengthen individual identities.

Social worker activities directed at the environment include "providing opportunities for action, decision-making, and mastery, and restructuring situations for a better adaptive fit" (Germain, 1979, p. 18). Procedures to strengthen and support informal social networks or to link isolated older people to existing or evolving social networks are also useful and appropriate in environmental activities.

## TYPES OF CHANGES OR LOSSES

### Biophysiological Declines

Normally, as people age declines in physical capabilities occur. According to Beaver, "changes in physical appearance and declines in physical ability are what people notice first" (1983, p. 57). There may be changes in facial features, skin resiliency, body posture, muscular strength, general body contour, and ability to see and hear (see Huyck, 1974). Huyck identified "slowed response" (1974, p. 29) or reaction time. Crandall described this phenomenon as "the length of time between the onset of a stimulus and the execution of a measurable response to that stimulus" (1980, p. 244). "For example, an older person crossing the street may find it difficult to get all the way across the street in the time allotted for one green light" (Huyck, 1974, p. 29). By the time the older person has registered the information that the light has changed, little time remains to cross the entire street.

Biological aging refers to those physical changes in the individual that have been found to be associated with aging (see Rogers, 1979). Such changes may occur in cell structures, organ systems, or their functioning (see Dibner, 1975). Many of these changes result in diminished physical capacities, disabilities, and health loss. (see Saul, 1974). Keller and Hughston state that "the most obvious biological declines are seen in the dramatic drop in reserve capacity" (1981, p. 19). Reserve capacity refers to the physical energy or reserve that individuals can call upon in time of need.

"Biological aging is a universal, unidirectional, and a multidimensional process. It is universal in that it happens to all living organisms. It is unidirectional in that there is only one way to go (i.e., a person cannot grow young). It is multidimensional in that it occurs in many areas" (Keller & Hughston, 1981, p. 19). For example, not only do the skin wrinkle and muscular strength decrease, but hearing, vision, taste, smell, and many other areas are also involved in this unidirectional, age-related change.

Fundamental to an understanding of the physical aspects of aging is the realization that there are "marked individual differences in the onset and rate of physical change with age" (Beaver, 1983, p. 58). Not only do individuals age at different rates with respect to different functions, but different organs and subsystems within the individual age differently (see Keller & Hughston, 1981). Even though most individuals definitely experience a physical decline as they grow older, they do not necessarily become incapacitated (see Crandall, 1980).

With the passage of time the individual undergoes a number of physiological changes. "The general pattern of change is a gradual reduction in the performance of organ systems; this reduction begins in the early 30s and continues throughout life" (Beaver, 1983, pp. 60–61). For instance, with increasing age the connective tissue (the substance that binds the body together and gives it support) becomes stiffer and less capable of allowing nutrients to pass (see Bromley, 1974). The cardiovascular system tends to become less efficient. The heart becomes flabby and circulates less blood throughout the body, which in turn affects important organs such as the brain (see Crandall, 1980). As people grow older the kidneys decline in functioning by as much as 50 percent.

The digestive system is one of the critical systems of the body. Food must be converted to a state that is capable of being taken into the cells by way of the blood plasma. This conversion process is known as digestion. Once food is digested it must be transferred to the blood stream. The process by which this transfer occurs is called absorption. Thus digestion and absorption are the two primary functions of the digestive system (see Memmler & Wood, 1977). The digestive system of an older individual will generally not function as efficiently as that of a younger person. Crandall states that "with increasing age, there is less gastric juice and less saliva to aid in digestion" (1980, p. 139).

While senescence is generally acknowledged to be a period of physiological decline, geriatricians agree that physiological changes are highly individual and point out that "there is a wide range of therapeutic and medical treatment to serve older people, to alleviate physical distress, to mitigate effects of illness, to offer rehabilitative services, to reverse certain correctible conditions" (Shanas, 1962, p. 61). In other words, "older people's physical circumstances are not uniformly inevitable or irreversible but are amenable to medical, surgical, psychiatric, and other kinds of treatment intervention" (Saul, 1974, p. 22).

## Psychological Changes or Losses

Beaver points out that "a number of changes are known to take place on the psychological level as the individual ages" (1983, p. 72). However, "to understand a person's behavior, one must know his present physical state, the way he senses, perceives, and organizes stimulation, his present environmental context, and the influences of his inner states" (Dibner, 1975, p. 69).

**Changes in Sensation.** Radical changes in vision are unlikely to occur before the age of 40–45. However, visual efficiency frequently declines in old age. For instance, "after the age of 40–45, the most common causes of blindness are those which predominantly affect the elderly" (Beaver, 1983, p. 83). Cataract formation is one such cause.

A cataract is a condition in which the eye's lens becomes opaque (cloudy) causing partial or total blindness. In those cataract cases where partial vision remains, frequent changes in eyeglasses may aid in maintaining youthful vision for some time. Cataracts can be removed successfully through surgery. In fact 95 percent of all cataract surgery has been successful, and such surgery has been successfully performed on persons well over 90 years of age (see Ernst & Shore, 1976).

Another leading cause of blindness in old age is glaucoma. Glaucoma is a "condition that is characterized by excess pressure of the eye fluid" (Memmler & Wood, 1977, p. 147).

General visual acuity (that is, the ability to see things clearly) also declines with age. "Visual acuity under most conditions is drastically reduced in old age especially after the age of 65–70" (Dibner, 1975, p. 70).

Farsightedness is another visual difficulty that may affect the aged. Farsightedness means that a person sees distant objects better than near ones, and is due primarily to the lens's loss of elasticity. Although this condition can be improved through the use of eyeglasses, many older people complain of eye strain and of not being able to see small details such as sewing thread, numbers on telephones and in telephone books, directions on medications, and so forth (see Ernst & Shore, 1976).

Decreased sensitivity to light and increased sensitivity to glare also change with age. Old people have more difficulty adapting to light changes. For instance, "the old person who enters a dark theater may experience a much slower adaptation to the light level than younger age groups. Also the older person who attempts to drive an automobile may have considerably more difficulty driving at night than in the daytime" (Ernst & Shore, 1976, p. 33). If older people take appropriate precautions, many of their visual impairments can be corrected with such aids as eyeglasses, "contact lenses, magnifying glasses, talking books, large-print books, proper lighting, or color coding" (Crandall, 1980, p. 142).

In summary, a number of visual changes occur with age. Some, like blindness, can seriously impair the older person's mobility and ability to manipulate objects, and can cause other difficulties.

**Hearing.**    Although hearing loss increases with age, the extent to which it does so has not been well documented. "The existing data show that the major functional changes in hearing are associated with disturbances in the inner ear and related neural pathways" (Beaver, 1983, p. 85).

Hearing loss may begin as early as age 20 and increase gradually throughout life. With advancing age the functional changes in hearing significantly interfere with the communication process. Older people who have hearing difficulties frequently ask others to repeat what they have said or to speak louder or more distinctly (see Kalish, 1975). Generally speaking "this is bound to effect how the older person feels about himself as well as his ability to communicate adequately with others" (Beaver, 1983, p. 85). Thus "To avoid being embarrassed the older person who has difficulty hearing may avoid social interaction, and thus become isolated and further alienated from the environment" (Crandall, 1980, p. 278).

It is easy to take good hearing for granted. In the world of the hearing impaired, words in a conversation may be misunderstood, musical notes may be missed, and a ringing doorbell may go unanswered. Hearing impairment ranges from difficulty in understanding words or hearing certain sounds to total deafness. Because of fear, misinformation, or vanity, some people will not admit to themselves or to anyone else that they have a hearing problem. It has been estimated, however, that approximately 30 percent of adults aged 65 through 74 and about 50 percent of those aged 75 through 79 suffer some degree of hearing loss. According to the National Institute on Aging (1983), in the United States alone more than 10 million older people are hearing impaired.

If ignored and untreated, hearing problems can grow worse, hindering communication with others, limiting social activities, and reducing constructive use of leisure time. As was previously pointed out, people with hearing impairments often withdraw socially to avoid the frustration and embarrassment of not understanding what is being said. Hearing-impaired people may become suspicious of relatives and friends who "mumble" or "don't speak up."

Hearing loss may cause an older, hearing-impaired person to be wrongly labeled as "confused," "unresponsive," or "uncooperative." At times the feelings of powerlessness and frustration experienced by elderly individuals trying to communicate with others result in depression and withdrawal.

While older people today are in general demanding and receiving greater satisfaction from life, those with hearing impairments often find the quality of their lives diminished. Fortunately, help is available in the form of surgery, treatment with medicines, special training, a hearing aid, or an alternate listening device.

**Other Senses.**   Taste, smell, pain, and touch have not been studied as extensively as hearing and vision. Some studies show decrements in each of the sensory modalities, whereas others show no changes. For instance, research indicates that "not only do individual taste buds become less sensitive with aging, but also the number of taste buds decline" (Atchley, 1980, p. 46). However, research on the sense of smell indicates little change with age (see Engen, 1977).

**Other Age-Related Psychological Changes**
*Intelligence.*   What is intelligence? Most people *seem* to know what is meant by intelligence, yet efforts to provide a formal definition that is both meaningful and useful are elusive. Some people view intelligence as an attribute, part or all of which is genetically given. Botwinick points out that "experience and biological change modifies the basic potentialities, but precisely how and how much is not easily determined. The emphasis is on capacity—a theoretical limit when health, educational opportunities, social background, motivation, and other factors do not detract from intelligence" (1977, p. 581).

Another definition of intelligence focuses on ability rather than on capacity; that is, what a person is able to do at a given time. Generally speaking, the term *intelligence* refers to abilities possessed by individuals—the ability to respond quickly and successfully to new situations, the ability to learn or understand from experience, the ability to acquire and retain knowledge, and so forth (see *Webster's,* 1970).

People's mental abilities have traditionally been measured by standardized psychological tests such as the Wechsler Adult Intelligence Scale (WAIS). Investigations concerned with whether adults become more or less intelligent or capable with age have generated an impressive body of research (see Whitbourne & Weinstock, 1979).

Psychologists frequently divide intelligence into two major types: crystallized and fluid. "Crystallized intelligence is believed to reflect the mental abilities that depend on the individual's encounter with the world—on both formal and informal experiences in everyday life" (Schaie & Geiwitz, 1982, p. 220). Fluid intelligence is "the major measurable outcome of the influence of biological factors on intellectual development—that is, heredity, injury to the central nervous system or to basic sensory structures, and so forth" (Horn & Cattell, 1966, p. 254). Riegel points out that "the intelligence of children is dominated by fluid rather than by crystallized functions. The former are already well developed early in life; the latter are not. In contrast, the intelligence of older adults is dominated by crystallized rather than fluid performances" (1977, p. 74). Abilities requiring language-learning skills, formal logic, and general factual knowledge are identified as crystallized. Abilities requiring sensorimotor coordination, new learning, and speed performance are identified as fluid.

An introductory question raised in early studies of intellectual abilities is: Does intelligence decline in old age? Nearly all earlier studies, including Wechsler's (1958), have shown that most human abilities—including intelligence—decline fairly early in adulthood. However, more recent literature indicates the following: (1) Declines in intelligence may start later in life than previously thought; (2) they may be smaller in magnitude; and (3) they may include fewer functions (see Botwinick, 1977).

The controversy as to whether there is an age-related decline in intellectual functioning frequently centers around the "research methods used and their pitfalls" (Botwinick, 1977, p. 580). For instance, cross-sectional studies of intelligence usually show that considerable decrement in intelligence accompanies old age.[1] Longitudinal studies, however, indicate a much lower loss of cognitive capacity.[2] Virtually no changes in measured intelligence were observed in one follow-up study of older individuals three years after initial testing (see Eisdorfer, 1963). Another study spanned an eight-year period and found decrement in only a few areas (see Jarvik, Kallman & Falek, 1962).

---

[1] "Cross-sectional methods use only two or more samples of persons representing different age groups who are studied at only one point in time. The groups are measured for a selected variable, or a series of variables which the investigator wishes to study" (Beaver, 1983, p. 78).

[2] "Longitudinal studies follow an individual or group of individuals over a relatively long period with repeated measures taken on selected variables at subsequent points in time" (Beaver, 1983, p. 78).

A dozen years later, when respondents were in their mid-80s, significant losses were found but these could be explained primarily by terminal decline[3] (see Blum, Fosshage & Jarvik, 1972).

K. Warner Schaie, former director of the Gerontology Research Institute at the University of Southern California in Los Angeles, recently completed a 21-year study of intellectual performance in aging adults.[4] Dr. Schaie and his colleagues examined several thousand healthy, community-living volunteers ranging in age from 22 to 81 years. Subjects were called back at seven-year intervals for retesting. The most positive and provocative finding is that at all ages the majority of people studied maintained their level of intellectual competence—or actually improved—as they grew older.

Between the ages of 60 and 67 fewer than 30 percent of the subjects showed a dropoff in psychological performance. Among the older age groups—subjects who moved from their eighth to their ninth decade during the course of the study—between 35 and 44 percent showed some decline. Interestingly, a significant minority in each age range continued to improve. Even those between the ages of 74 and 81—almost 10 percent of the people tested—performed better than they had at younger ages. Schaie's findings take us a long way from the previously held belief that intelligence peaks at very early ages and then declines because of aging.

Dr. Schaie's work has begun to shed some light on the factors that might play a role in individual variations. First, it appears that conditions such as cardiovascular disease can undermine cognitive functions. Second, it is clear that people who are raised in advantaged socioeconomic environments are more apt to attain high levels of intellectual functioning and to maintain such functioning into old age. Third, it appears that middle-aged people whose lifestyles and attitudes are flexible are likely to maintain their intellectual abilities later in life. The evidence that changes in environment and in education can affect intelligence in old age is of extreme interest to the scientific community and a source of hope for future generations.

*Memory.*　Memory refers to the retention of specific incidents and events that occurred at a given time in a given place (see Craik, 1977). Time and place are of the essence when an individual recalls a specific event; for example, who he or she ate lunch with last Friday or what he or she was doing on May 31, 1984. Adults rely heavily on memory in many aspects of their interactions with the environment. And often if a word, a name, a fact, or an event does not come to mind when the older person wants it to, the individual tends to think "I must be getting old." In each of these situations the older person is having difficulty recovering material from mem-

---

[3] The term *terminal decline* refers to "observations that individuals who show a notable change in any one of a variety of measures of cognitive performance are more likely to be dead within a few years than are those who show no particular change" (Kalish, 1975, p. 41).

[4] Most of the information on Dr. Schaie's scientific study was obtained from the National Institute on Aging's *Special Report on Aging,* 1982.

ory. In those situations where an event has had a significant impact on the person, the older individual has less difficulty remembering. Or the meaning the event has is very important in terms of whether or not it will be remembered. Unfortunately, as many people age they *expect* to experience memory loss, declining intelligence, and mental confusion, so their recall frequently matches their expectations.

The literature distinguishes between at least two types of memory: short- and long-term, or primary and secondary. Short-term memory refers to recall of material after a relatively brief delay (that is, from one hour to several days). Material can be "actively retained in short-term memory through rehearsal or internal repetition of the information" (Whitbourne & Weinstock, 1979, p. 31). Researchers have generally concluded that short-term memory is *not* impaired with aging. The older person who is in good health does not appear to have any particular problem recalling the immediate event (see Kastenbaum, 1979).

Long-term memory refers to the recall of events that occurred in the past that have neither been frequently rehearsed nor thought about (see Crandall, 1980). Some researchers believe that the older person can accurately recall events that occurred 50, 60, or 70 years ago (see Kastenbaum, 1979).

Depression is often linked to loss of memory and loss of other intellectual functions. This linkage needs to be given further attention, especially since depression may be related to loss of close relatives, retirement, or failing health—circumstances many older people face, often simultaneously.

**Learning.**   Although memory and learning are different aspects of the same underlying mechanism, it is useful to differentiate between them. Learning may be defined as the acquisition of general rules and knowledge of the world, while memory refers to retention of specific events that occurred at a given time in a given place (see Craik, 1977).

In studying the way people process new information, researchers have discovered that many of the problems older people experience while acquiring, storing, and retrieving information can be overcome with time, effort, and through training in the use of special and relatively simple techniques. Consider, for example, how many of us use simple tricks or clues to remember someone's name or some other kind of information.

Research shows that if older people are allowed to study new information in any manner they choose, they are unlikely to use any clues voluntarily. However, when older individuals are trained to organize new information in a certain way, to rehearse verbally, or to tie some information to a visual image, their performance on memory tests improves. Unfortunately, almost all current studies of learning and memory have taken place in laboratories where the focus of the research is upon fixed and uncomplicated questions outside the realm of day-to-day experience.

**Problem Solving.**   The literature on problem solving in old age is relatively sparse. Many cross-sectional studies have shown an age-related decline in problem-solving ability in both verbal and nonverbal situations (see Dibner, 1975). Old people have proven to be less able than younger people to reason logically, describe similarities, construct sentences from odd words, and perform tasks of analysis, synthesis, and inventiveness. The latter skills and tasks require that the older individual make abstract rather than concrete associations.

Early hypotheses suggested that older people perform relatively poorly on certain tasks due to rigidity—"functional fixedness" or "inability to abandon one scheme of organization in favor of another" (Rabbitt, 1977, p. 618)— and loss of abstractive ability. A more recent hypothesis, which has more support than the first, is that older people are "less able to integrate or organize information than the young" (Rabbitt, 1977, p. 619). That is, older people may require more information (regarded by young people as redundant) before they can make a perceptual judgment. Rabbitt succinctly states that:

> The young appear to be able to optimize organization to employ the least possible number of critical variables. The old may not be able to attain such selectivity and may persist in clumsy organizational schemes incorporating variables redundant to the classification required. (1977, p. 620)

Thus considerable evidence supports the hypothesis that older people accumulate more redundant information than younger people and may take longer to interpret data (see Bernadelli & Clay, quoted in Welford, 1958). And even if older people were given more time for data interpretation, there would still seem to be a decrement in their problem-solving ability (see Dibner, 1975).

**Psychomotor Performance Changes.**   Individuals first experience the environment through their sensory processes. They then give meaning to the sensory input through perceptual and integrative processes that may or may not signal the need to take action. If a physical reaction to stimuli is required, "the choice must be made of what reaction to perform and how it should be carried out" (Whitbourne & Weinstock, 1979, p. 26).

Psychomotor performance changes as the individual grows older. Reaction time (that is, the length of time between the presentation of a stimulus and the beginning of a response to that stimulus) increases with age. It is difficult to pinpoint precisely why changes in reaction time occur as people age. However, the nature of the stimulus and the complexity of the response appear to be causative factors.

Simple motor performance does not appear to be highly affected by age, but complex motor performance does. Simple motor performance requires that the older person have only minimal processing, decision making, or other skills (see Crandall, 1980). Some examples might be "pressing a button to turn on the television, turning off a light switch, or stepping on a spot on a rug" (Barrow & Smith, 1983, p. 226).

Complex motor performance requires more information processing, decision making, and complex skills than simple motor performance. Some examples might include "copying words or tracing patterns, riding a bicycle, or dancing" (Welford, 1977, p. 458). Generally speaking, studies indicate that both types of motor performance decline slightly as a person grows older.

However, "older people have found ways to compensate for their lack of speed" (Beaver, 1983, p. 83). For instance, whenever older people are confronted with complex tasks, they "may use such compensatory techniques as working more slowly, more carefully, or dividing the task into smaller units to be handled sequentially" (Dibner, 1975, p. 76).

**Psychological Implications of Changes or Losses.**    Loss, suffering, and human error are part of most lives. However, the elderly are confronted with multiple losses, some of which may occur simultaneously. Many of the losses and life events experienced by the elderly are stressful. Barrow & Smith point out that "stress undoubtedly ages people and is a well-documented cause of anxiety, depression, migraine headaches, and peptic ulcers" (1983, p. 15). In old age the stress can be more acute since immediate problems bring to mind earlier difficulties. The elderly person may be haunted by memories of stressful events and relationships that date all the way back to childhood (see Kastenbaum, 1979).

Faced with these lingering memories of the past, older people may feel helpless. They are also undoubtedly aware that there are fewer resources available to cope with problems in their immediate environment; that is, fewer people to share experiences with, less physical and natural control over the environment, and so on.

Age alone does not account for the losses that occur on the psychological level. Such losses are connected to a number of life circumstances that include but are not limited to poor or negligent medical care, stress, poverty, inadequate nutrition, lack of exercise, or excessive smoking.

Generally speaking, the decline with age of some sensory and perceptual functions results in less incoming environmental information and the consequent risk of maladaptive behavior. For instance, hearing losses can be detrimental to the elderly in terms of orienting them and keeping them in touch with their environment. Crandall points out that "hearing loss may cause individuals to misinterpret instructions, commands, or descriptions concerning their environment. Thus, they may act inappropriately or may engage in behavior that may be detrimental to their safety" (1980, p. 278). While gerontologists believe that compensatory adaptations are made to minimize the negative effects of loss of hearing, little is known about the process or extent to which such personal coping efforts succeed in counteracting maladaptation.

The way older people deal with loss may be the single most important factor in reducing tension, ameliorating the difficulty, and slowing the rate of their decline. Hurlock points out that "the psychological causes of aging, when combined with the physical, accelerate the aging process by speeding up the rate of decline" (1968, p. 786). However, reviewing the loss with a supportive person often aids in its resolution and gives both the person experiencing the loss and the listener a clearer picture of its significance.

Those people who have successfully lived through Erikson's eight stages of life (as described later in this chapter) and who have adjusted to life's major crises or critical events are often better able to accommodate the changes and losses that accompany old age. But those older persons who, for whatever reasons, have not gained emotional maturity or mastered the psychological tasks required of a productive adult have fewer inner resources to fall back upon (see Friedlander & Apte, 1983).

## Social Changes or Losses

Generally, "The changes that are often the most noticeable and the most feared are the biological and physiological changes" (Crandall, 1980, p. 130). However, a number of other losses are added to the biophysiological ones, including loss of role, activity, and status—quite unrelated to the limited *physical* decrements of normal, healthy aging.

Most people experience partings and separations repeatedly—both temporary and permanent—and throughout their lives. As one passes from childhood into adulthood, one loses playmates, friends, lovers, and often family members. Changes in residence, occupation, or place of business are also not uncommon, and such changes are not always easy, especially if a person has developed strong and affectionate ties (see Carr, 1975).

Retirement or loss of the work role is one of the major social-role losses that a person must deal with as he or she grows older. However, an understanding of the concept of social role must be provided before a discussion of retirement can begin.

**Social Role.**   A social role is a pattern of behavior that is expected of a person who occupies a certain social status or position in society. Social roles are linked to social norms, those conventions that prescribe, guide, control, or regulate proper and acceptable behavior.

Social roles should not be seen in isolation as they exist in relation to another role or group of roles. Consider for example a basketball team as a set of various *positions*—one center, two forwards, and two guards. It is also appropriate to speak of the *role* of the forwards, guards, or center. The center's role is not only linked to that of the other members of the team and vice versa: It also defines the specific behavior expected of the person playing or occupying the center position. In the area of employment, the role of supervisor has no meaning without the role of worker. In the practice of social work, the role of case worker takes on meaning when it is linked to that of client.

Anderson and Gibson point out that "roles exist prior to their present incumbents and continue to survive after an individual departs" (1978, p. 27). Therefore, individuals may retire from such roles as foreman, plant supervisor, teacher, or nursing home administrator, but each of these roles remains in existence and will be assumed by a different individual.

An established set of rules designates what behavior is expected in socially defined positions. For example, society has guidelines that spell out the behavior expected of postal carriers, nurses, school principals, students, and so on. Most people carry out their roles according to societal norms—appropriate modes of conduct between people. For instance, children know they should not be disruptive or belligerent in class, mature individuals know they should not dress like teenagers, and so on. When individuals do not perform their roles in an appropriate manner, sanctions of varying degrees (that is, reprimand, ostracism, demotion, fine, or imprisonment) can be applied.

People perform a variety of roles throughout their lives and usually assume more than one role at a given time. For example, individuals who are now old have acted in such roles as child, sibling, spouse, parent, worker, grandparent, widow(er), and so forth. Some of these roles may have had a certain amount of pain and trauma associated with them: Inherent in the role of widow or widower is the feeling of pain as well as loss. The transition from the active work role to that of retirement may bring with it a number of losses including loss of income, status, interaction with fellow employees, and the cessation of a productive working experience.

**Retirement.**   One of life's most significant changes or events is retirement. The term *retirement* generally refers to separation or withdrawal from work in which a person was gainfully employed. Retirement brings about a number of changes in a person's life. The retiree no longer goes to a daily job, has more opportunity to structure his or her own time, and has more time for personal growth and ongoing community involvement.

The transition from worker to retiree of course has a considerable impact on the elderly person's income, lifestyle, social status, and social role. Many people become poor when they retire. It costs money to live and with soaring inflation, the high cost of living, and fewer federal dollars spent on social programs, those older people living on fixed incomes are the ones that suffer the most. Moreover, limited funds may mean that the older person does not have the financial means to pursue hobbies, to travel, to visit children or grandchildren, or to entertain. Work has always been essential to an individual's survival. The puritan ethic made work the cornerstone of virtue, thrift a lofty measure of character, and independence the foundation of worthiness (see Feldman & Scherz, 1967). In fact, "the achievements and social status associated with occupation are major ingredients in the way we judge ourselves and others" (Kastenbaum, 1979, p. 62). Individuals who are self-sufficient and self-reliant are highly valued in American society. Feldman and Scherz point out that the common expression "worth his salt" attests to the prevalent regard for the person who earns his way, especially if he "pulled himself up by the bootstraps" (1967, p. 16). Older people who have retired—for whatever reason—are no longer able to produce and earn their way in the same way as those who are working in a full-time job.

No matter how far in advance an individual plans for retirement—and may be looking forward to it—when the actual moment comes that person also experiences the reality of no job to go to tomorrow, no organization or agency to be a part of, and no co-workers with whom to share easy and pleasant comradeship. There are those who believe it is "easy when an individual retires to feel unwanted, undervalued, and disposable. Self-approval, self-respect, and sureness of identity can be easily shattered" (Bradford & Bradford, 1979, p. 4).

Some people feel lost without the structured hours and familiar routine that regulated their lives while they worked. Some feel guilty about having so much time on their hands. Others experience feelings of goallessness, having little or no direction to guide their lives. The challenge for the latter group of retirees is to develop meaningful life goals and purposes for this period.

The transition from worker to retiree is not always a difficult experience. Atchley (1971) found that leisure could be a legitimate source of identity after retirement because: (1) individuals and their friends grow older and retire at about the same time; (2) even with retirement a number of other important roles continue (family, church, or community roles may still need to be filled); and (3) retirement and leisure are becoming socially acceptable in contemporary American society. Thus retirement does not have to result in any significant disruption of a person's social and interpersonal network.

Atchley's position notwithstanding, there are those who view retirement as a vehicle for social loss. According to Schwartz, "Many persons, upon retirement, lose not only a job with its attendant source of income, but at the same time, lose status as a co-worker or colleague with its attendant source of close contact and friendship. They also lose opportunities to participate in a number of valued activities such as membership in company bowling leagues, organizational picnics, and union meetings."[5]

Holcomb states that "In a culture in which one's status and one's identity is largely determined by what one does, the occasion of retirement may mean a greater loss of one's sense of identity than it means to one's economic conditions" (1975, p. 244).

Some believe that the biggest adjustment for the retiree is the emotional adjustment. Emotional adjustment to retirement is contingent upon the individual's attitude before the event took place. In fact, Hendricks and Hendricks point out that "if the individual perceives retirement negatively, fears the loss of work role or friends from the job, or is uncertain for any reasons about the future, adjustment may be problematic" (1981, pp. 288–289). Fears about retirement are frequently alleviated when the individual has accurate information about health, finances, and emotional or psychological problems that may arise. But the literature does not seem to place as much emphasis on this aspect of retirement as it does on such pragmatic issues as financial planning and management, developing hobbies, and drawing up a will. There are, however, a number of preretirement programs that deal with the emo-

---

[5] From A. N. Schwartz, *Professional Obligations and Approaches to the Aged* (Springfield, Ill.: Charles C. Thomas, 1974), p. 10. Courtesy of Charles C. Thomas, Publisher, Springfield, Illinois.

tional aspects of retirement adjustment such as how to effect more positive attitudes and how to develop useful coping strategies.

Retirement will continue to present future cohorts of older individuals and society with the challenge of finding meaningful ways to use leisure time. There is no question that given proper resources, opportunities, and motivation, older people can make a valuable contribution to society long after their working years have ended.

**Relocation.**   There is evidence that suggests that change of residence can cause serious stress for older persons, although not many older people choose to change residence—only a small proportion move each year. Of the older Americans who moved between 1975 and 1978, nearly one half remained within the same Standard Metropolitan Statistical Area (SMSA) while about one fourth remained outside SMSAs. During this 3-year period only about 14 percent of Americans 65 years old and over moved to a different house. Within this age group mobility was greater for those between 65 and 74 (15 percent) than for those 75 and over (12 percent) (see *Social and Economic Characteristics of the Older Population: 1978*).

Moving is disruptive at any age, but it is particularly difficult for the elderly. For the older person, moving is often compounded by social isolation, intergenerational conflict, or the feeling of imposing upon someone or being imposed upon (see Yawney & Slover, 1973).

A review of the literature on relocation research indicates a growing concern about the negative effects of moving older people involuntarily from one environment to another and speaks to the need for finding ways of counteracting those effects (see Liebowitz, 1974).

Negative effects such as increased mortality and/or morbidity rates have been attributed to such moves. A study by Aldrich and Mendkoff (1963) revealed that when disabled persons were transferred en masse from one institution to another for administrative reasons alone, there was a marked increase in the death rate. Miller and Lieberman (1965) describe another situation in which residents of an old age home were removed for administrative reasons. Twenty-three of the 45 subjects in their study were judged to experience serious physical or psychological deterioration after the move. Ferrari (1962) found a relationship between death among nursing home residents and their participation or lack of participation in choosing the home. Those residents who participated in the choice of a nursing home had lower mortality rates than those who did not.

"These findings have obvious implications for methods and techniques of managing moves and for the nature of the institutional environment" (Brody, 1977, p. 70). There is a belief among some researchers that social work help is beneficial and tends to reduce relocation stress (see Killian, 1970). A study by Blenkner (1967), however, found the exact opposite. The Blenkner study indicated that older persons who are not institutionalized may fare better without social work help than those who are institutionalized and who are provided with a high level of individual care.

Ogren and Linn (1971), who conducted a four-year study of the effects of transfer from one nursing home to another on 82 male veterans, disagree with Blenkner. Their findings indicate that the most important factor in good adjustment to a nursing home is the staff's understanding of the patients' needs for assistance and service. Ogren and Linn concluded that the social work help received by the patients and their families was of value.

Social workers and other human services practitioners should be aware that the home (house or other private dwelling) is a very important factor in the lives of the aged. Many older people spend 80 to 90 percent of their time in their homes (see Montgomery, 1965). Home is "a place where things are familiar and relatively unchanging, and a place to maintain a sense of autonomy and control" (Butler & Lewis, 1977, p. 211). For these and a variety of other reasons, some older people insist on remaining at home regardless of the consequences to their emotional and physical health and their personal security (see Butler & Lewis, 1977). Such a tenacious spirit is understandable in light of the following:

> The relocated person no longer has the support of familiar surroundings, friends, church, and other organizations to help him. He is faced with the dual task of familiarizing himself with a new environment and developing a network of social relations. All this may be complicated by a decline in functional abilities and by the limited opportunities in status offered to the aged in our society. (Yawney & Slover, 1973, p. 88)

Probably the most difficult type of relocation is from the community into an institution—especially if the move is involuntary. In these instances the older individual has little control over the situation and may experience a sense of helplessness and powerlessness mixed with anxiety. According to Lieberman (1965), there are indications that most elderly nursing home residents never completely accept their new world. Fortunately, families appear to place relatives in institutions only as a last resort.

**Widowhood.** The loss of a spouse through divorce, separation, or death can be devastating. The surviving spouse suffers pain, grief, and numerous deprivations that derive from the spouse's absence (Kalish, 1975). Loneliness, loss of sexual satisfaction, and loss of someone with whom to share one's most intimate self are some of the deprivations that accompany the death of a spouse. However, "any marriage that survives over the years will almost certainly end with one of the spouses, usually the woman, widowed. It is very rare that both spouses die simultaneously" (Beaver, 1983, p. 113).

According to *Social and Economic Characteristics of the Older Population: 1978,* the major reason for older women being unmarried was the death of their husbands. In 1978, 52 percent of the women 65 and over and 69 percent of those 75 and over were widowed. Among men the corresponding proportions were 14 percent and 23 percent respectively.

Like retirement the loss of a spouse results in profound changes in the older person's lifestyle and circumstances. Widows are faced with the loss of the breadwinner (in most instances), financial helper, lover, companion, and friend. Widowers are faced with the loss of the homemaker and house-keeper (in most cases), lover, companion, and friend.

Some widows may seek out a male companion, not necessarily for the purpose of marriage, but rather to have someone who will escort them to various places. The most common pattern among widows, however, seems to be a group of women getting together to provide one another with support and companionship and to have others to go places with. Men tend to remarry more frequently than women, and after they are once again part of a family their loyalties are to that family.

Retirement, relocation, and widowhood are three of the most challenging events that the older person can experience. Each involves loss and a certain amount of change, and each requires reorganization and the acquisition of new social roles. Kennedy states that "old statuses and roles are lost and new relationships must be substituted in order to effect a satisfactory adjustment to changed situations" (1978, p. 86). The older person who can find new activity patterns, friends, and gratification will no doubt make a successful adjustment to each of these inherently stressful events.

The latter statement is consonant with the activity theory of aging. Activity theory maintains that "there is a positive relationship between activity and life satisfaction and the greater the role loss, the lower the life satisfaction" (Lemon, Bengtson, & Peterson, 1976, p. 61). Social activity is perceived to be the essence of life for people at all ages. In fact, Decker points out that "social activity is so important that our level of social activity can determine whether we age successfully or unsuccessfully" (1980, p. 135).

## The Economic Situation of the Elderly [6]

Incomes drop sharply after people retire, and although most of the nation's elderly have retirement protection (through social security and other public and private programs), the benefits are frequently too low to provide an adequate income. This problem exists in spite of the fact that the proportion of elderly below the poverty level has been falling sharply in recent years. In 1974 only 16 percent of the elderly were poor as compared with 35 percent in 1959 (see *Current Population Reports, Special Studies, 1976*). However, almost 15 percent or 3.3 million persons 65 years of age and over were below the poverty level in 1976.

Soaring inflation and the rising cost of living have eroded the funds of most of America's elderly, especially those who live on fixed incomes. Skyrocketing health care costs are also a major contributor to income insecurity in old age.

In 1978, among elderly whites one of every eight (13 percent) was poor, but about 35 percent of elderly blacks and 28 percent of elderly Hispanics

[6] A substantial portion of the information in this section is derived from *Facts About Older Americans, 1978.* U.S. Government Printing Office, DHEW Pub. No. (OHDS) 79–20006.

were poor. The proportion below the poverty level was much higher for elderly persons living alone or with nonrelatives (30 percent) than for those living in families (8 percent). Persons 65 years of age and over who resided outside the nation's metropolitan areas were more likely to be poor (20 percent) than were elderly metropolitan residents (12 percent).

As with most elderly families nearly all (93 percent) income received by individuals 65 and over and identified as poor was from public sources. Only 15 percent was from earnings, while about 39 percent was from other sources.

Of the 4.2 million families who received more than half their income from public sources, only 15 percent were poor. However, 39 percent of the 5 million elderly individuals who received over half of their income from these sources were below the poverty level.

People must begin to economize skillfully and prudently long before their retirement years. Since life expectancy has increased significantly over the years, people can place value (cost of living) in both the present and the future. At least 25 years have been added to the average lifespan since 1900. Thus the individual has 15 to 20 more years of life after reaching age 65. Put differently, individuals currently have more nonworking time following retirement than they did in 1900. Therefore, people must use whatever income they have available to them as wisely as possible long before their retirement years, so they will have some kind of economic protection in their later years.

### Medicare

Medicare is a health insurance program for the aged and disabled that was enacted by Congress in 1965 as Title XVIII of the Social Security Act. Medicare was not designed to cover the total cost of medical care for the aged; rather, it was intended to help pay for medical services during acute illnesses.

Medicare is actually two distinct programs: The Hospital Insurance Fund and Supplementary Medical Insurance. Each of these programs has its own separate funding source. Medicare Hospital Insurance is financed by payroll taxes, and Medicare Supplementary Medical Insurance is financed by a combination of beneficiary premiums and general revenues.

The hospital insurance plan pays for inpatient hospital care, which may include a semiprivate room, meals, regular nursing services, operating room, special care units, drugs and medical supplies, laboratory tests, and rehabilitation services; nursing home stays (that is, extended care in a skilled nursing facility); and home-health services. The medical insurance plan covers physician services, outpatient hospital services, diagnostic tests, outpatient physical therapy, speech pathology services, medical equipment and supplies, and home-health services.

Part A Coverage (hospital insurance) is automatic for the following individuals: (1) those people aged 65 or over who are eligible for social security benefits; (2) those who are eligible for social security benefits for two years or more because of disability, and (3) those who have end-stage renal disease. Part B Coverage (medical insurance) is voluntary. Over 95 percent of the elderly in the United States are covered under Part A, and about 95 percent of the elderly elected to participate in Part B.

A number of services are not covered under medicare including dentures, hearing and eye examinations, eyeglasses and hearing aids, routine physical exams, and most routine foot care. Since the latter services are a form of primary prevention, it would be important to older people if they were covered under medicare.

The cost of health care in this country has reached an all-time high. When medicare was launched in the 1960s, its first-year cost was estimated at $3 billion. By 1983 that figure had reached a total of $47 billion and may well reach $112 billion by 1988 and a much larger sum by the year 2000 (see Scheibla, 1984).

A number of proposals have been advanced to prevent medicare from going broke. One proposal would raise the age for medicare eligibility from 65 to 67. Such a change would make it difficult for a worker to retire at age 65 because for two years that worker would not be covered by medicare, and adequate private medical insurance would cost between $3,000 and $4,000 a year. If individuals became seriously ill during that time, they would risk financial destruction. Other proposals include: greater individual payments for health care received under medicare; higher medicare premiums; small medicare payments for short-term illnesses and full payments for hospitalizations lasting more than two months; and an additional tax on both alcohol and tobacco to bolster the medicare fund. It is difficult to determine what the final solution or set of solutions will be, but the financial crisis must be dealt with if medicare is to remain solvent.

### Medicaid

The medicaid program, authorized under Title XIX of the Social Security Act in 1965, is a federal-state program providing medical assistance for low-income persons who are aged, blind, disabled, or members of families with dependent children. In 1983 medicaid covered about 22 million individuals, of whom approximately 3.6 million were elderly and 3.1 million were blind or disabled.

All states except Arizona, the District of Columbia, Guam, Puerto Rico, the Virgin Islands, and the Northern Mariana Islands currently participate in the program. The federal government's share of program costs is determined by a formula based on the per capita income of each state and ranges from 50 to 78 percent. Each state administers and operates its own program and, under broad federal guidelines, determines eligibility and the scope of benefits to be provided. As a result the programs vary considerably from state to state.

There are two categories of beneficiaries, one mandatory and the other optional. States must cover the "categorically needy," those individuals receiving assistance under the Aid to Families with Dependent Children (AFDC) or Supplemental Security Income (SSI) laws. However, states have the option of providing medicaid coverage to the "medically needy," those persons who are aged, blind, disabled, or members of families with dependent children whose income falls below the state standard for case assistance when medical expenses are deducted.

There are also two categories of services provided under medicaid, one mandatory and the other optional. Mandatory services, which every state must offer, include inpatient and outpatient hospital services, skilled nursing facility services for people over 21, home health services for those entitled to skilled nursing facility care, and physician services. Optional services include such items as intermediate care facility services, prescription drugs, eyeglasses, and dental care. All states (except Arizona) provide intermediate care facility services. Medicaid is the primary public health care program that addresses the long-term care needs of the elderly.

Despite medicare and medicaid the low income of many older persons prevents them from getting adequate medical attention because of the various deductibles, limitations, restrictions, and coinsurance provisions that limit the amount of health care for which medicare pays.

### Health Status and Health Problems of the Elderly[7]

Contrary to prevailing stereotypes, the older population as a whole is healthier than is commonly assumed. In 1981 8 of 10 elderly persons described their health as good or excellent compared with others of their own age, while only 8 percent said their health was comparably poor. About 40 percent reported that a major activity had been limited for health reasons (compared with about 20 percent of the age 45 to 64 population), but 54 percent reported no limitations of any kind in their activities. Not until age 85 and over did about half of the population report being limited or unable to carry on a major activity because of a chronic illness.

Persons 65 and over experience approximately twice as many days of restricted activity due to illness as those under 65 (almost 40 days for persons 65 and over versus 19 for those under 65 in 1981). But those elderly who worked in 1981 did not experience a marked difference in the number of lost work days—four or five days a year on the average for both the younger and older working population.

The very old do have more need for assistance than the "younger-old." For instance, in 1978 less than 1 percent of noninstitutionalized people age 65 to 84 needed help in eating, while about 4 percent of people age 85 and over required such help. About 7 percent of the very old needed help with toileting versus less than 2 percent of the younger-old. Eleven percent

---

[7] A significant portion of the material in this section comes from the U.S. Senate Report of the Special Committee on Aging, *Developments in Aging,* 1982, Vol. 1.

of the 85 and over group needed help dressing, and 18 percent needed help bathing, while the figures were about 3 and 4 percent respectively for the 65- to 84-year-old group. Based on these functional measures more than 80 percent of the noninstitutionalized very old were able to take care of their own daily needs.

**Chronic Conditions.**    The likelihood of developing a chronic illness increases dramatically with age. Most older persons have at least one chronic condition (over 80 percent according to a 1979 National Center for Health Statistics survey) and multiple chronic conditions are a common occurrence. In 1979 the most frequently reported chronic conditions in persons 65 and older were arthritis (44 percent), hypertension (39 percent), heart conditions (27 percent), visual impairments (12 percent), and diabetes (8 percent).

In general most older persons are capable of living independently despite these chronic conditions. According to the National Center for Health Statistics (NCHS), fewer than one in six older persons said they could no longer carry on normal activities because of chronic illness.

**Leading Causes of Death among the Elderly.**    "In order of frequency, the leading causes of death in the older population are: heart disease, hypertension, cancer, and stroke" (Barrow & Smith, 1983, p. 255). Accidents are another leading cause of death among the elderly. Barrow & Smith indicate that "most fatal accidents involving the elderly take place in the home" (1983, p. 262). This is ironic since the home is the most familiar and reassuring environment for older people. Nevertheless, some people may be accident-prone and may find themselves involved in a number of "freak" accidents; that is, getting out of bed too fast and twisting a heel, closing a window on one's finger, missing a step, and so on. These accidents almost always result in pain and/or incapacitation and frequently mean a visit to the doctor or even a stay in the hospital.

**Preventive Efforts.**    Older people must begin to find ways to counteract their propensity for injury by accidents. One way to minimize or even eliminate the number of accidents in old age is to take as many preventive precautions in and around the living environment as possible. There are a variety of design features that housing experts consider beneficial in the construction or installation of housing for the elderly such as adequate levels of light, including sunlight and artificial light to accommodate visual changes; and adequate control of sound and noise to help the elderly adjust to changes in hearing. Persons who already "have difficulty hearing should be provided with amplifying systems for doorbells, telephones, radios, television sets, and so forth" (Loether, 1975, p. 45). Other useful features for minimizing accidents in and around the home include guardrails for bathtubs, nonskid rugs, light switches placed at a level that can be reached (including from a wheelchair) without difficulty, access ramps, hand rails, and so on.

**Alzheimer's Disease.** Of the many disabling conditions of the aged, one of the most serious is Alzheimer's disease. Alzheimer's disease is a progressive, degenerative disease of the brain. The disease is characterized by microscopic lesions in the brain. It has an irreversible, progressive course and ends in complete mental and physical disability (see Fischman, 1984). Originally, scientists believed that Alzheimer's disease was caused by arteriosclerosis or "hardening of the arteries." However, researchers now believe that the disease is due to other causes—all of which are unknown. Unfortunately, there is no known prevention for Alzheimer's disease, no specific treatment, and no known solution. It is commonly believed that about 5 to 6 percent of the U.S. population age 65 and over is affected by Alzheimer's disease.

Alzheimer's disease is sometimes called *pre-senile dementia*. The disease is so named because it presents a syndrome of senile dementia that appears at a "comparatively early age, sometimes before the age of 50" (Colville, Costello & Rouke, 1968, p. 198). According to Butler & Lewis "the pre-senile dementias are a group of cortical brain diseases that look clinically like the senile dementias seen in older people but occur earlier, in the 40- and 50-year age groups. Intellectual deterioration and personality disintegration are two predominant features" (1977, p. 88). Also present are such symptoms as impairment of memory and judgment, incoherence in speech, disorientation, restlessness, delirium, and confusion. As the disease progresses individuals are less able to care for themselves. Butler & Lewis vividly describe the progression of Alzheimer's disease.

> The clinical appearance is one of rapid mental deterioration beginning with marked mental deficits and tendencies toward agitation. It proceeds toward more severe symptoms such as incoherence, aphasia, agnosia, apraxia, Parkinsonism-like gait and convulsive seizures. Later, the person becomes rigid and may become unable to stand and walk; eventually utter helplessness prevails, with incontinence and marasmus. (1977, p. 88)

***Effect of Alzheimer's Disease on the Family.*** Alzheimer's disease can have a devastating and long-lasting effect on families. Consider the following case example:

> Sharon Lofton's husband was vice president of a small manufacturing firm when he was diagnosed as having Alzheimer's disease. He was then 51 years old. His was a rather slow process of withdrawal from his job, his friends, and various social contacts. Mr. Lofton was forced to retire at age 58. The disease had depleted the family savings. As a result the family was forced to move to cheaper quarters, thus leaving behind established friendships and familiar surroundings. This pattern continued for the next five years as the Loftons moved four more times. The firm for which Mr. Lofton was employed terminated his pension, disability, and insurance benefits because he was forced to take "early retirement." Hospital costs, relocating costs, legal expenses, and living expenses depleted all of the Loftons' reserves.

As Mr. Lofton's health deteriorated his wife became his round-the-clock caretaker.
The stress and strain of caring for her husband left Mrs. Lofton physically and
emotionally exhausted. She confided in one of her friends that "it became frightening
living with this stranger who might push me or twist my arm or throw things at the
television. The loving, softspoken husband I once knew was no longer there."
The caretaking role became so exhausting and trying for Mrs. Lofton that she
eventually decided to place her husband in a nursing home—a decision that was
made only as a last resort.

Family members exhibit a range of feelings and reactions toward the
person with Alzheimer's disease. Some individuals experience feelings of
anger and resentment; others feel helpless and/or overwhelmed; and others
feel demoralized and devastated. None of these emotions is, however, out
of the ordinary. As the disease progresses and the ill person's health worsens,
family members experience the loss of a meaningful relationship; they mourn
for the way the person used to be.

**Discussion Questions.**  Mrs. Lofton learned that her husband had Alzheimer's disease when he was 51 years old. Considering the pervasiveness of
the disease and the heavy toll it exerts on families as well as on victims,
what kind of educational information and practical advice would have aided
the Loftons at the outset? Be specific in your answers. What kind of professional community resources should have been contacted by Mrs. Lofton
for her husband? For herself? How can clinical social workers plan to meet
the needs of elderly with problems similar to the Loftons'? What kind of
professional and community efforts are needed?

## ERIKSON'S PSYCHOSOCIAL THEORY

Of all the ego psychologists Erik Erikson is believed to have had the
greatest impact on the field of aging. Erikson postulated that development
occurs through a series of stages—from childhood through old age. Each
stage marks a major adjustment people must make to their social environment. Erikson identified eight stages of life. Each stage mirrors a crisis or
conflict in development (see Erikson, 1963). The critical factor is how people
adjust to each problem area, because some resolution of each age-specific
task or conflict must be found before a new stage can begin and a new
task is presented to the developing ego.

Erikson proposed that four stages occur during childhood. The first stage
(from infancy to about one year of age) is marked by the conflict of trust
versus mistrust. If infants' needs are met and attention and affection are
provided, they will emerge from this stage with the feeling that the world
is a safe place. Learning that they can cope with minor infringements on
their safety will enable them to feel they have qualities of worthiness.

Stage two deals with autonomy and doubt. During this period (about one to three years of age), children learn to master their bodies. They also begin exploring their world. Elkind points out that "if parents recognize that the young child needs to do what he is capable of doing at his own pace and in his own time, then he develops a sense that he is able to control his muscles, his impulses, himself and, not insignificantly, his environment—the sense of autonomy" (1977, p. 5).

In the third stage the four- to five-year-old has the task of building initiative rather than guilt. Children enter the preschool years with a body they "own" (are consciously aware of) and with the knowledge that they are independent persons. How others react to the child's activities during this period will influence whether a sense of pride and initiative is felt or guilt results.

The fourth stage occurs between ages 6 and 11. Children are confronted with the conflict of industry versus inferiority. Those who are encouraged to be interested in and explore things will leave this stage enjoying productivity and being industrious. If at this time children are given little encouragement and experience little success, they likely will feel inferior.

In stage five young people move into adolescence (roughly between the ages of 12 and 18). They are faced with the basic task of identity versus identity diffusion—an inner struggle. According to Evans (1967) "identity" means an integration of all previous identifications and self-images including the negative ones. Identity formation is the synthesizing of the basic drive, endowment, and opportunities. What emerges is an identity youths can recognize and accept. "During the late teenage years, young people struggle with such issues as achieving a sexual identity and thinking about a career choice" (Barrow & Smith, 1983, p. 52).

After ego identity is established young people once again turn their interests outside themselves. They are beyond the crisis of doubting what and who they are. They now have energy to push forward—toward the world. This is the sixth stage (commonly referred to as young adulthood) the time of dating, serious courtships, and early married life. Erikson believes that at this time the resolution of intimacy over isolation is important. Intimacy means the ability to fuse one's identity with another's without fear of losing oneself. It is the ability to be intimate that makes marriage possible as a chosen bond. Without intimacy marriage is meaningless.

The seventh stage occurs once individuals reach middle age. Erikson believes that middle-aged adults will either be preoccupied with themselves or become concerned about others. Thus Erikson refers to the task of generativity versus self-absorption. During this stage individuals begin to take their place in society and to help in the development and perfection of whatever society produces. To create, to take care of, and to share are the positive outcomes of middle adulthood.

By the time individuals move into the last stage of life, many of their major efforts are nearing completion. The task they must accomplish is to establish ego integrity. As used in Erikson's theory integrity refers to an ability to accept the facts of one's life and to face death without great fear. Older people who have achieved a sense of integrity look back on their lives with satisfaction. They genuinely appreciate themselves and know that their life experiences and their individuality are due to an accumulation of personal satisfactions and crises.

Integrity is "the acceptance of one's one and only life cycle as something that had to be and that, by necessity, permitted no other substitutions" (Erikson, 1963, p. 268). The older adult, in order to experience integrity, must accept a lifelong series of conflicts, failures, pain, and disappointment and incorporate them into his or her self-image. This is a comparatively difficult process (see Newman & Newman, 1975).

The other side of integrity is despair. Adults are much more likely to emerge despondent from the integrity versus despair crisis than are infants to emerge distrustful from the trust versus mistrust crisis. If individuals fail to achieve ego integrity, they will look back on their lives as a series of missed opportunities and missed directions: In their twilight years they will realize that it is too late to start again. For such individuals the inevitable result is a sense of despair about what might have been (see Elkind, 1977).

## SUMMARY

Gerontology is the systematic study of the aging process, a process that involves biophysiological, psychological, and social factors. Each of these factors is interdependent. For instance, one's physical condition affects social behavior and vice versa.

The physical, psychological, and social changes that accompany advancing age often place older people under stress. While some of the elderly can tolerate various situations with minimal stress, others are unable to do so. Although stress and adaptation to stress are necessary parts of living, an individual's capacity to deal with stress and resolve crises is quite different during different parts of the life cycle. Overall, however, stress greatly taxes the adaptive resources of the older person's biopsychosocial systems.

Change experienced as loss is viewed by the authors as a predominant theme in the lives of the elderly. Loss inevitably accompanies advancing age. Although each loss may be experienced as trying and difficult, older people are challenged to readjust and to find effective methods of dealing with their losses. The majority of the elderly are able to draw on years of experience and coping abilities that have held them in good stead throughout their lives.

All people as they age experience physiological changes. Such changes in the elderly result in a gradual decline in performance of the body's various organs and organ systems.

The behavioral aspect of the psychology of aging includes a number of areas. Among these we have discussed the following: the senses, intelligence, memory, learning, problem solving, and psychomotor performance changes.

Losses also take place on the social level. Some of the most obvious social losses are: retirement (which affects income, lifestyle, social status, and social role), widowhood, and relocation.

The most commonly reported chronic conditions by persons 65 and over are arthritis, hypertension, heart conditions, and visual impairments. If older people are to maintain optimal levels of health, they must begin to take advantage of those preventive strategies that are known to be effective.

Erik Erikson's eight stages of life provide the basic framework for viewing personality development from childhood through old age. Erikson recognized that personality development continued throughout the life cycle and that the "individual continues to establish new orientations to self and the social world" (see Barrow & Smith, 1983, p. 51).

# Chapter 2

# Chapter 2

# Intervention with the elderly: levels and roles

## INTRODUCTION

In this chapter we will discuss the three major levels of intervention—primary, secondary, and tertiary. These interventions are not mutually exclusive (see Goldberg & Deutsch, 1977).

Primary prevention is advanced actions aimed at stopping or forestalling something, and thereby rendering it ineffective. If, for example, people are careful about maintaining good dietary or nutritional standards throughout their lives, they may succeed in warding off the chronic conditions that characterize the aging process. By taking advantage of preretirement counseling programs, older people are able to plan more realistically for their financial, social, and psychological future, thereby reducing or eliminating much of the stress and resultant illness associated with aging.

Secondary or "remedial interventions can also be thought of as preventive in the sense that they have the secondary purpose of forestalling the subsequent development of even less desirable states" (Goldberg & Deutsch, 1977, p. 416). Interventions at the secondary level are designed to deal with a problem situation or condition that already exists. For instance, an elderly couple's marriage is threatened by the husband's retirement. A social worker—with the older couple's assistance—can initiate a set of change procedures designed to modify the situation and bring it back to a more effective level of functioning.

Interventions at the tertiary level attempt to ameliorate the effects of an already dysfunctional condition and help individuals or families regain as much of their typical functioning as possible. Tertiary interventions suggest more serious behavior problems or a more deteriorated condition than those found at the secondary level. Behavior problems at this level will require more intense remedial strategies. For example, elderly people in nursing homes often become totally dependent on the staff: many require custodial care. But there may be some things, however minimal, they can do for them-selves. To prevent total dependency staff needs to ascertain if these residents can take care of their own personal needs, walk for brief periods of time, participate in nursing home activities, and so on. Tertiary or rehabilitative interventions can be considered preventive since an effort is made to modify the effects of a problem or to modify the problem itself, so individuals can regain as much of their typical functioning as possible.

The most important goal for the helping professional is to endeavor to maintain older people at optimal levels of functioning. Yet it should be noted that such professionals as doctors frequently find that older patients have come to them at a very advanced stage in their illness. Visiting nurses seeing older persons in their own homes are often faced with two problems—a sick patient and the collapse of the social environment. Social workers frequently discover that the family has valiantly managed to keep the bedrid-den and/or mentally disturbed older person in the home until the only re-course is institutionalization. Finally, a concerned neighbor finds an older person sitting alone in a dimly lighted room and discovers that this person has not eaten in the past three days. In the face of an imposing array of age-linked changes and the consequent high risk for the aged of hazards that would be trivial for a younger person, it is incumbent that preventive measures for health maintenance be stressed.

The reader is challenged to consider the significance of preventive mea-sures to avoid, delay, or modify certain age-linked problems and/or changes.

"From its beginnings social work has seen its function as preventive as well as remedial" (Brill, 1973, p. 99). Richmond conceptualized prevention to be

> One of the end results of a series of processes which include research, individ-ual treatment, public education, and then (by retraced steps) back to the admin-istrative adaptations which make the intent of the legislation real again in the individual's case. (1930, p. 587)

Probably the best explanation of Richmond's statement comes from Witt-man, who pointed out that "a wise society would learn to apply knowledge about human behavior and social systems to develop humane social policies and create mechanisms that would eventually prevent the onset of prob-lems." (1977, p. 1052)

Although much has been written about the concept primary prevention, according to Roskin "most social work practice and training focused on early identification, limitation of disability, and rehabilitation" (1980, p. 192). At this point the reader may ask, "What is preventive social work"? Wittman clearly states that preventive social work is "An organized and systematic effort to apply knowledge about social health and pathology in such a manner as to enhance and preserve the social and mental health of individuals, families, and communities." (1977, p. 1049)

The kinds of activities that are essential here are those that can avert or discourage the development of specific social problems, or delay or control the growth of such problems when early symptoms present themselves.

Let us examine a hypothetical situation. Suppose people in various towns in the United States are concerned about improper diet, smoking, and lack of exercise among their elderly residents. Public and private funding have been made available to study the problem for the purpose of finding ways to improve the physical and physiological well-being of people as they age. People in three small towns in New Jersey are asked to become involved in a preventive project to test whether a mass media campaign alone or a mass media campaign combined with intensive, small-group discussions can affect behaviors associated with high rates of cardiovascular disease—improper diet, smoking, and lack of exercise.

Of the three towns involved one is selected as a control group. That is, this town receives whatever information about diseases related to the cardiovascular system that would customarily be made available to its citizens. The other two towns conduct a mass media campaign that emphasizes the linkages between personal habits (smoking, eating, exercise) over the course of one's life and the major cause of mortality, cardiovascular disease—particularly among the elderly. In addition, one of the two towns holds a series of discussion groups aimed at high-risk persons in which the content of these mass media ideas is brought home directly and personally. The results are very encouraging—especially when both forms of prevention are used.

Prevention or preventive activities can take different forms. Some activities are more complex than others and would require knowledge of a number of causal factors in order to be effective. Prevention at the level illustrated in the hypothetical example would require among other things knowledge of biological and physiological causal factors as well as an understanding of what individuals themselves contribute to their physical and physiological functioning.

In another prevention situation a number of preretirees, ages 55 to 60, were involved in an intensive preretirement program that provided information and education on retirement. The company-sponsored program lasted five years (until those aged 60 reached age 65 and decided to retire). The program was designed to test the hypothesis that involvement in a preretirement counseling program leads to a successful transition to retirement. The preretirees received every conceivable form of information and educational experience: personalized counseling and financial planning; information about health and health insurance; legal information about wills, probate, and so on; information about creative uses of leisure including volunteerism; consumer issues and concerns; mental health; concerns of widowhood or widowerhood; safety issues in the home and in the community; taxes—liabilities and benefits; jobs and earning opportunities; death and dying; care of pets; housing and moving; coping with crime in the home and on the street; and so forth. The sessions lasted 2 hours a day, 3 days a week for 60 months (plus a 3-year follow-up to observe how those who had retired were faring).

The preventers had a control group of preretirees who did not receive this enriched program but rather got whatever standard information about retirement the company had to offer. The results were very encouraging—especially for the preventers. There were significant changes in terms of the retirees' ability to assume new roles, use their leisure time creatively, develop positive attitudes about the future, sustain community involvement, and so on.

Social workers are not currently as involved in preretirement counseling activities as often as they should be. So often a social worker's contact with the elderly comes only after retirement, when people are experiencing difficulty making the transition to retired life. Involvement in preventive activities at an early stage can avoid the economic stresses, emotional conflicts, and interpersonal tensions that retirement often brings.

## DEFINITIONS OF PRIMARY, SECONDARY, AND TERTIARY INTERVENTION

According to Bartlett, intervention is the "action of the practitioner which is directed to some part of the social system or social process with the intention of inducing change in it" (1970, p. 161). "Intervention aims at making a difference in outcome and in the course of events. It is guided by a constellation of values, purposes, and knowledge and is based upon legal or institutional sanctions" (Lowy, 1979, p. 49).

Generally, when one thinks of prevention, terminology such as secondary and tertiary prevention come to mind, and these terms are frequently equated with treatment and rehabilitation—in that order. There is, however, less agreement about the meaning and nature of the term *primary prevention*. Bloom pointed out that "even a brief review of the literature reveals such a diversity of meanings of this term as to require a concerted effort at a common working definition" (1981, p. 6).

It is reasonable to assume, and most people would agree, that society would be better served if scientists were able to prevent a problem rather than cure one. Yet prevention as a concept, and perhaps as a strategy, is vague and is given a variety of meanings. A starting point is to present the lay meaning of the term *prevention*. One dictionary gives a series of related definitions including the following:

> Prevention implies a stopping or keeping from happening, as by some prior action or by interposing an obstacle or impediment; suggests advance action to stop something in its course and thereby make it ineffective; implies a making impossible by shutting off every possibility of occurrence; suggests the preventing of some unfavorable outcome by taking the necessary anticipatory measures; suggests a warding off of imminent danger or misfortune. (*Webster's New World Dictionary*, 1970, p. 1127)

But this definition is imprecise and suggests no specific directions or activities that would be useful in warding off unfavorable outcomes or the like. A more useful definition of prevention is found in Young's *Dictionary of Social Welfare*. Prevention is defined as "activities which are designed to establish wholesome or acceptable modes of behavior, especially as a means of preventing delinquency, disease, and so on" (1948, p. 157).

Bloom (1981) believes that Young's (1948) definition of prevention allows for a more conceptual analysis of the term. Even though the concept of prevention evolved several years ago, in only a few problem areas such as delinquency and child guidance has social work as a profession attempted to apply it (Friedlander & Apte, 1980).

In public health, however, prevention is given the highest priority. "Public health theoreticians have established a model that identifies level of prevention and specifies the interventions effective at each level" (Wittman, 1977, p. 1050).

In general, the public health approach represents a modification of what is usually referred to as the disease-medical model. In this model disease is perceived as a phenomenon that passes through defined and specified stages as it develops. Certain diseases have distinctive patterns in their natural histories. Bloom points out that:

> A specific microorganism causes specific pathologic changes that have characteristic and usually sequential signs (those events detectable by means of instruments) and symptoms (those events observable directly by the victim and others). Such a natural history of disease can be used as a frame of reference for mobilizing action. (1981, p. 9)

Causal factors in the disease-medical model are usually attributed to existing biological states and conditions. Thus Bloom observed that:

> The public health variation of the disease-medical model expanded the boundaries of possible causal factors to include not only the biological, but also the physical and social environments. It also investigated what the victims themselves contributed to their own problems, and how the causal agents and their vectors or carriers are implicated. (1980, p. 11)

There is a wide spectrum of preventive activities in the field of public health. For instance, Leavell and Clark (1958) specified a range of preventive activities along a continuum of problem severity with "absolute prevention at one end and rehabilitation (prevention of further disability) at the other" (see Friedlander & Apte, 1980, p. 370). Leavell and Clark (1953) divide this continuum into the following levels:

1. **Health Promotion.** The procedures employed in promoting health are not directed at any particular disease or disorder but serve to further general good health and well-being. Health education and motivation are vitally important in this connection. Procedures that promote good health

include maintaining a good standard of nutrition, which is adjusted according to the various developmental phases of life, and taking into account rapid growth and development in infancy and early childhood, the physiologic changes that are associated with adolescence, the extra demands of pregnancy, and the variations in nutritional requirements of the aged as compared with those of the young adult.

For instance, suppose people are concerned about improper diet and lack of exercise among the elderly. Public and private funds have been made available to study this problem. The funding agencies recognize that the provision of adequate nutritional care and appropriate forms of exercise are important to the total well-being of the elderly—their feelings, socioeconomic status, and health status. For instance, good nutrition "makes its greatest impact when a pattern of good eating has continued throughout a life span. The influences of eating practices are continuous and cumulative" (Marble & Patterson, 1975, p. 207).

Chronic conditions such as heart disease, stroke, and cancer are permanent and may incapacitate an individual for a long period of time. They are also physically, financially, socially, and emotionally taxing. Indeed, chronic illnesses impact upon the families of the elderly and upon society in general. Thus it is incumbent upon all helping professions to inquire how these debilitating conditions might be mitigated. Maccoby and Farquhar (1975) have successfully used mass media procedures on a communitywide level to inform the public of how personal habits—primarily dietary patterns, cigarette smoking, overeating, and exercise—heighten the risk of premature heart disease and to change longstanding risk-related behaviors.

Multimedia campaigns included television programs and spot announcements, radio programming, newspaper articles and advertisements, posters, and direct mailings. All of these techniques were used to create interest in the health program, which focused on personal habits. Instructional manuals and personal influence relying on modeling, guided practice, and feedback reinforcement were used to change habits injurious to health. Medical examinations of people selected from the community revealed that these media campaigns produced significant reduction in risk-related behavior.

2. **Specific Protection.** This is prevention in its strictest sense. It comprises measures applicable to a particular disease or group of diseases whose purposes are to intercept the causes before they involve man, such causes being those related to the agent, the host himself, or the environment.

Epidemiological surveys often provide information about differential risks older people face with respect to heart disease. Personal habits such as smoking, eating foods rich in cholesterol, and not getting sufficient exercise have been empirically associated with the health condition. Large numbers of older persons—the population at risk—have no doubt been exposed to prevention-oriented communiques emanating from the mass media. In addition, small discussion groups have been employed in a variety of settings (that is, multipurpose senior citizen centers, retirement communities, community colleges, and so on) frequented by older people regarding how to affect attitude and behavior change.

3. **Early Recognition and Prompt Treatment.**   The obvious objectives of early recognition and prompt treatment are to prevent spread to others if the disease is communicable; to cure or arrest the disease process; to prevent complications or sequela; and to shorten the period of disability. The foundation of the ideal control program is case finding in the early stage of disease when treatment is most effective.

   According to Crandall (1980) many of the physical conditions with which the aged are afflicted can be prevented or treated successfully after onset. A number of health problems experienced by the elderly are not necessarily a consequence of growing old. Instead, "factors such as exercise, diet, environment, health care, and stress are all related to health" (Crandall, 1980, p. 157). Even after older people develop certain chronic conditions such as heart disease, stroke, and arthritis, a regimen of regular and appropriate exercise can help to mitigate against such conditions.

   Crandall further points out that "whereas in the past exercise for the aged was believed to be dangerous, it is now widely believed that lack of exercise is dangerous" (1980, p. 157). Exercise is not just an activity for the young. It is believed to contribute to the healthy development of older people as well.

4. **Disability Limitation.**   This heading includes prevention or delaying of the consequences of clinically advanced or nonpreventable or noncurable disease.

5. **Rehabilitation.**   This is more than a disease-stopping process; it is the prevention of complete disability after anatomic and physiologic changes are no longer reversible, and its objective is to return the affected individual to a useful place in society.

   For years there was a tendency to perceive older people, particularly those in nursing homes, as not being amenable to therapy. The prognosis for any kind of positive change was poor. For example, an older person with a broken hip would probably never have been able to walk because the hip would never have healed. Furthermore, the older person's attitude toward his or her illness was negative and depressing. Why attempt rehabilitation?

   Now, however, new knowledge about hip injuries has emerged—knowledge that has made the fusion of broken bones in older people possible. Therefore, the prognosis, with healing through physical therapy, is now very good for the elderly. And casework with older people who have hip injuries is taking on more positive overtones.

   It is probably more beneficial and cost-effective if manpower and resources are aimed at prevention that occurs at the first level—health promotion.

From its inception, the orientation of public health has been to provide services to the community rather than services to the individual. But "in social work practice, the greatest effort is placed on individualizing the client for the purpose of care or treatment, and it is frequently suggested that this is the best way to help the individual change" (Friedlander & Apte, 1980, p. 371).

## PRIMARY PREVENTIVE INTERVENTION

Primary preventive intervention attempts to ward off or avert problems before they occur. In this respect primary prevention uses public health measures to protect the health of the community. The measures or activities essential for promoting community health are classified as (1) health promotion and (2) specific protection.

In the continuum described by Leavell & Clark (1955) the kinds of activities that would promote an active state of positive health and reduce the risk factors that contribute to functional declines include modification of diet, nutrition, exercise (activity level), dress, personal habits, health examinations, and so on. Factors such as these, along with others in the older person's environment, must necessarily be altered if primary prevention is to become a reality. Weg states that:

> If anything is to be learned from the long-lived peoples of the world, and from those older persons of this country who age "successfully," it would seem possible and desirable to alter those factors in the environment that appear to contribute to the declines in functional capacities with time. For instance, in a number of organ systems, such as the digestive, cardiovascular, pulmonary, and nervous systems, a percentage of the loss appears to be due to disuse or misuse, and thus susceptible to control or at least retardation.
>
> A careful examination of functional capacities emphasizes the continuum of life. The level of capacity available at 70 and 80 is a consequence of all that has gone before—one's heredity, the interaction with the human and physical environment, nutrition and exercise, intellectual and affective pursuits—in the total lifestyle to date. (1975, p. 250)

### Preventive Measures for Health Maintenance

A review of the variables below evokes possibilities for change long before the person reaches old age.

**Exercise.**   Exercise is physical exertion for the purpose of improving the physical appearance of the body or for the sake of enjoyment: It is important throughout life. Young boys and girls need exercise to properly develop their growing bodies. During the adult years exercise helps keep the body in good physical condition. Athletic activities such as hiking, dancing, golf, and calisthenics provide healthful exercise for older persons. Doctors often prescribe some form of exercise for older people who are overweight, constantly tired, and emotionally depressed.

Exercise aids health by improving blood circulation, breathing, digestion, and metabolism. Cureton points out that "all exercise provides the most benefits when combined with good diet, sufficient rest, and the proper medical attention" (1981, p. 339).

The kind of exercise engaged in should have meaning for the older person. Most older people dislike being busy for the sake of being busy. Therefore, the exercises should be purposeful and performed on a regular basis. Work activities performed around the house can provide exercise. Washing floors, painting walls, planting a garden, and weeding in the yard are among the home activities that can provide helpful exercise (see Cureton, 1981).

A person who engages in some form of exercise on a regular basis is likely to feel physically and psychologically fit. Landry advises the following:

> The exact nature and intensity of the program should, of course, be decided on an individual basis and, if necessary, with medical or other professional advice. An exercise regimen should be tailored to a person's age, sex, safety requirements, ambition, motivation, and perseverance (1980, p. 331).

While the importance of exercise is well recognized by almost everyone, the question of what kind and how much for the individual elderly person may be rather perplexing. Any exercise undertaken should help to maintain normal posture, correct joint alignment, prevent contractures, preserve strength or ambulation, stimulate circulation and metabolism, and provide emotional satisfaction (see Bierman & Hazzard, 1973). Certainly the individual's previous exercise history must be considered. If a man or woman is accustomed to walking at least one mile three times weekly and demonstrates no symptoms of cardiovascular or musculoskeletal distress, there is no reason why he or she should not continue this activity, regardless of chronological age. On the other hand, one would hardly prescribe such a regimen for an older person who after walking one block becomes short of breath.

**Accident Prevention.**   If accidents, especially in the home, are to be reduced then "the environment should be evaluated to determine what alterations are necessary to make it easier for the elderly to function and to remove hazards which are a threat to safety" (Bierman & Hazzard, 1973, p. 180). What kinds of accident prevention measures can be taken to increase safety in and around the home? Bierman and Hazzard state that

> Such measures as housing on one floor, stairs well lighted and with strong, easily grasped railings on both sides, night lights in bedrooms, bath, and hallways, and grab-rails beside bathtub, shower, and toilet in [the] bathroom are obvious precautions and their use should be more commonplace. (1973, p. 180)

**Diet.**   Good nutrition contributes to a person's physical and emotional well-being, although the nutrients required by each elderly person vary widely. Nonetheless, "in general, older people need about the same amount of protein, minerals, and vitamins as adults of all ages" (Marble & Patterson, 1975, p. 196).

Doctors usually advise people to reduce their caloric intake as they grow older because their activity level decreases and their metabolic requirements lower. In addition to changing to a diet that is low in calories, many older people are beginning to increase their mineral, protein, and vitamin intake.

In those instances where older people are taking drugs for some health condition, diets may need to be modified to increase the intake of minerals such as potassium. Food intake for older people is frequently lessened after a spouse dies. Eating alone may depress one's appetite. Real effort, ingenuity, and increased motivation may be needed to help older people overcome and deal with loneliness. Marble & Patterson point out the following:

> For the person with lessened food intake, nutritional care can contribute to well-being. Nutritional care means considering the person first with all his qualities—strengths, disabilities, fancies, and foibles—as well as the food he needs. (1975, p. 202)

There is no question of "multiple benefits in prevention or modulation of a number of the age-associated disorders" (Weg, 1975, p. 251).

**Stress.**   There is no question that stress has been identified as a major and predisposing factor in cardiovascular dysfunction: We refer particularly to atherosclerosis, coronary heart disease, and hypertension (see Weg, 1975). Stress is increasingly present in the fast-moving business and industrial worlds where deadlines and high levels of production are paramount. Weg has observed that "the noticeable absence of this kind of stress among the long-lived peoples and the absence of low level organic disturbances are suggestive of the serious consequences of the pace of most Americans' lifestyles." (1975, p. 252)

How can people be reached before they encounter problems? One approach is to provide knowledge about the life changes, both biological and psychological, that people experience as they enter the various stages of life. Another is to increase awareness of social and economic environments that produce significant stress, especially in the lives of older individuals.

Stress management seminars could be (and are) held for people who have experienced one or more major life changes such as the death of a spouse, family member, or close friend, a major illness or accident, retirement, relocation, divorce, or separation. Attendance at an educational seminar consisting of a specified number of sessions, certain topics of discussion, and so forth could be encouraged.

Another useful approach is to make the kinds of community and life-enhancing programs available that are helpful in reducing the incidence of a particular problem. We will identify and describe below several preventive services that fall into this category.

### Primary Interventive Services to Meet Community Needs

**Information and Referral.** Frequently older people do not know where to seek assistance and are uninformed about what services are available. And even in cases where people know that services are available, they may not know what to ask for. Schmandt et al. point out that "the best service system will be of little use if people do not know how to enter the system or to receive a package of services addressed to their particular needs" (1979, p. 23).

Information and referral services identify and evaluate existing programs, refer older people to requested and/or needed programs, utilize flexible and creative outreach methods, determine whether or not the older person received the needed service, and evaluate whether or not the service was useful. The existence of an information and referral system should reduce wasteful wear and shopping around by persons who are not informed.

The direct outreach approach is expensive and unfeasible for a number of programs due to limited funds. Direct outreach is an attempt to reach isolated or unattached older people through door-to-door canvasing and other outreach efforts of churches, senior citizens' groups, and various community organizations to make services more available. Thus the "use of the media appears the best way to reach isolated elderly populations" (Gelfand & Olsen, 1980, pp. 69–70). The success of an information and referral program, of course, is dependent, at least in part, on the extent and quality of the service system to which it refers.

**Rural versus Urban Elderly.** Information and referral services are especially needed in rural areas. Older people living in rural areas are generally more isolated, have a lower standard of living, and are more likely to live in one place longer than their urban counterparts. In addition, older rural Americans are in poorer health (Ellenbogen, 1967; Youmans, 1974; Schooler, 1975) than the urban elderly. The assumption that the more dispersed patterns of population, distribution, and the lack of public transportation—especially in many rural areas—result in lower service utilization by the rural elderly may be incorrect. The data presently available are too sketchy to present a clear picture of rural/urban utilization differentials (see Krout, 1983).

However, if older people in rural areas are to maintain the quality of their lives at a satisfactory level, a variety of services that can be easily and effectively delivered must be made available. Nevertheless, even this approach to services has problems because as Harbert and Ginsberg point out:

> Rural aged are apt to be less knowledgeable about available social services, more indifferent or hostile to government-supported programs, more difficult

to mobilize for participation in social programs, and less receptive to community action that supports social legislation. (1979, p. 64)

**Health Programs.**  As people grow older they are bound to suffer from a variety of chronic illnesses. Thus older people are among the major consumers of health care in this country. Geriatric health clinics—where they exist—should contain elements of both primary and secondary (treatment) prevention. Such programs could provide a wealth of information on various health conditions, as well as conduct basic screening of blood pressure, vision, and hearing. It seems reasonable to point out that any local primary prevention program could be built around educational programs informing the elderly about nutrition, care of chronic illnesses, correct drug usage, and a variety of other medical issues. These educational programs have been run at senior centers, nutrition sites, and adult day care centers. Short television and radio announcements have also been utilized in efforts to alert the population to potential health problems and appropriate treatment.[1]

**Crime Prevention.**  Because of their advancing age and physical weakness, the elderly are more vulnerable (at-risk) to violent crimes and confidence schemes than those in other age categories. Many older people are so afraid of being victimized when they go out that they become virtual prisoners in their own homes. Loether states that "criminals lie in wait and victimize them when they leave their homes to shop, go to church, or even to the mail box" (1975, p. 114). There are those who believe that because older people "may fear dealing with the police or attackers who live in the neighborhood, they often do not report crimes of which they have been a victim" (Gelfand & Olsen, 1980, p. 96).

While crimes against the elderly are a cause for serious concern, studies using data from large national samples have shown that the elderly are the least likely age group to be victimized in such serious categories as burglary, theft, rape, robbery, and assault; and they are no more likely than other age groups to be victimized in the criminal category personal theft (Cook et al., 1978).

Although there is some uncertainty about how much older people are criminally victimized, there appears to be little question about their physical, psychological, and financial vulnerability. The authors pointed out in the previous chapter that as people age, they are afflicted by a variety of physical ailments, aches, and pain. Because some of their ailments are terribly painful, many of the elderly look for a quick cure at any cost. This makes them an easy target for the con artist who is astute at sizing up the older victim and picking out his or her points of greatest vulnerability.

Loether indicates that "there are many confidence games in common use, and more are being invented all the time" (1975, p. 116). Although older

---

[1] From Donald E. Gelfand, *The Aging Network: Programs and Services*, 2d ed., p. 68. Copyright © 1984 by Springer Publishing Company, Inc., New York. Used by permission.

people fall prey to a number of confidence games, not all such games are directed at or limited to the elderly. Mail order frauds, however, may be targeted specifically at the elderly because this particular form of criminal activity lends itself to the sick, handicapped, immobile, and isolated—those who cannot get out of the house and find it easier to conduct their business through the mail.

"Con games are so prevalent among the elderly that it was the focus of the 1976 House Select Committee on Aging" (Lester, 1981, p. 37). Women are especially vulnerable to this type of consumer fraud because they frequently outlive their spouses, who leave them insurance benefits and/or an inheritance. Many of these women do not have the necessary financial knowledge to recognize the con artist. As a result, many can be swindled out of their entire life savings.

Since older people are especially vulnerable to various crimes, confidence schemes, and frauds, the logical solution is to develop crime-related educational programs for the elderly. Some such programs are currently in existence. Gelfand & Olsen describe these programs as follows:

> These educational programs focus on informing older residents about how to avoid street crimes and recognize confidence swindles. A second type of program related to crime prevention encourages increased cohesion in the community and the implementation of support services, such as escort service. Finally, most areas have some form of victim assistance programs that provide financial compensation and counseling to victims of crime.[2]

The first two programs are in the nature of primary prevention because they are intended to obviate crimes against the elderly. Well-informed elderly people are less likely to be victimized by con artists and swindlers than those who lack knowledge of the pernicious schemes commonly in use. The third approach is aimed at compensating and treating the older victim after the crime has occurred, as well as at preventing further breakdown.

**Transportation.**  A critical problem facing the elderly, especially those 75 and over, is that of transportation (see Beattie, 1976). An adequate transportation system must be considered essential because it gives older people access to services beyond their home.

Delegates to the 1971 White House Conference on Aging "recognized that the ability to function within society-at-large is significantly dependent upon one's access to adequate transportation" (1971, p. 63). A large percentage of the population frequently relies on private transportation. However, as people grow older the private means of transportation on which they relied most of their lives is no longer available to them. Thus alternatives must be available to enable older people to reach their destination.

---

[2] From Donald E. Gelfand, *The Aging Network: Programs and Services,* 2d ed., pp. 93–94. Copyright © 1984 by Springer Publishing Company, Inc., New York. Used by permission.

An adequate transportation system is vital to the existence of the community. Older people, like everyone else in society, are dependent upon the ability to travel to acquire "the basic necessities of food, clothing, and shelter as well as employment and medical care" (White House Conference on Aging, 1971, p. 65). If the elderly are to participate fully in the spiritual, cultural, recreational, and social activities of the community, they must have access to an adequate transportation system.

An effective transportation system enhances independence, mobility, and free choice among the elderly. For example, "an effective, regular transportation service that provides access to a social agency or a senior center prevents older people from being helpless, lonely, or isolated" (Lowy, 1979, p. 79). It also keeps them from being restricted in their daily activities. Transportation is also a crucial factor in enabling the elderly to "maintain relationships with family and friends" (Gelfand & Olsen, 1980, p. 84).

**Housing.**   The vast majority—70 percent of older people—own their own home (see Huttman, 1981). Regardless of whether older people own a home or rent, many live in units that have glaring deficiencies. Eight percent of the older people in the United States lived in housing without plumbing in 1970. Many of these same people lived in older units, and some lived in very overcrowded, unsafe neighborhoods. If the housing needs of the elderly are ever to be met, housing assistance programs such as property tax relief must continue to be available to assist them in keeping up their monthly payments, making the necessary repairs, and maintaining a secure and comfortable dwelling.

As people grow older their physical health becomes problematic. This is why it is so important for people to begin anticipating certain problems and to have those design features installed in their homes or apartments that will mean less exertion in their old age. Comfortable housing should include indoor plumbing, an adequate electrical system, and an adequate heating system. The dwelling unit should be easy to clean and manage. And older people should be able to maintain the full and independent lives they desire. Wilma Donahue, testifying before the Senate Special Committee on Aging, said:

> Specially-designed housing with a variety of associated services is needed by many older people who must now live under growing apprehension of having too soon to seek refuge in long-term medical facilities as they progress through the later years of their lives. . . . And who must struggle against rising odds to maintain themselves in the community. . . . Assisted residential living, especially congregate housing, would extend significantly the period of time impaired elderly could remain in the community, though not all older people are able to remain in the community enjoying the independence, autonomy, privacy, and social relationships that constitute the essence of meaningful life. (1975, p. 894)

These, then, are some of the programs and services that have within them a preventive component. In some instances primary preventive activities are geared toward the promotion of "an active state of positive health which involves promoting optimal life conditions at the pre-onset stage of problem or symptom development" (Parad, 1965, p. 287). In other instances they offer specific types of protection against particularly stressful agents. Thus, we rely on generalized institutional forms of primary prevention" (Parad, 1965, p. 287). Educational programs on crime prevention, better transportation, information and referral services, as well as specific protective devices such as outreach services are all examples of this kind of prevention.

For preventive efforts such as the ones discussed above to be effective, there must be a wide range of services in the environment that focuses on development or potential development of human problems. According to Fischer, "the goals of preventive intervention involve attempts to build strengths into individuals and systems as a means of avoiding problems" (1978, p. 38).

At this point it is necessary to point out that if the older community is not geared toward prevention, some concerted effort must be made for spelling out the importance of the preventive service or program. Older people may feel they are getting along quite well and may perceive a new service as a threat to their independence. Therefore, whenever a new service is introduced, it must be accompanied by community education so the older person will perceive it as valuable and not shun it as a threat (see Saul, 1974).

## SECONDARY PREVENTION

Secondary prevention is oriented toward the earliest signs of problem onset. This type of prevention targets early diagnosis and prompt treatment. Secondary prevention focuses on (1) avoiding the development of further breakdown in any given situation, and (2) aiding people in developing coping methods that will help them to avoid the occurrence of similar future dysfunctional situations (see Fischer, 1978).

"Early secondary prevention may be approached by two basic social routes: First, voluntary application for help at traditional agencies" (Parad, 1965, p. 288), such as family counseling in a family agency. Family counselors can benefit the elderly in many ways. They can assist in preventing premature institutionalization of an aged parent by fostering sound attitudes to help very old people manage their lives relatively comfortably while remaining in the community. Moreover, they can help the very old to understand why certain of their behaviors, which are actually functional, are often incorrectly perceived as dysfunctional or pathological. The second route is case-finding or outreach efforts experimentally launched in a variety of settings including multipurpose senior centers, nutrition sites, public welfare agencies, and so forth. Thus the major emphasis is on intervention with older people who already have problems in order to prevent the growth of an undesirable condition or situation. The kind of intervention that flows from secondary prevention is treatment or therapy, which is expected to improve, neutralize, or even eradicate the noxious, causative agent and to promote health.

In the previous chapter old age was identified as the period of life in which a person experiences the greatest number of significant losses or profound crises. Often these losses occur in succession and with a high rate of frequency. The death of a spouse, relative, or longtime friend is frequent among the elderly. Loss of health, status, accustomed role in life, and loss of possessions and belongings are some of the other significant events experienced by the older person. Generally, such losses or events are dealt with by a series of adaptive mechanisms that can either lead to mastery of the new situation or failure accompanied by impairment of functioning. Even though these situations may be stressful to most people, they become crises to those individuals who are particularly vulnerable because of personality factors and/or unduly taxed emotional resources.

Losses such as the ones referred to above tend to disturb the homeostatic balance of the elderly and put them into a vulnerable state. Rapoport points out that "throughout the life span many situations occur which lead to sudden discontinuities by which the homeostatic state is disturbed and which result in a state of disequilibrium" (1970, p. 276). This state is marked by heightened tension and anxiety. To regain their equilibrium older people generally resort to their customary problem-solving mechanisms. However, "in a state of crisis, by definition it is postulated that the habitual problem-solving activities are not adequate to the task for a rapid reestablishment of equilibrium" (Rapoport, 1970, p. 276). If the familiar coping mechanisms are not successful, upset increases and people begin to mobilize untried, emergency coping methods. If the problem continues and cannot be resolved tension rises to a peak. Golan, who has written extensively on the crisis approach, states:

> At this point, a precipitating factor[3] can bring about a turning point, during which self-righting devices no longer operate and the individual enters a state of active crisis, marked by disequilibrium and disorganization." (1979, p. 500)

Three interrelated factors are believed to produce a state of crisis. According to Rapoport (1970), the following factors must be considered. "(1) one or a series of hazardous events[4] which pose some threat; (2) a threat to current or past instinctual needs which are symbolically linked to earlier threats that result in vulnerability or conflict; and (3) an inability to respond with inadequate coping mechanisms" (Rapoport, 1970, p. 277).

[3] "The precipitating factor or event is the link in the chain of stress-evoking happenings that brings tension to a peak and converts the vulnerable state into one of crisis" (Golan, 1979, p. 516).

[4] "The hazardous event is a specific stress-producing occurrence, either an external blow or internal change, which occurs to an individual or family in a state of relative stability in terms of biopsychosocial situations initiating a chain of reverberating actions and reactions" (Golan, 1979, p. 514).

Individuals may respond to the hazardous event in their own unique way depending on whether they perceive the event as a threat, a loss, or a challenge. If the event is experienced as a loss, the effect tends to be depression or mourning. An experience that threatens an individual's instinctual needs, integrity, or autonomy is generally accompanied by a high level of anxiety. Golan states that a "challenge stimulates a moderate degree of anxiety plus elements of hope, excitement, and expectation" (1979, p. 515).

Crisis theory recognizes that during emergencies people are more receptive to help and more amenable to change. Thus, quick and effective responses on the part of the social worker can have a great deal of influence, for the client is both suggestible and vulnerable. Stated another way "a crisis is any time-critical state or condition of a person or family that requires a prompt or effective action to avoid or quickly alter it" (Goldberg & Deutsch, 1977, p. 416). If, for instance, an older man responds to his wife's sudden death by considering suicide, immediate and effective intervention is necessary.

Secondary prevention is thus intended to correct an existing dysfunctional state or condition. Intervention at the secondary level helps to solve the problem as much as is possible. For instance, if, following a husband's retirement, an older couple identifies a marital problem and decides to seek help, a set of change procedures would be initiated to address the problem in a fashion that would enable the couple to again enjoy their marriage.

## CASE ILLUSTRATIONS OF SECONDARY PREVENTION

### Case Situation of Mrs. Holmes

The kinds of situations for which secondary intervention would be appropriate are described below. These case examples should give the reader an opportunity to think about the problems older clients present at this level and to decide upon the most effective intervention strategies.

Mr. Holmes, age 72, was formerly a plant supervisor and is now retired, married, and living with his spouse in a comfortable apartment. His health is good and his activity level has been high. A week ago, Mr. Holmes came to the Family Service Agency for counseling. When seen by the social worker, he complained of continuing depression and loss of interest in activities. His physician had indicated that no organic problem was causing the depression.

The social worker felt that more information about Mr. Holmes's depressed feelings was needed. Upon further exploration the worker discovered that Mr. Holmes's wife had been in the hospital for over a month due to uncontrollable diabetes. In order to stop the spread of gangrene, which had resulted from the diabetes, Mr. Holmes and his wife had agreed to the doctor's recommendation that Mrs. Holmes's left foot be amputated. This has been an extremely difficult period for both Mr. Holmes and Mrs. Holmes. Nevertheless, Mrs. Holmes made a relatively good adjustment to the surgery and was returned home for further recuperation three weeks prior to Mr. Holmes's first counseling session.

Mr. Holmes's depression began about two weeks prior to his coming in for counseling. More information revealed that Mr. Holmes's two daughters, who lived over 500 miles away, had spent two of the last three weeks with him and his wife. While at home the daughters had cooked the meals and taken care of the housekeeping details. Both Mr. and Mrs. Holmes felt comforted and relieved by their daughters' presence and were reluctant to see them leave.

However, the daughters were now gone and Mr. Holmes's depression seemed worse. Mrs. Holmes was still weak, and her husband felt that she still needed rather constant care and close observation.

Due to the intensity of Mr. Holmes's depression, the social worker spent time being as supportive, empathic, warm, and understanding as possible in an effort to encourage Mr. Holmes to talk openly about his feelings. However, the worker was also concerned about the fact that while Mr. Holmes seemed willing to care for his wife during this post-operative period, his depressed feelings seemed to indicate that he did not want the responsibility.

The worker was aware that if Mrs. Holmes was to make a successful adjustment and avoid the development of a more serious medical problem, Mr. Holmes had to be helped out of his depression. And the way things stood, as his wife's recovery period was extended, Mr. Holmes's depression worsened.

As Mr. Holmes continued in therapy, he became more aware of how his depressed feelings were interfering with his wife's recovery. The worker encouraged Mr. Holmes to become more understanding of Mrs. Holmes's situation, to communicate more with her about her feelings, and to become more involved with her care. Mrs. Holmes in turn was encouraged to be warm and understanding toward Mr. Holmes and to allow him to assist in caring for her. The worker suggested that Mrs. Holmes be specific about the kinds of household activities (i.e., cooking, washing dishes, running the vacuum cleaner, shopping, etc.) that Mr. Holmes could carry out. The worker felt that as Mr. Holmes became involved in the household chores, he would feel more helpful and needful and, subsequently, less depressed. Mrs. Holmes was also advised to compliment her husband for his help. Mr. Holmes was encouraged by the worker to talk about his interests and concerns with his wife. Mrs. Holmes was advised to listen—really listen—to what her husband was saying and to allow him to express himself without criticizing him in any way. The worker's intent was to provide help to both Mr. and Mrs. Holmes that was practical, specific, and realistic.

The worker hoped that by helping both Mr. and Mrs. Holmes deal with the reality of their current situation, they would know how to avoid the occurrence of similar dysfunctional situations in the future.

**Discussion Questions.**   If you had been the worker in this case situation, what would you have done differently? In other words, how can this couple best be helped? What are the inner pressures to which Mr. Holmes is responding? Are these pressures realistic? What about his depression? How depressed is Mr. Holmes, and how is he handling his depression? What about Mrs. Holmes? To what extent is her physical health interfering with their relationship? Can you think of any novel ways in which Mrs. Holmes can be encouraged to allow her husband to participate in her care? What kinds of in-home services can be used to supplement the help provided by the social worker?

### Case Situation of Mrs. Cummings

Mrs. Cummings, a 73-year-old, attractive widow, was accompanied to the Community Mental Health Clinic by her neighbor. Mrs. Cummings has lived alone for the past two years since the sudden death of her husband. Her closest relative and only son lives 350 miles from her and comes to visit her about every six months.

When seen by her physician Mrs. Cummings complained of blackout spells. The diagnosis was simple: inadequate diet. The doctor recommended a diet for Mrs. Cummings that would include all her daily requirements. To support his efforts, he called the nutrition site center and asked for help in signing Mrs. Cummings up for the hot meal program. (The doctor believed that participation in this program would be helpful in counteracting Mrs. Cummings' isolation and loneliness.)

A staff person was assigned to and called on Mrs. Cummings, told her the bus schedule for the noon meal, and invited her to participate. Mrs. Cummings said she would come to the nutrition center if she could get her neighbor to come with her. The neighbor agreed that this kind of program would be in Mrs. Cummings' best interest, so she agreed to go.

After Mrs. Cummings began participating in the hot meal program, the staff person had an opportunity to talk with her about her diet and found that, despite her doctor's advice, Mrs. Cummings was eating no more than one hot meal a day and was getting by on snacks or nothing at all the rest of the day. When asked about the inadequate diet, Mrs. Cummings said she couldn't cook for just herself now that her husband had died. She knew she should eat better, but couldn't motivate herself to do so.

Since the staff person found herself continually reminding Mrs. Cummings to watch her diet, she felt that additional professional help was needed. Mrs. Cummings' neighbor also expressed concern over her friend's unwillingness to take better care of herself and suggested that they go together to the Community Mental Health Clinic to find out what to do about the situation.

In a case such as this the help of a supportive person may be what the client needs to begin to deal constructively with a problematic situation. Obviously, Mrs. Cummings still has unresolved grief over her husband's death that needs to be worked through if she is to build strength into her life and go on with the business of living. Supportive persons such as the social worker and Mrs. Cummings's neighbor can help her to eliminate these destructive coping strategies and develop healthier problem-solving patterns, thereby reinforcing her capacity to cope with life. Secondary interventive

efforts such as this should enable Mrs. Cummings to develop coping strategies that will enable her to avoid the occurrence of similar dysfunctional
situations.

Social isolation following bereavement can be prevented through support
given at the time when grief is at its peak. A close, personal relationship
is especially important in an older person's life. In a study of adult life
stages, Lowenthal and her colleagues (1967) pointed out that men, especially
in late middle age, regretted the lack of depth in their friendships. Women,
on the other hand, were able to establish and maintain close relationships
with someone of the same sex more readily than men.

With advancing age people experience a decline in the number of roles
they can assume (that is, few networks to which the individual relates), a
reduction in the amount of their interactions, and less variety in their social
contacts. A close, personal, and meaningful friendship would be invaluable
to Mrs. Cummings, who is undergoing what may be the most trying and
stressful experiences of her life. Even if she does not have such a friendship,
there may be other meaningful people in her life who can be helpful and
supportive. For instance, Lowenthal and Robinson stress that "regular contact with a hairdresser, a barber, a bartender, a delivery boy, or a public
health nurse may be construed as having a confidant" (1976, p. 434).

Social workers can help older people—at the time of their greatest grief—
by shoring up their social networks including family, friends, and neighbors.
As in Mrs. Cummings' case, they can also encourage and facilitate the intake
of an adequate diet.

The importance of family in the life of the elderly should not be underestimated. The family is one of the most influential and significant networks
in the individual's life. It has the task of providing care and socialization
for the young, and providing a network of interpersonal support and identity
for its older members. Even after children leave home to establish their
own families, they still maintain close and meaningful relationships with
their parents. Adult children provide financial assistance, emotional support,
and help with household chores for their elderly parents. And older parents
provide love, assistance with babysitting, timely advice, and financial aid.

Another way to enhance the life of older, lonely people is to provide
them with a pet.[5] Current researchers are finding that more older people
feel better about themselves and more satisfied with their lives after they
have taken a pet into their home. Pets allow older people to share their
time and themselves with a significant other and to accept the affection
of another living creature. No doubt Mrs. Cummings could benefit from the
presence of a warm, affectionate pet in her life.

Early diagnosis and treatment of a potentially dysfunctional condition
(such as social isolation) is of vital importance to the future well-being of
the elderly. Anderson points out that "It is well-recognized that social isola-

---

[5] See also Chapter 7 for additional information on pet research.

tion increases the chances of admission to a mental hospital, especially among the elderly" (1978, p. 786).

## TERTIARY PREVENTION

Tertiary prevention—at the far end of the continuum—also includes primary prevention at the opposite end and secondary prevention somewhere in the middle. Tertiary prevention encompasses and includes both disability limitations and rehabilitation. Each level of prevention is characterized by varying degrees or amounts along the continuum because as people age, changes, declines, or deterioration are bound to occur, however imperceptible. Thus older people can only exhibit relative portions of wellness or sickness. Tertiary prevention, like primary and secondary prevention, has a preventive element. According to Parad:

> Activities in this category are usually labeled *intensive treatment* or rehabilitation; the aim is to control the spread of disability and, while avoiding further deterioration in social functioning, to strengthen the client to make the best use of his available resources. (1965, p. 288)

Tertiary prevention includes both disability limitation and rehabilitation. Disability, as it applies to the elderly, has been defined as inability to live at home without help. F. Anderson points out that "the prevalence of this condition increased from 12 percent at age 65'to 69 to over 80 percent at the age of 85 and above" (1978, p. 784). The important conditions leading to disability include the following: neurological, cardio-respiratory, arthritic, and psychiatric with obesity and visual impairment.

## CHANGING PATTERNS OF CARE

In recent years, emphasis has been placed on helping the elderly to live in their own homes and encouraging them to live as independently as possible. There is every indication that all people are happier and healthier in their own home (see Butler and Lewis, 1981). If, for whatever reasons, older people are unable to maintain themselves in their own home, they may have to move into a long-term care facility. This may mean care in a nursing home, a state mental hospital, a home for the elderly, or a foster home.

## DEFINITION OF LONG-TERM CARE

Long-term care has generally been thought of as care provided in an institutional setting for an extended period of time (see Cohen, 1975). However, long-term care is often required for individuals who live in the community, in their own homes, or under other types of long-term care arrangements. Thus there is no single plan that can be called "long-term care."

Living in a long-term care facility represents a radical departure from living in a family setting or in the community. Even though the quality of care and approaches to treatment in the facility may be high, the older person's range of choices including food, bedtime, rising time, dressing or not dressing, ambulating, bathing time, taking part in or refraining from activities, and a host of other details of everyday life are fairly limited (see Cohen, 1975). To adjust to changes such as the ones mentioned here makes severe demands on the individual.

## REASONS WHY OLDER PEOPLE ARE IN LONG-TERM CARE FACILITIES

Most older people are in long-term care facilities for two basic reasons: "First, they are likely to be suffering from one or more disabling chronic conditions. Second, they are likely to lack the psychological, social, and/ or economic means for dealing with their condition outside of an institution" (Gottesman & Hutchinson, 1975, p. 27).

At any one time between 4 percent and 5 percent of the elderly reside in institutions of various kinds. Since most persons are admitted to nursing homes and other institutional facilities when self-care and home care is difficult or even impossible, we cannot know how many of these people would have been able to remain in the community for a longer period of time had appropriate services been made available.

Most older people spend their whole lives in the community. Decisions to place someone in a nursing home are made reluctantly and only as a last resort. In a comprehensive study of the reasons why older people become residents of nursing homes, Tobin and Lieberman (1976) discovered three significant variables: increasing physical deterioration; inability or unwillingness of those responsible to provide the care that they or the older person perceived as necessary; and lack of community services to support independent living.

Perhaps the most common difficulty among nursing home patients is mental illness, which affects more than half of the patient populations. Butler and Lewis point out that "nursing homes tend to select persons with the kinds of psychiatric symptoms that cause the least problems" (1977, pp. 245–246). Those older persons whose behavior is considered unmanageable (that is, those who smoke in bed, are hostile, or are addicted to various kinds of substances) are rejected (see Butler & Lewis, 1977). By and large, older people do not frequent mental health facilities or seek out mental health personnel for help with their emotional problems.

Community mental health facilities have been severely criticized for their contribution to the elderly's mental health difficulties. Butler and Lewis point out that community mental health centers "have never been adequately funded, housed and staffed. There are no standards. Inservice training and personnel development have lagged. Racism and stereotypes about the poor have been negative influences" (1977, p. 228). These are undoubtedly some of the major reasons why community mental health services are underutilized by the elderly.

Many nursing home patients have other conditions, either alone or in combination with mental disorder. According to Gottesman and Hutchinson (1975), the most common of these are heart disease, stroke, or speech disorders associated with stroke—all of which are disorders of the circulatory system. About 25 percent of these patients are somewhat physically handicapped by permanent stiffness (that is, paralysis not due to stroke), back disorder, physical deformity, and arthritis. Finally, a small number of patients have disorders of the digestive system such as diabetes.

Gottesman (1971) believed that roughly one third to one fourth of nursing home patients are likely to be confused most of the time, while nearly two thirds are alert and are confused only occasionally.

## CIRCULATORY AND PHYSICAL INFIRMITIES

Disturbances of the circulatory system and physical infirmities are likely to affect ambulation and self-care. The most common ambulatory aids include wheelchairs, walkers, and crutches or braces. However, Grintzig (1970) and Gottesman (1971), in two separate studies, reported that most of the patients (80 percent and 60 percent respectively) were ambulatory without such aids.

Thus while many older nursing home patients are disabled in certain ways, they are not incapable of doing things for themselves or without help. If older, community-based residents in need of help could have access to appropriate services that would aid them in their daily living activities, certain deterioration in social functioning could be avoided. Appropriate services include such things as help with dressing, bathing, eating, medications, diet, sterile dressings, injections, and so forth.

While the intent of this chapter is not to debate the issue of home health care versus institutional care, there are those who believe that comprehensive and high-quality home-care services can be provided at about one half the cost of nursing home care. Yet because medicare offers only minimum coverage for home-care services, "twice as many older persons are permanently imprisoned in nursing homes as need to be there based upon the level of care which they require" (Odell & Odell, 1980, p. 104).

This medicare nonprovision is unfortunate, especially since the costs of health care have skyrocketed at a tremendous pace and substantial numbers of older persons (particularly those with chronic conditions) are in no position to pay for home-care services. Recognizing this, many public officials are calling more and more for a comprehensive national health insurance program. Moreover, significant breakthroughs in medical and biological research could go a long way in reducing the cost of health care and the length of stay in long-term care facilities.

Meanwhile, preventive maintainence is perhaps the most effective approach to lessening the damaging effects of a variety of illnesses. And even this—prevention of illness and early treatment to prevent exacerbation of existing illnesses—is still underemphasized (see Butler, 1975).

## Case Example of Miss Perkins

Miss Perkins was a very small, seemingly fragile woman who dressed in a stylish but dated fashion. She had been living in the same house for over 40 years. After the deaths of her two older, unmarried sisters (who had shared the home with her), she continued to live alone. In spite of her many eccentricities Miss Perkins was likable and personable. A well-to-do, socially prominent first cousin helped her financially, but took no sustained personal interest in Miss Perkins.

Spry and active all her life, Miss Perkins became increasingly anxious as she felt herself growing older and less steady on her feet. At the age of 75 she reached out for help by applying for admission to a nearby nursing home. The idea of planning for the move was distasteful to her. The prospect of dismantling her beloved home, with its accumulated and cherished possessions of over half a century, was overwhelming and threatening to her.

Miss Perkins was quite lonely, had little money, and was undergoing tests for bleeding from the bowel. When the tests proved negative she decided not to enter the nursing home. Nevertheless, she was afraid to withdraw her application for fear she might need to be admitted at some future time. The social worker at the nursing home offered her deferred status. This meant that the nursing home encouraged her to remain in the community for as long as possible, that the social worker would be available to her when needed, and that she could be admitted if and when her circumstances required.

At intervals during the next few years, Miss Perkins' bowel problem would flare up; a flurry of phone calls and home visits would ensue and help to alleviate it. With each such incident Miss Perkins went through the process of conflict, doubt, hesitation, and indecision. She would review a number of alternatives and express her fears about group living—especially with people she didn't know. Repeatedly, the situation was resolved in favor of Miss Perkins staying in her own home a little longer. During this period the nursing home provided Miss Perkins with a variety of supportive services including telephone reassurance, friendly visiting, a hot lunch program, homemaker, and transportation services whenever she needed to go to the doctor.

Miss Perkins was sustained by the knowledge that she could enter the nursing home if and when it became necessary. With the help of supportive services she remained in her own home for the next nine years, at which time she suffered a massive stroke and was immediately hospitalized. She died in the hospital less than three weeks later.

It is doubtful that without the continuous supportive and practical help of the nursing home staff, Miss Perkins would have been able to function in the community for as long as she did. Their understanding approach to Miss Perkins' needs enabled her to maintain as much independence as possible and, given her rather tenuous situation, helped her to avoid rapid social deterioration.

**Discussion Questions.**  As you know by now, a number of physiological changes impact upon the behavior and adaptive capacities of people as they grow older. Most older people compensate for the changes in a number of ways. Rectal changes such as bleeding from the bowel that Miss Perkins was experiencing were cause for concern. This is understandable, especially since she lived alone, had little money, and was uncertain about whether she should or should not remain in her own home.

Although Miss Perkins has been able to manage reasonably well on her own all these years, what primary preventive efforts (particularly health educational) could have been utilized by her in late middle age that might have warded off some of her health concerns in later life? Are you convinced that the caseworker provided an adequate diagnostic assessment of Miss Perkins' case situation? If not, what facts are needed to make the diagnostic assessment adequate? How do you feel about the interventive strategies used by the worker in Miss Perkins' behalf? Can you think of ways such interventive strategies can be improved?

An older person's need for casework services can come to the attention of the social worker in a number of ways. A citizen may call the local public welfare department about an older neighbor who needs food, clothing, or shelter. A doctor may contact the social worker in a hospital to help making living arrangements for an elderly patient. A nutrition program employee may note the absence of a regular client. And, of course, elderly people or their families may request help. Many of the problems for which the elderly seek help are common to people of all ages. Some representative examples are problems related to emotional and physical health, finances, housing, marital and family relationships, and the structuring of time.

The caseworker helps clients use their own resources to find solutions to their problems: Encouraging clients to help themselves whenever possible is an important part of the caseworker's job. Caseworkers may also urge clients to seek outside help from health, social service, and recreation services.

The social worker's first priority is to help elderly people achieve the best possible emotional and physical health in order that they may remain in their own homes for as long as possible. If the older person has health problems that can be handled at home, the services of a visiting nurse might be arranged for, supplemented by a homemaker service and telephone reassurance. If there are family conflicts arising from the new roles family members must assume following retirement, counseling may be necessary.

Elderly people cannot always cope with or adapt to their environment. They may need to move to a new setting where their needs can be adequately met. Social work assistance may be required to find alternative living arrangements when serious conflicts arise between parents and their adult children with whom they live.

Casework with the elderly can be frustrating at times. The resources or services that might be helpful in reducing an older person's problems often are not available. And many problems associated with aging are simply facts of life for the elderly—problems that a caseworker cannot hope to solve. Casework with the elderly can, however, be both challenging and rewarding.

## Group Work with the Elderly

Just as individual counseling services have been offered to the elderly and their families, so too have group services been made available. Burnside asserts that "group work is one form of treatment that is effective with the elderly and that should be considered in prevention and maintenance aspects of the health care of older persons" (1978, p. 3). Group work is conducted by a diverse occupational group that includes nurses; recreational, occupational, and physical therapists; psychiatrists and psychologists and social workers; and administrators of long-term care facilities.

Though social workers have led groups of people (especially adolescents) for years, Jerome Kaplan (1953)[6] was one of the first social workers to write about group work with the elderly. Group services have been offered to older people in a number of institutional settings and in the community in such places as churches, settlement houses, and multipurpose senior centers. Groups for the elderly vary from recreational, occupational, and educational to those focused on counseling and therapy. Brody points out that "group services are accessible to those who are relatively intact mentally, physically, and functionally" (1977, p. 73).

Group work with older people who live in the community is often conducted in a range of settings such as multipurpose senior centers, highrise retirement apartments, YMCAs and YWCAs, churches, Jewish community centers, and so forth. The purposes for which groups are conducted vary and may include some of the following: (1) to educate and inform older people about available federal, state, and community resources to which they can turn for information, advice, and help in the solution of problems; (2) to provide information on diet, nutrition, money management, community services, safety, emotional and mental health, consumer tips, and so on; (3) to bring together socially isolated older individuals enabling them to be members of a cohesive group, so they can give each other mutual help as well as an opportunity for social contact; and (4) to enhance feelings of self-confidence and self-competence.

Community-based groups are often organized around such topics as pretirement counseling, widowhood, income tax information, crime prevention, and consumer protection. Older people who participate in groups find them challenging, stimulating, and rewarding. Many older participants do not look forward to seeing the group end.

Other types of groups such as reality orientation, remotivation, and the more traditional psychotherapy groups are more appropriate for confused, disoriented, and disturbed elderly. Such groups, where they exist, should

---

[6] See, for example, Jerome Kaplan, *A Social Program for Older People,* (Minneapolis, Minn.; University of Minnesota Press, 1953).

be conducted by a group leader who is well educated about the elderly and about group dynamics.

A brief discussion of selected groups and group methods for the elderly is discussed below.

### Groups and Group Methods for the Elderly

Reality orientation groups are very popular and have been used as the first step in treating regressed elderly persons diagnosed as having Chronic Brain Syndrome (see Burnside, 1978). Talbee, who has been instrumental in developing and refining this technique, indicated that "the reality orientation program was developed to improve the quality of care for patients with a nursing diagnosis of confusion, defined as disorientation with respect to time, people, places, or things. Confusion may have multiple causes in the elderly. Knowing the causes helps with preventive measures" (1978, pp. 206–207). Since reality testing is an important aspect of reality orientation groups, correct information must be constantly given to the confused, disoriented elderly person (see Burnside, 1978). It is especially important to reduce disorientation as much as possible in the three spheres of time, place, and person.

To be most effective reality orientation techniques must be applied consistently by everyone in the hospital setting—clinical therapists, dietetic personnel, maintenance men, volunteers, visitors, medical technicians, social workers, and nursing staff—on a 24-hour basis.

### Case Example[7]

The reorientation began at 6 A.M. when the patients were awakened. The nursing assistant called them by name and told them the time, the day, and what time breakfast would be served.

The assistants serving the breakfast trays continued reality orientation (R.O.) by calling the patients by name, introducing themselves to the patients, explaining the food on the trays, and perhaps introducing the schedule for the day—especially what the patients would be doing in the next several hours. The nursing assistants, while giving the patients their baths or taking them to a clinic, continued the reorienting process. If a patient seemed confused during a conversation, the staff member would take a few extra seconds to reality test. The process continued all day and through the evening and night shifts.

Nursing home staff who incorporate this type of therapeutic group activity into their programs for elderly persons have begun to report progress in individual patients. Some patients have become more alert and have begun to assume more responsibility for themselves. Talbee believes that "such

---

[7] This case example was taken from Irene Mortenson Burnside, *Working with the Elderly—Group Processes and Techniques* (Duxbury Press: North Scituate, Mass., 1978), p. 209.

a program may also be effective in health maintenance for aged citizens" (1978, p. 206).

Reminiscing groups are seen as a way of capitalizing on the strengths and the wisdom of the elderly. Anyone can reminisce—even older individuals with physical, emotional, and cognitive handicaps.

Ebersole (1978) identifies the following nine major reasons for encouraging reminiscing among a group of older people: (1) to develop or enhance cohort affiliation; (2) to increase opportunities for socialization; (3) to encourage a meaningful exchange of ideas; (4) to develop the ability to articulate one's thoughts in a group situation; (5) to promote intergenerational understanding; (6) to enhance recreation (reminiscing can be recreation in its most fundamental sense); (7) to share the life review;[8] (8) to develop tools for moving into other types of groups; and (9) to promote self-actualization and release creativity.

Many subjects can be discussed in a reminiscing group including holidays, birthdays, major events, families, geographical places, travel, modes of transportation, and so forth (see Burnside, 1978).

Topic-specific groups such as music groups can be both helpful and useful in bringing about positive changes in older group members. Music has generally been thought to soothe the mind and body. Hennessy acknowledges that "the use of music in groups of elderly people is considered therapeutic and can enhance the day-to-day existence of the institutionalized aged" (1978, p. 256).

The goals of music groups vary, but among the most common are the following:

1. To improve the quality and enjoyment of daily living.
2. To increase body movement.
3. To reach withdrawn members.
4. To provide props in group work.
5. To increase or enhance reminiscing within the group through music.
6. To increase feelings of relatedness to cohorts through familiar music.
   (Burnside, 1978, pp. 13–14)

## SOCIAL WORK ROLES

In an effort to effect change in individuals and in some part of the social system or social process, social workers developed casework. The social caseworker attempts to "work with individuals and families toward the goal of enabling them to cope with the reality of their existence and recognize the need to realize their own potential" (Brill, 1973, p. 100).

In casework, social workers use interviews to identify the problems of individuals and families. Once facts and feelings are brought out the case-

---

[8] "The life review is the process by which each person comes to terms with the totality of the life experience and fashions a meaning acceptable to the self" (Ebersole, 1978, p. 242).

worker can help people understand and solve their problems and, if necessary, can secure additional services. Caseworkers are employed in nearly all of the agencies that provide social services to the elderly including senior centers, public or private social service agencies, community mental health agencies, nursing homes, and family service agencies.

Change in casework is also brought about through active intervention in the environment. Hollis points out that "when the worker actively intervenes in the environment he may play many different roles" (1970, p. 63). For instance, if the worker is trying to obtain needed resources, the type of role played may vary from *provider of a resource* to *locator of a resource* or *interpreter* of the client's need to *mediator* on the client's behalf to *advocate* when the resource is resistive to the client's need (see Hollis, 1970).

Hollis goes on to say: "When some change in the environment rather than a resource is needed, the worker may take the role of modifier of the situation (1970, p. 63). Sometimes older people, as well as those in other age groups, are forced to relocate for a number of reasons, one of which may be substandard living conditions. When such relocation occurs older people are often confused, bewildered, and uncertain about what to expect. If the housing authority has had difficulty communicating with the older person about why the move is necessary, the worker may be able to clarify any misunderstanding between the parties involved by providing essential information about the meaning of the move to the older person. The worker may also suggest what can be done to ameliorate this situation. In another situation, the worker may help a landlord understand why an older tenant decided to withhold payment of the rent, by interpreting the older person's actions.

When the worker is interacting directly with the client, the process almost always includes helping the client to be aware of the available options in his or her environment. That is, "the client is most often being put in touch with a resource system which he/she will need to go on using" (Hollis, 1970, p. 63). Thus the worker will be instrumental in helping clients to learn what the resource system has to offer, what services or programs they are eligible for, and how they can best use that system.

Older people may have little knowledge about a particular program because they have never needed the service it offers. An educative process by the worker to inform the older client of what the service has to offer and how to go about using it would be helpful.

Information about social work roles comes from a variety of sources including Hollis (1970), Federico (1973), Loewenberg (1977), Baer and Federico (1978), Fischer (1978), Baer (1979), Teare (1979), and Zastrow (1981). While some writers have identified the roles and activities of social workers, others have described the essential skills, competencies, or specific tasks they perform.

Since the list of roles and activities engaged in by social workers is lengthy and varied, the authors have attempted to tease from the various extant lists those that are particularly germane to primary, secondary, and tertiary intervention.

### Primary Intervention Roles

**Consultant-Educator.**   The primary social work role, which has the potential to impart information or knowledge about health standards and effective health practices before a condition is manifest, is that of consultant-educator. This role combines two essential activities—consulting and educating. The essential task of the consultant is to work with other professionals for the purpose of helping them to be more effective in providing services.

The educator aspect of this role can include a variety of activities such as participating in leadership seminars, making appearances on television and radio, writing articles for newspapers, magazines, journals, or other publications. The type of format available to the educator is almost limitless. What is most important here is that the educator imparts information to a wide variety of older people before a condition or problem is manifest.

In the combined consultant-educator role the caseworker may function to provide information, interpret rules or regulations, teach and transmit knowledge, and so on. This role is bound to be even more central in the future, especially since professional schools of social work "do not have the resources to supply a sufficient number of professionals to conduct all the front line activities necessary to deal with the huge amount of social and personal dysfunction present in our society" (Fischer, 1978, p. 19).

The consultant-educator may provide services to other professionals, non-professional workers, or people identified as clients. Functioning in this role the worker can give guidance to agencies and organizations by suggesting ways to increase the effectiveness and efficiency of their services. In addition, Fischer points out that as social workers function in the consultant-educator role they "can provide a whole range of caretaking (or mediating) personnel such as teachers, parents, and nursing staff with the basic tools necessary to deal with problematic situations in the natural environment" (1978, p. 19).

This role is especially important when one considers that only a relatively small number of professional social workers are needed to participate in programs involving the training of people who are engaged in care-giving.

**Advocate Role.**   Typically, social workers in the advocate role have been client-focused, and with this focus they have defended clients, helped them to "cut the red tape," and attempted to fight their battles for them.

However, in recent years the advocate role has expanded as social workers have directed more of their attention toward changing the system. Consequently, the social worker as advocate has been instrumental in influencing a policy change or changes in the community. This is, of course, a broader approach to advocacy, because the individual's problem or potential problem is viewed in light of the sociopolitical system from which it emerges. Fighting for the client's cause in this fashion, the advocate takes on an extended and broader battle, one that may eventually result in relief for many (see Harbert & Ginsberg, 1979).

## Secondary Intervention Roles

The main emphasis in secondary prevention is on early diagnosis and treatment. The kinds of social-work roles that best illustrate recognition and prompt treatment are those that will, for example, stop the spread of disease as quickly as possible, prevent complications, and shorten the period of disability. Treating successfully after onset is a primary goal. Successful treatment includes spelling out the kinds of regimes that will improve and enhance the older person's well-being. Those social-work roles that facilitate successful treatment at the secondary level include the following: the clinical role, the broker-advocate, the enabler, and the outreach worker. The first three roles are discussed in detail below.

**The Clinical Role.**   The clinical role in social work has been emphasized over the years, sometimes to the exclusion of other practice roles (see Fischer, 1978). The clinical role in social work involves direct work with the client on a one-to-one basis. The caseworker's function is to provide this individualized service. Social workers are change agents and their goal "is to bring about positive changes, either directly in the client's functioning or in environmental factors immediately impinging upon the client's functioning" (Fischer, 1978, p. 12).

In the clinical role the worker works directly with individuals, families, and small groups on problems they may be experiencing in their daily lives. The worker's strategy may involve facilitating changes in attitudes and feelings, "behavior change, provision of advice, crisis intervention, counseling, or therapy" (Fischer, 1978, p. 17). This is an extremely crucial role because "even major and effective social reforms will not completely obviate the pressing needs for individualized services" (Fischer, 1978, p. 17).

Baer and Federico have identified three major purposes of social work:

1. "To enhance the problem-solving, coping and developmental capacities of people.
2. To promote the effective and humane operation of the systems that provide people with resources and services.
3. To link people with systems that provide them with resources, services, and opportunities." (1978, p. 61)

Broadly speaking, social work is concerned with interactions between people and the various institutions of society that affect people's ability to accomplish their life tasks, realize their aspirations, adhere to their values, and alleviate their distress. The kinds of interactions referred to above, between people and the social institutions in which they function, take place within the context of the larger society.

**Broker-Advocate Role.**  The broker-advocate role is a traditional one, social work having begun in part as an attempt to mediate between individuals and societal institutions. Over time this role took on lesser importance as the clinical role grew. It reemerged in the 1960s as a primary role because many people recognized that "clinical services alone were insufficient to overcome the effects of an oppressive environment" (Fischer, 1978, p. 21).

When a client or group is in need of help and the existing institutions are uninterested in (and sometimes openly hostile to) providing services, the advocate's role may be appropriate. An advocate provides impetus for collecting information, arguing the validity of a client's need and/or request, and challenging an institution's decision not to provide services.

The broker, on the other hand, brings together individuals and groups who need help, but do not know where to turn to get it with available services.

The broker-advocate role can be focused on either individuals or institutions. Some of the characteristic ways in which social workers can carry out their advocacy functions are by: (1) helping older clients wind their way through a bureaucratic maze; (2) providing concrete and material aid; (3) providing referrals and then following up to see that the services are made available and utilized; (4) locating resources; (5) mediating or negotiating between a client and a specific system; (6) identifying a specific problem; and (7) fighting to help clients obtain needed services or resources (see Fischer, 1978).

Perhaps a more useful approach to an understanding of the broker-advocate role is to look at its separate components.

**Broker.**  All too often people have no idea what services are available in the community and have little or no knowledge of where to turn when they need help. "A broker links individuals and groups who need help and do not know where help is available with community services" (Zastrow, 1981, p. 14). For instance, a neighbor, concerned about the welfare of an older widowed woman who lives alone, may be referred to the protective services unit of a public welfare department.

In many parts of the country lack of transportation constitutes a major handicap for the elderly. If there is no way for them to move around, in or out of a community, healthy and physically mobile persons can be isolated as completely as if they were bedridden. Without mobility older people often abandon the idea of visiting friends, relatives, and senior centers, or engaging in other social activities.

## Case Example of Alvin Peters

Alvin Peters, age 73, has high blood pressure and a troubling hip condition. He could use free medical services but finds traveling to the clinic very difficult. He would also like to go to church on Sunday, but that's three miles from his home. How can he get around?

Through the help of the nearby social services agency, Mr. Peters' son learned that the local Red Cross has set up a transportation clearinghouse for the elderly that provides door-to-door service when needed. The worker linked the son to the local Red Cross agency, and the father is now provided with transportation that enables him to go to the clinic as well as to church every Sunday.

## Case Example of Myra Burton

After her stroke 77-year-old Myra Burton became a burden to her daughter and son-in-law, whose home in Los Angeles she was sharing. Mrs. Burton could move about to a limited extent but needed help and rehabilitation. Her family felt she should not be left alone: the constant demands on them were a strain.

Highly sensitive, Mrs. Burton feared being put in a nursing home, which to her meant the "end"—being cut off from her beloved family. But her family was more than willing to keep her in their home—if somehow the pressures could be reduced.

A call to Information and Referral Services proved to be very helpful. The worker was knowledgeable about the day-care program that had recently been set up at a Los Angeles geriatric center and hospital. This information was communicated to Mrs. Burton, her daughter, and her son-in-law. Now, each weekday morning Mrs. Burton and seven other older people are picked up by a van-type vehicle fitted with a lift to accommodate those who would otherwise find it hard to get into it. At the center's affiliated hospital Mrs. Burton receives treatment from a physical therapist, who follows a program prescribed by her own doctor. A nurse is there to observe her, carry out the doctor's orders, and give her medication on time.

Social workers must become as knowledgeable as possible about the total service network that exists—especially in their own area—if they are to carry out the role of broker effectively.

**Advocate.**   Advocacy is another strategy for change and deals with certain kinds of situations such as special needs of patients in long-term care facilities (particularly nursing homes) and the specific needs of older people. The latter needs are often handled through ombudsman programs, whose purpose is to cut the red tape. Included here would be such situations as: social security or pension claims, welfare rights, medicare and medicaid benefits, and eligibility for special housing; as well as problems related to probate and estate planning, making a will, taxes, disability insurance, a driver's license, apartment leases, credit arrangements, consumer contracts, and so forth. Gelfand and Olsen point out that "Today, the ombudsman programs are affiliated with the state unit on aging and work through the Area Agencies on Aging" (1980, p. 220).

In fact, one of the major responsibilities of aging networks is that of advocate for older people. State advocacy assistance programs have enhanced the advocacy efforts of the networks by providing additional support for a number of activities. These include the maintenance of a state legal services developer who provides assistance to area agencies on aging in developing legal service programs; simulates the involvement of the private bar in serving older people; and identifies and analyzes regulatory and legislative issues related to securing the rights and benefits of older people. The programs also supplement funding for state long-term care ombudsman programs and provide support for developmental efforts related to protective services.

Patti describes the advocacy system as follows:

> The advocacy system may be an individual practitioner, ad hoc group of colleagues, or the formal subunit of an organization, such as a supervisory unit or department. Its purpose is to gain administrative approval for the proposal that seems to benefit all or some portion of the organization's clientele. (1977, p. 1540)

According to Zastrow:

> [The advocacy role] is an active directive role in which the social worker is an advocate for a client or for a citizen's group. When a client or a citizen's group is in need of help, and existing institutions are uninterested (and sometimes openly negative and hostile) in providing services, then the advocate's role may be appropriate. In such a role, the advocate provides leadership for collecting information, or arguing the correctness of the client's need and request, and for challenging the institution's decision. (1981, p. 15)

**Enabler.** The worker engaged in this role helps individuals, groups, or families in a variety of ways. For instance, the worker helps to articulate client needs, clarify and identify client problems, explore resolution strategies, and select and apply a strategy. He or she also helps clients develop their capacities to deal with their own problems more effectively (see Zastrow, 1981). The role of enabler is no stranger to the social worker, who makes frequent use of it when working with individuals, families, and groups. Zastrow points out that "the model is also used in community organization, primarily when the objective is to help people organize to help themselves" (1981, p. 14).

**Outreach Worker.** Outreach worker activities include those that primarily involve going out into the community to identify needs and make follow-up referrals in a variety of service contexts.

### Tertiary Intervention Roles

Interventions on the tertiary level mainly stress delaying the consequences of that which is already clinically advanced, as well as prevention of complete disability. Disability limitation and rehabilitation are useful goals that should be pursued because of their emphasis on the potential for change—regardless of the seriousness of the older person's condition. The available medical techniques allow for healing and real (not false) hope.

At this point the reader is probably aware that the roles discussed as being useful at the secondary level of intervention are also appropriate and useful at the tertiary level.

The authors have identified some of the social-work roles that are useful at the three levels of intervention. There are others such as teacher, mobilizer, community planner, care-giver, and so on that may also be skillfully applied at the various levels. While roles and levels of intervention have been identified and discussed, we do not suggest that they are or should be rigidly applied to the various levels. The social worker's knowledge and skill are critical factors in determining the appropriateness of a particular role or roles in a given situation.

## SOCIAL WORK PREVENTION AND THE ELDERLY

Aging is inevitably accompanied by decline and changes that have negative consequences. Thus it is imperative that preventive measures of various kinds be stressed. According to U.S. census data, people age 65 and over (and especially those age 75 and over) are the fastest growing demographic group in the population. Their burgeoning ranks mean that social workers and other helping personnel must be cognizant of the problems and issues that affect the various areas of their lives.

Throughout this text our emphasis is on making helping professionals knowledgeable about those programs, activities, and preventive interventions that will effectuate positive changes in the lives of older people. This emphasis is consistent with the prevailing awareness in our society of the importance of health—or wellness.[9]

The well-elderly is one target population that could benefit from preventive efforts at the primary level of intervention, since these efforts stress health promotion and specific protection. These people are motivated and wish to acquire up-to-date information on how to maintain their current level of wellness. Health education programs designed for the well-elderly can stimulate their interest in wellness and provide information they frequently seek on such topics as how to stay fit, nutrition, suitable exercises, and the local facilities available to them.

Many older people become involved in health advocacy programs. Staying healthy while conserving finances is a prime concern for older Americans, who pay more per capita to maintain good health than any other age group (see AARP Educational and Service Programs for 1984). Thus volunteer health advocates help their friends, neighbors, and other older persons understand the medicare system and other health care entitlement programs.

---

[9] "Wellness" refers to an individual's positive, ongoing commitment to become healthier and to stay healthy.

Sometimes they address large groups of people or organize exhibits at health fairs and elsewhere. Advocates may also acquaint community groups with various film resources on preventive health care and chronic diseases, so people can better recognize their own health needs and secure timely medical treatment if problems arise.

A major role for the social worker at the primary level of intervention is to provide education and training for older volunteers, so they can better perform their tasks and skills in relation to the older people they serve. Since most people learn best by doing, social workers must be skillful in showing older people how to go about their tasks. They must also inform the older volunteer how a specific activity (or activities) contributes to the success of the whole prevention program.

Another elderly target population that could benefit from preventive efforts at the secondary level of intervention are those persons who are "at-risk" due to episodes of acute illness, but have limited access to services; or those who have experienced stressful situations such as widowhood, relocation, or retirement and do not know where or to whom to turn for help. Many of these people feel socially isolated, and social isolation increases the likelihood of admission to a mental hospital—especially among the elderly.

Preventive efforts aimed at early diagnosis and treatment may mean new interests, new hope, new knowledge, new friends, and stronger family and friendship supports. The social worker can, for example, encourage the intake of an adequate diet and shore up both formal and informal support networks at a time when the older person is most vulnerable.

A number of older people are at-risk because they are experiencing serious physical and/or emotional health problems. Most elderly people with serious chronic disabilities and impairments are able to continue to live in their own homes if the kind of assistance they need is available to them over an extended period of time.

Types and amounts of assistance needed may vary widely. One impaired older person may need help with meals and home chores, another with household management, and another with shopping trips and visits to doctors. Others need regularly scheduled in-home assistance with personal hygiene and health-care routines.

Disabled and impaired persons who require such help are sometimes referred to as "functionally dependent," which means that they cannot perform all the basic tasks and functions of daily living and are dependent on others for assistance with one or more of these essential tasks. It does not mean that they need medical attention or must live in an institution such as a nursing home, a state mental hospital, a home for the aged, and so forth. Many of these people could benefit from long-term care[10] in the community.

---

[10] Long-term care is care needed by persons who, because of physical and/or mental conditions, are unable to perform the tasks of daily living for an extended period of time without assistance.

Most older people who are functionally dependent prefer to remain in their own homes. However, one reason so many older persons go to nursing homes and other institutional settings is that they and their families do not know enough about the possibilities of in-home care.

Functionally impaired older people often give up their chances of being cared for at home without even trying to find out what those chances are. Consider the case of Louise Atkins:

> Mrs. Atkins was about to be discharged from the hospital. Her greatest wish was to return to her own home. But her doctor said she could not go back to living alone unless her condition greatly improved. The doctor recommended she live with relatives or in a nursing home. But her family felt they could not cope with the problems of caring for a functionally dependent person, no matter how much affection they felt for her. They decided the nursing home was the only possible answer. And that is what they told her doctor.

Therefore, Mrs. Atkins was sent to a nursing home without ever receiving advice or counseling from anyone knowledgeable about the kind of care she needed. The social worker who specialized in problems of personal care, the home health care specialist, and the visiting nurses' association counselor were never consulted or brought into the picture for Mrs. Atkins. The social work staff at the area agency on aging for the community in which Mrs. Atkins lived was not asked for its suggestions about available community-based services.

In order to meet the needs of the elderly in an efficient and appropriate manner, various helping professionals who have expertise in certain areas of aging must be involved. Each member of the team of helping professionals including physicians, nurses, social workers, home health care specialists, and so on has a role to play in the health care of older people.

While the emphasis in this book is on the types of roles that social workers at the master of social work (M.S.W.) level play in the care of the elderly, we must point out that baccalaureate level workers also play a vital role in their care. A number of social workers with undergraduate degrees are working with the elderly in a variety of roles such as advocate, counselor, broker, and case manager. Although we have not discussed the skills needed for social work practice at the baccalaureate level, we presume that they are being taught in practice or methods courses. Social workers with undergraduate degrees have played and continue to play a vital role in the social functioning of older people. If we are to upgrade the quality of life for the elderly, a variety of trained personnel is needed. No older person should have to undergo the kind of ordeal experienced by Mrs. Atkins.

## SUMMARY

Primary prevention focuses on conditions essential for healthy and successful living and includes the identification of the following: harmful influences in the environment, forces that support individuals in resisting those influences, and environmental factors that increase the resistance of a population to future disturbances (see Caplan, 1964). Primary prevention requires identification before a problem or disease manifests itself, and the implementation of effective interventions to reduce the incidence of a problem or disease in all population groups.

Primary preventions are, therefore, preferable to secondary and tertiary interventions because they are intended to forestall or prevent problems. Given the growing numbers of older people in our population and the limited number of resources, it is incumbent upon social workers—primarily those who work with the elderly—to have a basic understanding of preventive methods of intervention and to know how and when (that is, at what point in the older person's life) to intervene. For instance, if accidents are known to be a major cause of disability among the aged, the environment should be evaluated to determine what alterations are necessary to make it easier for the elderly to function safely and to remove hazards that are a threat to their safety.

For primary prevention to be effective, it is important to know the causes of certain dysfunctions. Brill states, "We can interrupt the course of an ongoing event effectively without knowledge of basic causation, but we cannot do effective prevention" (1973, p. 78). The meaning here is that if information about basic causation is missing, "then even well-intentioned preventive programs will not be successful" (Goldberg & Deutsch, 1977, p. 415).

It is quite possible, for example, that efforts to prevent the development of marital problems among the elderly often failed because the root causes are neither known nor understood. As a result practitioners interested in working with older couples who have marital problems are often forced to employ secondary (remedial) and even tertiary (rehabilitative) interventions to modify the condition or its effects. What this suggests, of course, is that it would be preferable to investigate the etiology and origins of marital problems.

However, it is quite possible that we will never have a complete or comprehensive body of knowledge about the complexities and processes of aging and old age. Therefore, our efforts at prevention at the highest (primary) level will undoubtedly be based on what we currently know, no matter how imperfect that knowledge may be.

A number of roles such as that of broker, consultant, advocate, educator, and enabler have been identified and discussed in this chapter because of their obvious utility in working with older people at the three major levels of intervention—primary, secondary, and tertiary.

# Chapter 3

# An eclectic perspective to clinical social work practice with the elderly

## INTRODUCTION

The eclectic practice perspective to clinical social work with the elderly is defined in terms of technical flexibility. Thus we will identify and discuss five theoretical approaches to clinical social work in this chapter.

The psychosocial approach to clinical practice is summarized with attention given to its procedures for client engagement, case assessment, and treatment planning. The direct and indirect treatment techniques used with this approach are also discussed.

A discussion of the crisis intervention approach to practice is included because of its unique and effective use of brevity, intensity, and duration in helping those elderly who experience fairly sudden episodes of severe emotional distress and behavioral dysfunction.

Relationship development and relationship as a treatment procedure are outlined as they are used in the client-centered approach. The central concepts of cognitive theory, as well as a selection of cognitive treatment procedures are addressed in terms of their implications for work with the elderly. Attention is also given to the learning/behavioral school of thought. Respondent, operant, and imitative learning are defined, and a number of operant and respondent treatment procedures are identified, defined, and discussed as they relate to direct practice with the elderly.

The chapter concludes with a case example that illustrates the application of a variety of assessment and treatment procedures drawn from the five treatment approaches. This case discussion demonstrates the technical flexibility that characterizes the authors' definition of eclectic intervention. A number of practice roles are also reflected in this case illustration.

## KNOWLEDGE FOR ECLECTIC PRACTICE

A professional endeavor such as clinical social work practice (casework) with the elderly must be guided by established knowledge. Practice knowledge for casework is drawn from many different academic disciplines and professional fields. This wide range of knowledge which is available to the caseworker includes both explanatory and interventive knowledge. Explanatory knowledge helps to answer why questions: It is useful in the case assessment process wherein caseworkers seek to understand the dynamic dimensions and elements of a client's problem situation. Interventive knowledge helps caseworkers to answer what and how questions and provides guidelines and techniques for conducting all phases of the interventive process. Formalized treatment approaches (also referred to as treatment systems or theories) contain both kinds of knowledge. Reid and Epstein (1972) point out that a treatment approach contains a supporting theory (explanatory knowledge) and a treatment model (interventive knowledge).

Until recently the custom had been for caseworkers to become schooled in one or, at most, a few treatment approaches and to use only one approach per case. Today there is a growing tendency for workers to learn a wide range of approaches and to utilize a mixture of approaches in any one case. This flexible use of treatment procedures is referred to as *eclectic practice. According to Theodorsen and Theodorsen, "in an applied field, eclecticism involves the use of any procedures, concepts and theoretical principles that seem appropriate to solve a particular problem, whether or not they form an integrated system" (1969, p. 123). The authors encourage an eclectic orientation of this nature to casework practice with the elderly. Fischer points out that "the essence of eclectic practice involves technical flexibility, selecting interventive procedures on the basis of the specific client/problem/situation configuration and, to the extent possible, on the basis of evidence of effectiveness" (1978, p. 237).*

Technical flexibility applies to all phases of the interventive process. The worker may use concepts and procedures from a number of approaches to establish rapport with the client, conduct a case study and assessment, develop a treatment plan, and conduct definitive treatment. There are two major advantages to eclectic intervention versus the single approach orientation. (1) Outcome goals may be defined in a number of different ways, thus maximizing the chances of achieving compatibility between the client's wishes, strengths, and external resources on the one hand, and the stated outcome goals on the other. (2) The availability of a wide range of treatment procedures from many different approaches increases the chance of selecting specific treatment procedures that are known to be effective in accomplishing specific ends.

Eclecticism as defined here requires that an orderly and thoughtful process of intervention be followed in each and every case. Regardless of how many different concepts about the nature and causes of problematic behavior are applied in producing a case assessment (diagnosis), the worker must use the laws of logic in formulating assessment hypotheses. In so doing he or she cannot stray from the objective facts of the case.

The authors have chosen five social work practice approaches to examine in conjunction with selected interventive procedures. An attempt is not made to summarize any one of these approaches in its entirety. The focus of discussion is on those procedures that are considered to be useful in light of the range of problems and conditions commonly experienced by the elderly, and the nature of human functioning in the later years of life.

Although the procedures discussed on the following pages reflect a considerable diversity, as do the approaches from which they are drawn, their premises reflect a common foundation. This foundation stresses the importance of the individual's right to self-determination and to the opportunity to realize his or her innate potential for self-realization.

### The Psychosocial-Systems Approach to Clinical Social Work Practice

This approach to casework has been a traditional hallmark of the social work profession. It is an open and general treatment theory that incorporates concepts from numerous behavioral and social sciences. Its supporting theory about the nature of human growth, development, and functioning and the nature of adaptive and unadaptive behavior draws heavily from both sociology and psychology. In recent years the sociological and psychological underpinnings of this approach have been enriched and balanced with the addition of social system theory. According to Hollis, the most notable of the psychosocial theorists, "today the psychosocial view is essentially a system theory approach to casework. The major system to which diagnosis and treatment are addressed is the person-in-situation gestalt or configuration" (1970, p. 35). It is not unusual today for practitioners to refer to this model as the psychosocial systems approach.

In the authors' opinion the interventive process of this approach offers a generic set of guidelines that can be followed in all cases. The major elements of this process are: (1) engaging the client in treatment, (2) conducting the case study, (3) formulating the assessment (diagnosis), (4) formulating a treatment plan, (5) implementing the treatment plan, and (6) terminating and evaluating the case. Engaging the client in treatment is a process whose goal is to establish a relationship between client and caseworker that enables the client to use the worker's help. The activities of case study involve the gathering of case facts. The next task is to formulate a problem assessment (diagnosis). This formulation consists of a systems assessment of the client's physiological, psychological, and social functioning. The systems view of human functioning or the ecological perspective (Germain & Gitterman, 1980) sees man as both cause and effect. That is, the nature and quality of the individual's total "here and now" behavior is influenced by the external environment, which in turn influences the environment.

An assessment of this kind locates the various sources of the problem and it helps to pinpoint which intervention targets are within the client and which are rooted in the social and physical environment. The desired changes in client functioning are formulated in terms of specific outcome treatment goals. Some of these goals may call for specific changes in one or more aspects of the client's internal makeup. For instance, the client may have to change attitudes and/or customary ways of coping with the demands of daily living. Other outcome goals may pertain to changes that must be made in the client's environment. For example, various people may have to modify their attitudes toward the client and/or the habitual ways in which they interact with him or her.

The task of constructing a treatment plan or strategy opens the door to eclectic practice. At this stage of the interventive process the worker is at liberty to select treatment procedures from any known approach that he or she has reason to believe can be used effectively to achieve the specified treatment goals. This technical flexibility is limited only by the nature of the targets and goals, the client's acceptance and approval, and the worker's ethical code. The worker should look to the published professional literature for those relevant treatment procedures reported to be effective with similar clients, similar problems, and similar outcome goals.

Conducting the treatment involves putting the plan into action. This is done with the awareness that the plan may have to be modified at times throughout the treatment phase because of changes that occur in the client's condition, and/or the recognition that the procedures are not affecting the desired changes. Thus although treatment should be as well planned and orderly as possible, it must be flexible and open to change.

When the outcome goals have been attained the planned, systematic treatment has come to an end. The ending of a formal intervention should be handled in an orderly fashion with special, sensitive attention given to the ending of the client-worker relationship. The worker should gradually prepare the client for the termination of their interaction, and together they should summarize and evaluate the goals that were accomplished.

That which is learned from the outcome evaluation can enhance the ability of the client and the worker to cope with similar problem situations in the future (see Pincus & Minahan, 1973). Progress should be evaluated at every stage of the interventive process. Fischer (1978) believes that a formulated treatment plan should include a strategy for evaluating the impact of treatment applications. He recommends that rigorous methods of evaluation be used to the extent permitted by available time and resources.

The psychosocial treatment procedures are grouped into two broad categories. One category contains procedures for intervention in the environment, and the other contains procedures for direct intervention with the client.

Environmental intervention is undertaken to obtain needed resources for the client and/or to modify the client's environment. In securing resources the worker may be required to perform the roles of locater, interpreter, moderator, and advocate. Environmental modification involves the inducement of change in some aspects of the client's social configuration. For example, the attitudes of others toward the client may have to be altered, or the worker may have to help people who are close to the client learn how to relate more effectively to the client. Environmental modification in essence includes working for the client's benefit with family members, friends, neighbors, members of informal organizations, and/or members of formal organizations. Specific and unique procedures for modifying the environment are not defined by the psychosocial approach.

The three major types of direct treatment procedures are called reflective worker communication, nonreflective worker communications, and procedures of direct influence. Nonreflective communications are also referred to as the sustaining techniques because they sustain the distressed client by helping to modify feelings about the self and others.

The chief sustaining procedures are communications such as acceptance, reassurance, encouragement, concern, understanding, and empathy. The term *sustaining casework* has been traditionally used when referring to the type of case in which the client experiences multiple and severe distresses along with impaired functioning. In such a case the prognosis is poor for total restoration of functional capacities and removal of all subjective emotional distress. Therefore, the goals of sustaining casework are to minimize distress and prevent further loss of functional capacities.

The sustaining casework techniques (nonreflective communications) are used extensively with long-term care of elderly clients who are functionally impaired and who are either institutionalized or housebound. In many housebound care situations sustaining casework procedures are beneficial to the emotional well-being of both the client and the significant others such as spouse, children, siblings, and/or friends who serve as daily caretakers. The caretakers of severely functionally impaired clients are often heavily burdened and need casework attention to help them cope with their stressful situation.

Psychosocial treatment may at times systematically utilize the relationship between the worker and the client as a primary treatment tool. Here the relationship experience itself serves as the therapeutic agent. Often, for example, the lonely and socially isolated elderly client can be helped considerably by his or her relationship with the worker.

The work of Hollis (1964) spells out in detail the category of direct treatment procedures best known as the "reflective worker communications." These procedures form the heart of psychosocial casework as a therapeutic intervention. The worker's questions and empathic comments help the client take a close look at the person-in-situation configuration. Reflective discussions promote self-understanding of the client's contribution to the problem and the distress of others. Insight is gained about one's past experiences, personality patterns, and current experiences, as well as from the ways in which factors are related to the client's problem. Direct treatment procedures rest on the assumption that insight promotes improvement in a client's condition or problem.

Direct influence procedures are worker actions that advise, instruct, suggest, and prescribe how a client should behave in order to solve a problem. The psychosocial approach minimizes the importance of these procedures. Contrary to traditional belief, many psychosocially oriented caseworkers use direct influence procedures. However, they combine direct influence with reflective procedures and use extreme care in order not to impose unwanted actions on the client.

### The Crisis Intervention Approach to Clinical Social Work Practice

This approach is essentially an eclectic one because it permits the use of concepts, procedures, and treatment principles taken from a variety of treatment approaches. According to Golan crisis theory is not a theory in the strict sense of the word: She calls it a "discernable framework within which to examine stress situations, as well as a body of guidelines and techniques for intervention at such times" (1974, p. 420).

The crisis approach has its primary connections with ego theory, stress theory, and learning theory. It is also related to communication theory, Eriksonian personality development theory, psychoanalytic theory, and systems theory. The major guidelines for crisis intervention have been summarized in considerable detail by many writers; among these are Rapoport (1970), Parad (1971, 1965), and Augilera and Messick (1974).

According to crisis theory all individuals, as they grow, develop, and function day-to-day throughout the course of the life cycle, are subject to stress. At times the impact of internal and/or external stressors is severe enough to cause a loss in a person's homeostatic balance, thereby thrusting that person into a state of crisis. A state of crisis is not an illness or form of deviance. Rather, it is a struggle with current life situations in which the individual experiences considerable subjective emotional distress and demonstrates behavioral disturbances. The crisis is initiated by an individual's experience with a hazardous event, which can be an external force or an internal change that triggers a chain of emotional and behavioral reactions. Events may be either anticipated such as the social transition of retirement, or they may be unanticipated (unpredictable changes that occur without warning) such as the sudden death of a loved one.

If customary and new coping mechanisms do not bring about a restoration of a homeostatic balance, the crisis state intensifies and functioning becomes more impaired. The person in crisis may perceive the event as a threat to autonomy, self-control, and/or as a profound sense of loss. The kinds of losses frequently experienced in the later years of life are identified and discussed in Chapter 1. Although these major losses represent setbacks and produce distress for all older people, they do not all or always result in a crisis reaction. In other words, all crises are stressful but all stress experiences are not crises.

The common characteristics of a crisis reaction are anxiety, depression, disorientation, confusion, physical discomfort, and a general inability to cope adequately with the usual demands of daily life. A crisis is time-limited. The intense state of distress usually dissipates within four to six weeks. As the state of active crisis diminishes, some form of reorganization takes place: This restoration of equilibrium may be adaptive, integrative, maladaptive, or even destructive (see Caplan, 1964). If individuals perceive the threat and/or loss as a strong challenge to master life, they may come out of the crisis experience with a higher level of functioning than the one they had prior to the crisis.

The aim of crisis intervention is to intervene with and on behalf of the client before maladaptation sets in. The timing of a crisis intervention is the heart of this approach. The overall intervention must be brief since the crisis reaction is by nature a time-limited phenomenon. To proceed with crisis intervention the worker's assessment must establish that the client's reaction to a hazardous event has resulted in an active state of disequilibrium, and that some form of reorganization or reintegration has not taken place. Workers can make the mistake of conducting crisis intervention after the client's crisis has passed.

Because crisis intervention is a brief form of treatment, the worker must be simultaneously engaged in fact-finding, assessment, and treatment. A major assessment activity is the identification of the specific problem-solving tasks that need to be accomplished if the crisis is to be resolved. The assessment provides the worker with an understanding of the nature and process of the crisis experience, identifies the specific areas of functioning that are most negatively affected, and defines the range and severity of the client's subjective distress. The worker determines which of the client's customary coping mechanisms are working and which are not working.

Treatment focuses on the here and now and is intense. For example, the client may be seen once a day for several weeks along with frequent telephone contacts. Treatment is reality oriented. It addresses the real here and now feelings and dysfunctional behaviors. The worker must establish rapport within a short period of time in order to give the client an opportunity to ventilate emotional distress. Interpretations are kept at a minimum; however, it is important to help the client understand the connection between the crisis reaction and the hazardous event. As the worker reviews the client's current problem-solving strengths and weaknesses, the client may be in a position to gain some understanding of weaknesses in coping mechanisms that existed prior to the onset of the current crisis.

Crisis treatment is also reality oriented because the worker gives the client specific advice and instructions about how to deal successfully with current problems. Often the worker is required to take strong, direct action because the client in crisis may not be able to make decisions and does not have responsible relatives who can act on his or her behalf. When the client has a social network of significant others, the caseworker attempts to elicit its support. Crisis intervention can utilize procedures from any treatment approach if they are compatible with a short-term format.

## The Cognitive Approach to Clinical Social Work Practice

A cognitive approach asserts that an individual's motives, emotions, and behavior are primarily determined by thinking. As a treatment approach the focus of intervention is on the client's cognitive processes—to induce changes in thinking, feeling, and behavior. The cognitive approach embraces a general body of concepts, principles, and procedures, as well as a number of cognitive treatment models. The best known models are: rational emotive therapy (Ellis, 1962), reality therapy (Glasser, 1965), rational casework (Werner, 1965), and problem-solving casework (Perlman, 1957).

With the exception of Perlman's casework approach, cognitive models and/or selected cognitive procedures have not been widely acknowledged by the social work profession. But in Werner's opinion, "whether identified or not, methods flowing out of cognitive theory are widely used by social workers today" (1974, p. 250). For instance, cognitive assumptions are implied when the caseworker proceeds as follows: (1) views behavior, thinking, and emotions as conscious phenomena rather than as manifestations of unconscious forces; (2) includes in the diagnosis attention to distortions or limitations in the client's thinking; (3) looks for the client's strengths and puts them to use; (4) involves the client in life experiences to alter inaccurate perceptions; (5) works toward client-desired goals by expanding the client's conscious awareness of self-reality and of the environment; and (6) encourages the client to take some responsibility for his or her behavior.

The central principle of cognitive theory asserts that thinking determines emotions, motives, and behaviors. When a person's thinking is distorted and emotions are disturbed, reality may be perceived inaccurately. Faulty perceptions of reality lead to more irrational thinking and continuing emotional distress.

Fischer points out that a wide range of cognitive treatment procedures "have been applied in four basic areas: (1) changing misconceptions and unrealistic expectations; (2) changing irrational self-statements; (3) enhancing problem-solving and decision-making abilities; and (4) enhancing client self-control and self-management" (1978, p. 176).

Whenever a problem in thinking is due to a condition other than organic brain damage and/or sensory impairment, the worker almost always addresses some intervention to the client's cognitive activities. Treatment procedures constructed on cognitive assumptions seem to be advantageous because they call for specific, concrete, and realistic worker activities applied directly to the designated cognitive difficulties. Most treatment theories acknowledge that some emotional and behavioral problems or parts of a problem may be caused by an individual's lack of information and/or lack of *accurate* information about reality. When such deficiencies are detected, the simple task of providing didactic information is a treatment priority.

When the assessment of functioning suggests problems in the client's thinking, the worker should give consideration to directly modifying these distortions. Many clients have serious misconceptions of reality. These distortions may cause emotional distress and/or maladaptive behavior. They may result from the client's failure to observe and attend to a sufficient number of pertinent stimuli or significant variables in the physical and social environment. In other words, individuals may have a distorted view of reality because they lack sufficient information to conceptualize reality accurately. If this is the crux of a client's problem, the worker should make this known to the client, provide him or her with examples and illustrations of the deficient perceptions, and proceed to teach the client some observational skills.

For some clients the primary cause of distorted thinking is erroneous beliefs. The faulty beliefs produce a misconception of objective reality. When this is the case, the worker must point out the incorrect beliefs and provide the knowledge required to formulate accurate conceptions of reality. When misconceptions of reality are eliminated, clients can let go of their unrealistic expectations and the accompanying distress of disappointment will diminish.

Raimy (1975) discusses the use of vicariation (modeling) for modifying client misconceptions. For example, a lame, elderly woman who has an unrealistic fear of participating in a carefully supervised physical therapy exercise may overcome her fear after observing someone very similar to her participating comfortably in the same exercise.

Ellis (1973) hypothesizes that an individual's strongly held ideas about the quality of life transactions greatly determine the nature of the emotions associated with those experiences. Much distress may be produced because an individual holds irrational beliefs about life experiences. For example, it is irrational for an individual to believe that it is necessary to be liked by everyone for everything he or she does. Ellis's treatment approach involves getting the client to recognize irrationality, to give it up, and to replace it with a rational idea.

An individual's emotional distress and maladaptive functioning may be a consequence of unrealistic and/or inappropriate goals. A goal is unrealistic if neither the individual nor the environment have the resources required to achieve it. When people establish unrealistic goals, they set themselves up for failure. In such instances cognitive treatment focuses on helping the client to establish realistic goals and identify to the tasks that must be accomplished to achieve those goals.

Behavioral dysfunction and emotional distress for some elderly individuals stem from a lack of or a deficiency in the problem-solving skills that are needed to cope successfully with the normal problems and demands of daily living. Such individuals can be taught how to apply a systematic problem-solving model to the problems of daily living. The professional literature offers many variations of the generic problem-solving process. Any of the models that are used to guide casework treatment can in most cases be translated into comprehensible language and taught to the client for application in coping with the problems of daily living (see Carkhuff, 1973). In the words of a client, the problem-solving process might sound as follows:

1. I have a problem(s). I have to do something about the situation, take some responsibility.

2. I must clearly define and describe the nature of each problem, its extent, what does it look like.
3. I must understand my problem. What makes it a problem, the things in me, the things outside of me that produce the problem.
4. What will I be like without the problem? How will I be different? How will I feel? How will I think? How will I behave?
5. What things can I do, what can be done to end the problem? What can I do, what can others do to make things change to the way I want them to be?
6. Of the possible ways to solve my problem, which way will be best for me and for others?
7. I must make a decision to take one course of action and work out the problem.
8. I must plan carefully what I will do first, second, third, and so on.
9. I must put my plan into action and stick with it step by step as long as it is succeeding.
10. I must clearly know and understand how my success came about in the solution of my problem and be ready to recognize how other problems now and in the future might be dealt with in a similar fashion.

The foregoing monologue scratches only the surface of the vast reservoir of cognitive concepts, principles, and procedures. What is most essential to understand is that a cognitive procedure may be any worker-designed, concrete technique that serves to bring about a change in one or more aspects of a client's thinking process.

Cognitive procedures have not been widely used in social work and other counseling professions. This may be due to a lack of familiarity with or understanding of the basic cognitive principles. For instance, many students and workers who are familiar with reality orientation, a technique used with many nursing home patients, are not aware that this technique is based on cognitive theory. The reality orientation technique is discussed in Chapter 7.

The reader is referred to Beck (1976) and Raimy (1975). Beck provides a clear explanation of the basic cognitive principles and compares them with those of other theories. Raimy provides a number of guidelines that help the worker avoid specific hazards when focusing on cognitive variables. Finally, we refer you to Zastrow (1981, Chapter 7) for a summary of two cognitive treatment models: rational therapy and reality therapy.

## The Client-Centered Approach to Clinical Social Work Practice

Carl Rogers (1942), the founder of client-centered therapy, believes that the focus of treatment should be on the client's immediate feelings (affects or emotions) about here and now life experiences. Rogers (1957) contends that a client gains knowledge and comprehension about personal and inter-personal difficulties, and is motivated to take problem-solving action as a result of receiving understanding and respect from the therapist. The immediate emotional transactions between worker and client are considered to be the most important treatment variables. Over the last 25 years Rogers and his followers have researched and refined the original client-centered tenets. The Rogerians' major contribution to contemporary practice is their definition of the essential core of therapeutic conditions (see Truax & Carkhuff, 1967; Carkhuff & Berenson, 1977). These core conditions are viewed as worker capacities or skills. The following definitions of the essential therapeutic core conditions are modifications of those offered by Truax and Carkhuff (1967, pp. 47–72):

1. **Accurate Empathy.** This is the helper's (worker's) ability to perceive accurately and with sensitivity the client's immediate feelings and to understand their significance. The worker must then communicate to the client in such a way that the client knows that he or she is being understood.
2. **Respect.** This refers to the worker's ability to communicate a feeling of warmth and the attitudes of concern and acceptance to the client.
3. **Genuineness.** This refers to the worker's ability to behave as an open, honest, and congruent person whose feelings about the here and now interactions between himself or herself and the client are real.

Research has shown (Carkhuff, 1969) that when the worker possesses adequate levels of these conditions or qualities, the chances of successful intervention outcomes are increased. According to Carkhuff (1971) it is possible to train workers to develop these qualities. Such training is done through structured role-playing workshops in which simulated worker-client interactions are taped and then carefully analyzed for the quality of the worker's responses to the client. Through these repetitious exercises, trainees learn to recognize and understand the difference between quality responses to clients and responses that are lacking in empathy, respect, and genuineness.

The core conditions (also referred to as facilitative core qualities) are, in essence, the worker's capacities, which bring about a relationship of rapport and trust with the client. When the client perceives the worker's understanding, respect, and genuineness, he or she feels more at ease and becomes more willing and able to openly explore thoughts and feelings with the worker. The client's expanded self-exploration promotes an expanded and deeper understanding of self. These gains increase the client's motivation and ability to take specific actions to solve problems and to satisfy needs. The core conditions are essential to effective relationship building and the continuing intervention with all cases, regardless of the client's age or problem.

## The Behavioral Approach to Clinical Social Work Practice

There is no single behavioral approach to interpersonal treatment. Many authorities have contributed different theories of behavior: All share the basic assumption that human behavior is the product of learning. Behavior is learned through one's life experiences in the social and physical environment. These learning processes and experiences are also referred to as conditioning processes and experiences. The basic position taken is that if behavior can be learned, it can be unlearned. Or, if certain experiences can result in the development of specific behavioral tendencies or habits, then other experiences can serve to extinguish or eliminate these tendencies.

According to the behavioral/learning school of thought, behavioral tendencies and patterns are viewed as being adaptive (functional) or maladaptive (malfunctional) and not as mental illness or disease. Maladaptive behavior is not seen as a symptom of some underlying problem, disease, or illness; rather, the behavior in question *is* the problem.

There are three kinds of learned human behavior:

1. **Respondent Behavior.**   Elicited by a stimulus that immediately precedes the behavior, this kind of behavior is automatic in nature and is mediated by the autonomic nervous system and the smooth muscles. Respondent behaviors are involuntary responses such as perspiring, blinking, twitching, blushing, salivating, and becoming pale, fearful, and anxious.

   When respondent behavior is elicited by a natural stimulus, the behavioral response (UR) and the eliciting stimulus are referred to as unconditioned variables. For example, fear in response to an unanticipated loud noise or a threat of physical harm is an unconditioned response (UR) to an unconditioned stimulus (US)—the noise or threat. A response such as anxiety or fear can also be a learned or conditioned response (CR).

   When a response such as fear has become a learned one (CR), that response can be elicited by a stimulus that would typically elicit little or no fear: This kind of stimulus is called a neutral stimulus (NS). But when the stimulus automatically elicits a learned fear response it is referred to as a conditioned stimulus (CS).

   Respondent behavior is learned through experiences that take place over a period of time and in which the frequent pairing of an unconditioned stimulus (US) and a neutral stimulus (NS) occurs. The following example shows how stimulus pairing is involved in the establishment of a learned fear (conditioned) response, and how a neural stimulus becomes a conditioned stimulus:

   Mrs. Jones, age 70, lived alone in an old neighborhood that in recent years had become rundown. It was an area with a high crime rate. Over a period of one year Mrs. Jones had experienced two attempted purse snatching by teenagers; she had observed numerous episodes on the street involving young people pushing, shoving, and taunting elderly people; and she had heard about many cases of mugging and burglaries that were committed by the juvenile delinquents of her community. All of these experiences had elicited fear and lingering anxiety in Mrs. Jones.

   The purse-snatching attempts, observing threats to others, and hearing the accounts of crime were the unconditioned stimuli that had elicited fear (unconditioned response) in Mrs. Jones.

As time passed Mrs. Jones began to experience frequent episodes of intense fear and lingering anxiety for no apparent reason. These fear experiences occurred almost every time she was in public places and occasionally when she was at home. To avoid the painful fear and anxiety Mrs. Jones secluded herself in her home.

The caseworker carefully studied and assessed Mrs. Jones's anxiety problem and concluded that the anxiety reaction was a conditioned response (a learned anxiety condition). In this case the anxiety was being elicited by the presence of teenagers (conditioned stimulus).

Teenagers had always been part of the stimulus field in each of the previous threatening episodes experienced by Mrs. Jones. Thus in the past teenagers had been a neutral stimuli for Mrs. Jones's real fear response. However, now a teenager who was doing nothing that would suggest threat or potential danger elicited an intense anxiety response (conditioned response).

2. **Operant Behavior.** Voluntary and purposeful, this behavior operates on the environment. Operant behavior involves the central nervous system and the gross muscles. This kind of behavior includes the activities of walking and talking. The bulk of human behavior is operant in nature. Operant behavioral tendencies are learned primarily as a result of the stimuli which immediately follow the expression of behavior. The strength, frequency, and type of stimuli greatly influence future behavioral expressions. For example, outgoing behavior at a party will become a tendency if that behavior is warmly received; however, if the behavior is coldly rejected or ignored, the individual will have a tendency to refrain from outgoing behavior at parties or will stop attending such social events.

While specific stimuli do not automatically elicit operant behavior as is the case with respondent behavior, the events and social contexts which precede the occurrence of operant behavior are significant because they provide cues for what kind of behavior is appropriate. For instance, late nighttime and a bed are, for most people in our society, the cues for the time and place for sleeping; but these stimuli do not automatically cause us to fall asleep. Cues for operant behaviors are referred to as antecedent stimuli.

3. **Imitative (Modeled) Behavior.** This is behavior that is learned through the experience of observing the behavior of others: It is learning by vicarious experience or imitation. Many of our social behavioral tendencies are acquired through our interpersonal relationship experiences in family, in school, in friendships, and in small groups. People in our lives who are perceived as important, desirable, and valuable strongly influence our behavioral tendencies. We *model* their behaviors. The reader is referred to Bandura (1971) for a detailed coverage of the principles of social learning and modeling.

When the caseworker's assessment and treatment plan includes target problems and outcome goals that are described in specific behavioral terms, the worker should give serious consideration to using treatment procedures that are based on the principles of learned behavior. The worker can turn to the rich literature on respondent, operant, and modeling procedures in search of tools that will fit the conditions of a particular case. The worker can also choose to design original techniques that are guided by the basic scientific principles of behavioral change. Wolpe's definition reflects the versatile nature of behavioral-based treatment. "Behavior therapy consists of applying experimentally established principles to overcoming these persistent maladaptive habits, scanning the whole range of the behavioral sciences, if need be, to obtain relevant principles" (1973, p. 1).

Operant conditioning attempts to shape new behavior tendencies, strengthen weak tendencies, maintain strong tendencies, or eliminate undesirable tendencies. These operations require some control and manipulation of the environment of antecedent stimuli (behavioral cues), as well as the environmental stimuli that immediately follow the occurrence of operant behaviors. The stimuli that are presented are called reinforcers.

A positive reinforcer is one that is perceived as rewarding and pleasant and therefore strengthens a weak or new behavioral tendency. The procedure of presenting rewarding stimuli is called positive reinforcement. The worker must select positive reinforcers that are known to be perceived by a client as strongly rewarding. Strong positive reinforcers for most people are verbal expressions of approval, affection, praise, recognition, and acceptance. Tangible objects such as food, money, and gifts are also strong reinforcers for most individuals. Sometimes appropriate or adaptive behavior is not shown because an individual is not aware of, or is unsure of, the expected behavior. For instance, sensory impairment can prevent an older person from picking up the cues (antecedent stimuli) for the required behavior in a social situation. An elderly person may not understand what is expected in a particular social context and therefore may not participate. Thus the worker must provide strong and clear behavioral cues (antecedent stimuli) when conducting behavioral treatment.

The procedure of *negative reinforcement* involves the removal or withdrawal of a stimulus that follows a behavior and has the tendency to discourage that behavior. For example, elderly Mrs. Jones may be inclined to attend weekly clinic more often if the intense heat in the waiting room and the nasty receptionist are removed. In the case of negative reinforcement, behavior is encouraged by removing unpleasant conditions or stimuli.

The operant procedure known as *extinction* involves the withholding of positive reinforcement for a response that a worker wishes to discourage from reoccurring. Extinction is most directly accomplished by ignoring the unwanted behavior when it occurs. Ignoring means making no response whatsoever. For example, when the elderly Mrs. Smith, an ambulatory resident of a nursing home, engages in her nasty gossiping (which upsets everyone), her behavior can eventually be extinguished if everyone totally ignores her gossip.

When positive reinforcement and extinction are both utilized with a client, the treatment procedure is referred to as *differential reinforcement.* This involves the positive reinforcement of a desired behavior and the withholding of reinforcement for maladaptive behavior. For example, the worker may succeed in elevating a client's poor self-concept by ignoring all of the client's self-devaluing expressions and by highly rewarding all self-worth statements.

Two types of "punishment" are used in operant conditioning. The objective of positive punishment is to present an aversive stimulus immediately following a behavior in order to decrease its occurrence. For example, a nursing home patient who refuses to eat the main course of dinner is severely scolded. Negative punishment (response cost) consists of removing some privilege or desired object contingent on the occurrence of an undesired behavior in order to decrease that behavior. For example, every time a nursing home patient refuses to eat a meal, she is not permitted to watch television for a designated period of time. The authors do not condone the use of punishment with older clients, and caseworkers are alerted to the fact that some nursing home staff members and family caretakers employ punishment techniques on a regular basis.

Many behavioral techniques are based on principles of respondent conditioning (learning) and involve counterconditioning and response extinction. Respondent extinction involves continuing presentation of the conditioned stimulus without any further pairing with the unconditioned stimulus. For example, in the case presented above Mrs. Jones's conditioned anxiety response may be extinguished by having her frequently interact with (be exposed to) only well-behaved and friendly teenagers.

*Systematic desensitization* and *in vivo desensitization* are two well-known counterconditioning techniques. They are used primarily to decrease and extinguish learned anxiety reactions. These techniques derive from the principle of reciprocal inhibition defined by Wolpe. "If a response inhibiting anxiety can be made to occur in the presence of anxiety-evoking stimuli, it will weaken the bond between these stimuli and the anxiety" (1973, p. 17). Assertive responses and relaxation responses are two kinds of responses that are known to successfully inhibit anxiety (see Wolpe, 1958).

*Systematic desensitization* consists of three phases: (1) the client is trained in deep muscle relaxation; (2) the therapist constructs an anxiety hierarchy; and (3) the client is presented—through imagery—with the anxiety-provoking stimuli while he or she is in a state of relaxation. If one is totally relaxed one cannot feel anxious; thus, the more pleasant response of relaxation inhibits the experience of anxiety. The basic assumption here is that one cannot be relaxed and anxious at the same time. Using a modification of Jacobson's (1934) relaxation procedures, the client is trained to relax through a series of practice exercises wherein muscles are tensed and then relaxed.

These exercises progress through all muscle groupings of the body. After practice at home and several training sessions in the therapist's office, the client is usually able to relax quickly through imagery.

The second phase of treatment involves anxiety hierarchies developed from carefully questioning the client about the stimuli that elicit fear reactions. The major themes of the anxiety-producing stimuli are determined, and for each theme a list of stimuli is compiled in order of potency of the anxiety reaction. In the final stage of treatment the client—while in a very relaxed state—is presented, through his own imagination and descriptions from the therapist, the anxiety-provoking stimuli from the hierarchy. When the client can be exposed in this fashion to a stimulus and not feel anxious, the therapist moves to a more potentially potent anxiety stimulus on the hierarchy. For a detailed discussion of this treatment procedure the reader is referred to Wolpe (1973, chap. 6).

*In vivo* (from the Latin "in life") *desensitization* is a treatment procedure wherein the client is desensitized of an anxiety reaction by being exposed, while in a relaxed state, to the real-life events, situations, conditions, stimuli, or encounters known to evoke anxiety. In this procedure the worker arranges anxiety-provoking stimuli on a hierarchy from least to most potent. After the client has been trained to relax through imagery, he or she is exposed to the least anxiety-provoking stimulus. When anxiety dissipates the client is exposed to the next stimulus on the hierarchy. This process continues until the client is able to face the most potent stimulus, the one at the top of the hierarchy, without experiencing anxiety. For example, an elderly client who has been isolated in her home for a long period of time might be extremely fearful of the outside environment. If her anxiety reaction was strictly related to distance from her home, a simple design of in vivo desensitization would involve the following steps: (1) The worker helps the client reach a state of relaxation (absence of anxiety); (2) the worker holds the client's hand and they walk out onto the porch while they talk about pleasant and familiar things; (3) if the client remains relaxed (free of anxiety), they then walk from the porch in the direction of the front sidewalk, again engaged in pleasant social conversation and talk of how safe the client feels; and (4) if the client continues to feel relaxed with each new distance gained, then greater distances from the home can be attempted. At any step along the way, when the client reports strong anxiety, client and worker return to a safer spot closer to the house, a spot where the client no longer feels nervous. A number of home-visit sessions will usually be necessary to successfully complete this kind of treatment. During each home visit a certain distance is covered; and the distance is increased with each successive visit. For a detailed discussion of in vivo desensitization and some case examples, the reader is referred to Wolpe (1973, chap. 7) and Watson and Tharp (1972).

*Assertiveness training* is a widely used procedure with the individual or with groups of clients. People who are timid or overly aggressive in their interpersonal transactions are inhibited by neurotic anxiety from making the normal productive responses that are called for in a social entercounter. Assertive behavior is defined by Wolpe as "the proper expression of any emotion other than anxiety toward another person" (1973, p. 81).

For many older people the anxiety associated with daily encounters in the social environment is caused by the complex and confusing nature of today's world. The older person may be fearful of making a mistake and being ridiculed, and therefore may avoid assertive behavior. Some older people's strict moral values prevent them from acting assertively. For instance, one may not be able to complain about the bad service received in a restaurant, from a sales clerk, or from a home repairman because to do so is considered to be in bad taste.

The first step in assertiveness training is to teach the client the difference between assertive and aggressive behavior. The client is encouraged to accept the value that everyone has the right to be assertive. The worker then helps the client identify and analyze the areas of life in which he or she is nonassertive. A strategy is then developed that includes descriptions of assertive behavior for the client to perform in specific daily-living encounters.

Through role-playing exercises the worker models assertive behavior and the client practices assertive responses.

Assertiveness training may also employ muscle relaxation techniques to help the client counteract anxiety. For a more detailed description of assertiveness training procedures, the reader is referred to Wolpe (1973, chap. 5) and Zastrow (1981, pp. 112–116).

For a more detailed coverage of the basic principles of learning theory and behavioral treatment procedures, the reader is referred to Craighead, Mahoney, and Kazdin (1976), Kanfer and Phillips (1970), O'Leary and Wilson (1975), Rimm and Masters (1974), Morrow (1971), and Leitenberg (1976). The reader is referred to Thomas (1967, 1970) for a discussion of the integration of behavioral techniques with the traditional methods of social work practice. Fischer and Gochros (1975) should be consulted for a good presentation of a variety of operant, respondent, and modeling treatment procedures.

### Case Illustration

The following case illustration is provided to illustrate the nature of eclectic casework with an elderly client. Some of the interventive procedures from the five treatment approaches are reflected in this example. Also illustrated is the use of the range of practice roles that were identified in Chapter 2.

> Mrs. M., an 82-year-old widow who lives alone in her own home in a rundown section of an old northeastern industrial city, was referred by a pastor to a nearby multipurpose community program for older adults. The pastor, after making a recent visit to Mrs. M.'s home, phoned the agency and suggested that Mrs. M. be contacted about the possibility of providing her with home-bound meal delivery services.

Armed with only the above information, the caseworker (hereafter referred to as C.) phoned Mrs. M. (hereafter referred to as M.) to make an appointment for a home visit. This was accomplished with difficulty because of M.'s impaired hearing and reluctance to talk to anyone who was "handing out charity." Only after a careful explanation about C.'s purpose for making a visit was M. willing to accept a definite appointment.

**First Home Visit.**   With her limited information about M., C. made the scheduled home visit prepared to begin the process of conducting a systems assessment of M.'s current state of functioning. From the few available facts about M. (age 82, widowed, living alone, impaired hearing, rundown neighborhood, and possibly in need of nutrition services), C. could predict the likelihood of a client with numerous unmet needs, specific functioning problems, and someone in a state of general functional vulnerability, if not severe impairment.

Repeated heavy knocking for five minutes finally brought M. to the door. A few minutes of conversation through the locked door was required to assure M. that it was safe to invite the worker into the house. M. moved slowly with a walker to her nearby wheelchair while she offered C. a seat. As C. began her process of study and assessment of the immediate presenting situation, she moved slowly and calmly, keeping in mind the necessity of establishing a relationship of trust and comfort, so M. would become engaged in the helping process.

C. took care to listen intently to M. and to choose her responses carefully, so M. would receive the message that C. was interested and was attempting to under-stand M. C., a facilitative person, conveyed herself in a warm, empathic, and genuine way through both her verbal and nonverbal expressions. During 15 minutes of conver-sation, which was a combination of reestablishing the purpose of the visit and a warm social exchange, C. observed a gradual but steady easing up of M.'s tenseness and reluctance to engage in spontaneous conversation.

After carefully and slowly explaining the meal program available to M., C. asked if she could tell M. about some of the other available services that might be of interest to her. M. was willing; she listened with close attention and displayed interest and comfort. C. made certain that M. was able to hear her clearly. With about 10 minutes remaining in her planned 1-hour visit, C. advised M. of the fact that she needed to leave soon. She used the remaining time to recap what had been decided upon earlier in the interview about when and how the meal delivery service would take place, and to ask M. if she could return one week later at the same time to continue their discussion about other services, needs, and interests. M. quickly agreed to the next meeting. She then had a severe coughing episode that lasted for several minutes. When it subsided she apologized for not getting up to see C. to the door. M. said that her legs were bothering her somewhat as a result of the recent damp weather. C. asked M. if she needed anything right then. M. thanked her and said no.

As C. made the trip back to her office she fixed in her memory the many observa-tions she had made about M.'s physical appearance, emotional expressions, manner of speaking, the condition of her home, and the attitudes, opinions, and values that were implied in M.'s verbal and nonverbal expressions. From these data C. began to formulate some beginning assessment hypotheses that would guide the focus of the next interview.

**Second Home Visit.** The second home visit began with C.'s inquiry about the meal service, which had started a few days earlier. As a monitor of the services provided by others C. needed feedback and impressions from M. All was well in this respect. C. then cautiously, but comfortably inquired about M.'s cough and legs. M. described minor discomforts in these two areas. She then opened up and spoke voluntarily about many aspects of her past and present life. C.'s close and empathic attention seemed to encourage and facilitate informative self-expression by M.

Using carefully selected and timed questions presented in such a way that they would not break M.'s voluntary flow of information, C. was able to secure detailed information about numerous areas of M.'s current functioning and social situation. From the wealth of information secured directly and indirectly by C. during this hour-long visit, C. was in a position to expand and refine the overall assessment picture of M.'s biopsychosocial functioning within the current social systems configuration.

**Case Facts to Date.**

1. Very limited income from social security. After utilities and property taxes are paid, very little remains for other things.
2. Owns the home, which is in need of repairs.
3. Husband died six years ago.
4. Has no close living relatives. Distant relatives do not contact her.
5. Has no close friends other than middle-aged, next-door neighbor who does some shopping for her and checks in on her occasionally.
6. Hasn't left the house since her husband's funeral six years ago.
7. Wheelchair and walker belonged to her husband who was an invalid for the last five years of his life. M. had cared for him in the home.
8. Watches television, does some knitting, and reads the daily newspaper.
9. M. complains of arthritis, chronic coughing, hearing loss, fading vision, circulation problems, and general aches and pains. Considers herself to be in good health and attributes the physical discomforts to the normal problems of old age.
10. Walks slowly with the walker and uses the wheelchair most of the time.
11. Sleeps downstairs because she cannot negotiate the stairs.
12. Hasn't been to a doctor in years but denies the need to see one.
13. Takes a lot of over-the-counter medication for her numerous discomforts.
14. Is receiving no social services or supplementary benefits.
15. Has a savings account—amount unknown.

**Worker's Speculations to Date.**

1. M. is depressed but attempts to hide this from the worker. Depression seems to be related to loneliness and continued grieving for the loss of her husband.

2. May have serious health problems as indicated by: chronic cough, circulation problems, difficulty walking, arthritic pain, general sickly physical appearance, and poor nutrition prior to meal service.
3. Hearing impairment may be aging related. Visual difficulties may be due to cataracts and/or the fact that her eyeglass prescription hasn't been changed for many years.
4. Because of poor health, absence of medical care, depression, loneliness, social isolation, limited income, and deteriorating house, M. is considered to be in a general and serious state of functional vulnerability. She is in serious risk mentally and physically. She is vulnerable to experiencing a functional crisis and the onset of very serious debilitating chronic illness. She is a likely candidate for institutionalization in the near future or early death if medical care is not secured.

**Worker's Plans.**

1. Priority short-term goal is to motivate M. to secure medical attention and to assist her in that pursuit.
2. Continue study and assessment in greater detail in order to determine the nature and extent of all client needs relevant for intervention.
3. Formulate a better understanding of M.'s depression and other possible psychological difficulties.

**Third Home Visit.**   C. devoted the initial few minutes of this visit to friendly, casual conversation and a general inquiry about M.'s well-being. C. (remembering that during the second visit she had not talked further with M. about the social services she had mentioned during the first interview) brought up the subject of home repair services, homemaker services, and chore service. She explained in detail the nature of each of these services, pointing out that there was no cost for such services because of Mrs. M.'s limited income status. She encouraged M. to ask questions and was careful not to sound as if she was trying to force the services on M. She concentrated on giving M. illustrations of how these services might be beneficial.

C. asked M. to think about taking advantage of these needed services and to give her a decision at the time of her next visit. C. also pointed out that if M. accepted a service and then decided she didn't want it, the service could be discontinued immediately upon request.

C. carefully explained that M. was eligible for a rebate from the county on her real estate taxes due to her limited income status. M. said she had heard something about that on TV but had not understood how to go about getting the refund. M. gave C. permission to secure the necessary forms and to help her apply for her tax rebate.

C. returned the focus of the interview to M.'s health by asking about her arthritis and cough. She gently asked many questions about the duration of M.'s numerous discomforts and their intensity. At first M. tended to minimize the health problems, but C.'s gentle persistence (taking advantage of her good, trusting relationship with M.) eventually allowed M. to admit that she was quite worried about her health, but was afraid to consult a doctor for a number of reasons. M. went on to talk about her general mistrust of doctors, who had never done much to help her husband when he was so ill; about her not being able to afford doctors' fees; and about her fear that most doctors just want to put old, sick people like her into a nursing home.

C. carefully and slowly addressed each of M.'s concerns—one at a time—in an empathic manner. During this process C. attempted to assure M. that medical expenses could be managed and that M. was not in danger of a doctor forcing her into a nursing home. She asked M. if she would seriously consider getting a medical checkup sometime soon. C. promised M. that she would help her arrange the doctor's appointment.

C. ended the interview with a brief recapping of the many things they had talked about. She reminded M. that M. had a lot of things to think about in preparation for C.'s next visit such as whether M. might be ready to accept some or all of the services for which she was eligible and whether she would be willing to see a doctor.

**Fourth Client Contact.**   One day before the scheduled fourth home visit, C. was informed by the meal service worker that M. had been admitted as an emergency case to the hospital. M. had been discovered in an unconscious state on her living room floor. C. made a very brief visit later that day to the intensive care unit. She saw M. for only a few minutes. M. had regained consciousness, but was not alert and probably was not aware of C.'s presence. C. inquired about M.'s condition.

*Worker's Collaborative Activities.*   C. collaborated with the hospital's medical caseworker who was assigned to M.'s case. It was agreed that C. would continue to see M. while M. was hospitalized and that the hospital social worker would assist C. in whatever ways possible.

**Crisis Intervention.**   During the first week of M.'s hospitalization C. made three very brief visits. M.'s serious physical condition did not permit any kind of interviewing activities. Each day C. checked on M.'s condition with hospital staff. After 10 days of hospitalization M.'s medical condition was stable and she was resting quite comfortably. Examinations had determined that M. was suffering from diabetes, high blood pressure, some permanent visual damage due to advanced, untreated diabetes, a congestive heart condition, early signs of arteriosclerosis, and the first stage of emphysema. All conditions were being treated, and the prognosis was that all could be stabilized in time with proper, ongoing medical attention and good health care practices at home on a daily basis. The hospital staff reported to C. that M.'s psychological condition was not good.

The first time M.'s condition permitted an interview (on the 11th day of hospitalization) C. found M. to be extremely confused and unwilling to be questioned or engage in conversation. For several days M. had been experiencing intense crying spells and had vacillated between episodes of begging to be allowed to go home and expressing fear of hospital personnel. On several occasions M. had accused the nurses and the doctor of keeping her prisoner and attempting to murder her. At other times she refused to talk to anyone.

The worker concluded that M. was experiencing a crisis reaction to a hazardous event: the medical emergency. When M. first regained consciousness in the hospital and was aware of the seriousness of her condition, she perceived the situation as a potent threat to her ability to survive outside of an institution. The tremendous fear that she would never get well enough to be permitted to return to her home threw her into a state of emotional disequilibrium. Her anxieties increased, her depression deepened, and her thinking became irrational.

Together the hospital staff—nurses, social worker, and doctor—and C. mapped out a crisis intervention strategy. Frequent but brief contacts by all caretaking staff were carefully spaced to ensure that during M.'s wakeful hours throughout the day she would not spend any long period of time without hearing the same reassuring message from a caretaker. The message was that M.'s health was gradually and steadily improving, and that she must start talking to the staff about making plans for her eventual return home. M. was shown genuine warmth and empathy, but all caretakers refrained from acknowledging any of her irrational verbalizations about being locked up or being put away in a nursing home. This portion of the treatment strategy employed the operant conditioning procedure of extinction.

The latter procedure was combined with positive reinforcement of any rational statement or response that M. made. The positive reinforcement took the form of smiling at M., reassuring her that she was getting better, and reminding her that she would eventually return to her home. Additional worker activities were directed at M.'s cognitive functioning on a daily basis to eliminate both her confusion (misperceptions of reality) and her erroneous beliefs. All staff members were careful to state their names and the purpose of their visits. For example, "Good morning Mrs. M., I am Sally Newman, your day-shift nurse. It is nine o'clock now and time for your morning bath." Or, for example, C. would say: "Good morning, Mrs. M., I am Mrs. Cook. I'm here for our afternoon visit; it's two o'clock. Shall we talk about preparing for your return home?" This practice of telling the confused person the facts of person, time, place, and purpose of contact is the essence of the reality orientation approach, which is frequently used with confused clients in institutions. Because there was no organic reason for M.'s confusion and distorted perceptions of reality, these cognitive and behavioral procedures helped to improve her condition within one week. She stopped expressing fear of not being able to ever go home and her confusion disappeared. The crying episodes ended, but a general depression continued that was similar in degree to the depression M. had displayed prior to the onset of the crisis.

During the first two weeks of the crisis reaction, C. arranged for M. to receive visits from her next-door neighbor and her pastor. These two individuals were the only members of M.'s informal social network. (It is important to make use of a client's informal supports during a crisis.) These contacts were very reassuring to M.: They were evidence that the outside world was still there for her to return to. The neighbor who was looking after M.'s house brought M. her knitting, her favorite pillow, and the picture of her husband that always stood on M.'s end table next to the wheelchair. Having these important personal articles from home with her during the remainder of her stay in the hospital served as further reassurance that M. had links to her home and the outside world.

As soon as M.'s thinking became clear enough for her to engage in reasonable and productive conversation and her emotional reaction calmed, C. initiated a very crucial part of the crisis intervention approach. She began a fairly intense, carefully organized problem-solving discussion. Now it was time to impress upon M. the necessity of engaging in serious preparation for her return home. Although C.'s position with the neighborhood agency and her time limitations did not permit her to directly conduct all of this phase of intervention, she was allowed and had the time to oversee and coordinate the direct, intense intervention provided by the hospital's medical caseworker and the other hospital staff including the nurses, nutritionist, and physical therapists. These personnel were responsible for preparing M. to return home.

This preparation entailed teaching M. how to give herself the required insulin shots, teaching her how to practice the required exercises, and teaching her the required diet to follow. The staff's work also involved motivating M. to follow numerous, general health practices on a daily basis for the rest of her life. And most important, they had to convince her to accept the visiting nurses service upon her return home, and to see the medical doctor for ongoing checkups for the treatment and management of her several chronic conditions.

During the remainder of M.'s hospital stay, C.'s contacts with her were very brief— twice a week. They served to reassure M. that C. was still concerned and would be her caseworker on a regular basis after M. returned home. C. advised M. that she would arrange to have all the home-delivered services begin upon M.'s return home. M. asked if C. would visit her on the very first day that she was back home. C. promised to do so.

*First Post-Discharge Home Visit.*   As promised, C. visited M. on the day she went home. It was a brief but satisfying visit to M. because C. assured M. that she would visit at least once a week, on the same day of the week, for about an hour each time. As C. was leaving M. said, "There are a lot of things I want to talk to you about if you will listen. I know it's safe now."

**Worker's Updated Assessment/Diagnosis.**   M. had come through a crisis that had been precipitated by her physical collapse and subsequent emergency hospitalization. Intensive, supportive, and reality-oriented treatment by the hospital staff and C. had helped M. through the crisis. M.'s postcrisis level of functioning was significantly higher than it had been before the crisis. Her health was greatly improved as a result of receiving ongoing treatment for a number of serious chronic conditions. M.'s physical and mental health had begun to decline more than six years earlier when she had been burdened with the hard and sad work of caring for her terminally ill husband. Following his death M. apparently had been unable to accept the loss: she became chronically depressed. Her depression and social inactivity kept her isolated from the mainstream of life. M.'s unresolved grieving for her husband continued over the years. When C. first met her the center of M.'s daily existence within her home seemed to be in the corner of the living room with her husband's wheelchair, walker, and picture. She had shut herself off from the outside world.

Upon her return from the hospital M. was in a state of good physical functioning and she displayed a mobility in the home that she had not had for a number of years. Because she felt much better physically, had experienced extensive medical attention, and was now home, M. no longer feared that accepting help from professionals would lead to rapid institutionalization. As a result she was much more open to social interactions. During the last two weeks of her hospitalization M. had become more and more cooperative and was motivated to learn to care for her health on a daily basis. In her many contacts with the hospital staff she had shown little if any confusion, and had begun to display more and more evidence of regaining the coping and problem-solving skills that she had possessed in the past. Although her psychosocial coping and adaptational capacities were now much improved, M. needed some concentrated help in two areas: (1) the lingering submerged depression associated with her unresolved mourning for the death of her husband; and (2) her long-standing social isolation and loneliness.

**Worker's Treatment Plan.**

*Primary Goals.*

1. To lift M.'s lingering depression, which is attached to unsuccessful mourning of husband's death.
2. To resocialize M. to the physical and social environment, so M. will no longer be isolated and lonely.

*Treatment Procedures to Combat Depression.*

1. Psychosocial procedures of ventilation, reassurance, acceptance, empathy, and respect (the sustaining, nonreflective procedures). These procedures will facilitate M.'s active expressions of grief and sustain her through the painful process of coming to grips openly and deeply with her real pain.
2. Psychosocial procedures of reflective communications. The reflective discussions of M.'s loss, the memories (good and bad) of her life with her husband, the ways in which she avoided effective grieving, and the ways she denied the reality of her loss should result in expanded self-insight about her past and present emotional needs.
3. Positive reinforcement in the form of warm verbal praise each time M. gains an insight, expresses genuine grief, and avoids denial.

*Treatment Procedures for Resocialization.*

1. In vivo desensitization of M.'s anxiety associated with the social and physical environment.
   a. Start weekly counseling session at home.
   b. Move sessions to C.'s office at neighborhood center.
   c. Follow-up office interviews by involving M. in brief social or recreational group activity at the center.

   *d.* Involve M. in expanded center programs on the day of the office counseling session.

   *e.* Involve M. in center programs on days other than the counseling day.

   *f.* Link M. to a carefully selected, trained senior volunteer who performs the role of friendly visitor or companionship therapist. The friendly visitor will, on the first few occasions, accompany M. to her doctor's appointment and on short shopping trips. Later the volunteer will accompany her only to the doctor's office and to the store. M. will make the return trips by herself.

2. Role play exercises to demonstrate or model for M. certain assertive social behaviors for negotiating those areas of daily living that M. still finds anxiety provoking such as dealing with bank tellers, store clerks, door-to-door salesmen, and so on. Role playing exercises will also give M. the opportunity to practice assertive behavior.

3. Teach M. the basic steps of a generic problem-solving process to help her see how this approach can be applied to the normal problems of daily living and how this approach makes good use of her problem-solving skills.

**Additional Intervention Plans.**

1. Monitor and coordinate all of the services that are currently in place for M. Assure their effectiveness and their immediate termination when no longer needed.

2. Contact local civic groups and organizations that are interested in local community organization and improvement. Ask that they advocate for M. and other residents on her street who together are not getting their fair share of public and community services such as adequate police protection, garbage collection, street cleaning, and street lighting.

**Closing Summary upon Termination of Planned Treatment.**　Counseling was terminated when the primary treatment goals were successfully attained. M. had overcome her long-standing depression. The depression had gradually dissipated over a period of five weekly counseling sessions in which the worker had encouraged and reinforced M.'s expression of anger and sadness about her husband's death. This ventilation of pent-up sadness (through the shedding of tears) had helped M. accomplish the kind of mourning she had been unable to do six years ago. This had been M.'s first opportunity to talk to anyone about her husband's death, the funeral, and the terrible sadness and helplessness she had felt following the loss. Sharing her feelings and experiences with the worker had greatly influenced the lifting of the depression.

   The careful and detailed follow-up, reflective discussions with M. had helped her to arrive at an understanding of how her long-standing depression and associated self-imposed social isolation had come about. She came to understand that by denying and repressing she had blocked her emotions and thereby become depressed. She came to realize how her fear of the outside world had developed, and how it had isolated her and prevented her from getting the help and resources she needed over the years, particularly with respect to her personal health. She also gained the insight that as a result of her many years of isolation, she was no longer sure if she knew how to cope with the environment and the people in it. She was able to acknowledge and understand her anxiety about getting involved once again.

The assertive training through role-playing exercises and the in vivo desensitization procedures had been successful. At the time of casework termination M. was active on a regular basis in numerous programs at the senior center. She was no longer anxious about moving about in the community. With the help of transportation services, she was able to do her own shopping, banking, and other routine chores outside of the home. She was also attending church and visiting neighbors. Her chronic health conditions were much improved as she was carefully following all of the doctor's instructions and keeping all her appointments. In her last session with the caseworker M. stated she was confident that she could cope with the routine and small problems associated with daily living—which seem numerous when one is as old as she. She said she knew that in the future she would seek outside help any time a major problem occurred.

**Discussion of the M. Case.**   The caseworker initiated the intervention within the framework of the psychosocial systems approach to the process of study, assessment, and treatment. The worker used her facilitative capacities to develop a relationship of trust with the client. While assessing the client's survival needs and developing a diagnostic understanding of the client's psychological problem of depression and social isolation, the worker linked the client to needed, concrete services as soon as possible. Before the worker had completed the needs assessment and the overall (biological-psychological-social) functioning assessment and problem diagnosis, the client experienced a crisis reaction.

The worker performed the roles of crisis intervention coordinator and consultant to the hospital crisis team. She also continued to provide sustaining casework throughout the client's stay in the hospital. Upon the client's return home the worker arranged for the resumption of concrete services and continued to monitor those services. Since the client came out of the crisis with a higher level of psychological functioning than she had had before her crisis, the worker could move quickly to initiate intensive one-to-one counseling that focused on the client's lingering depression and need for resocialization.

At this point in the case, with definitive outcome goals established and a clear understanding of the client's strengths, weaknesses, and personal characteristics, the worker was in a position to apply numerous treatment procedures from a variety of approaches. The systematic counseling that the client received made use of behavioral, cognitive, and psychosocial treatment procedures. This technical flexibility is a good example of the meaning of eclectic casework practice.

## SUMMARY

This chapter defines the meaning of eclectic practice in terms of conceptual and technical flexibility. The authors promote the use of this practice perspective with the elderly. Five well-known theoretical approaches to treatment are identified that provide many approaches and procedures for eclectic practice with the elderly. The central concepts of the approaches presented are: psychosocial, crisis intervention, client-centered, cognitive, and behavioral. The psychosocial system's intervention process is viewed as generic to all cases. The sustaining, reflective, and indirect psychosocial procedures are defined and illustrated for their application to the elderly client.

The nature of crisis reaction is defined and the procedures for conducting crisis intervention are spelled out. The eclectic nature of crisis intervention is acknowledged. Treatment procedures from any source may be utilized if they conform to the short-term, intense, and reality-focused format of crisis intervention.

The client-centered approach is discussed because of its excellent conceptualization of the core conditions that promote and facilitate the client-worker relationship. These conditions—empathy, respect, and genuineness—are defined in terms of worker capacities.

Cognitive theory, as it relates to the nature of maladaptive behavior and emotional distress, is described. The reader is encouraged to use cognitive treatment procedures when intervention is focused on bringing about some change in the elderly client's thinking content and/or processes. Cognitive restructuring and problem-solving activities are addressed and briefly illustrated for their utility with the elderly client.

Behavioral theory is discussed with respect to three perspectives on learned behavior: respondent, operant, and imitative. The respondent treatment procedures of desensitization and assertiveness training are explained and illustrated. The operant techniques of positive reinforcement, negative reinforcement, and extinction are defined and brief case applications of each are presented.

The case narrative at the end of this chapter demonstrates the conceptual and technical flexibility that characterizes eclectic practice. The following elements, drawn from the five treatment approaches, are illustrated in this narrative: (1) psychosocial systems assessment, (2) facilitative relationship core qualities, (3) sustaining procedures, (4) reflective discussion procedures, (5) crisis intervention, (6) in vivo desensitization, positive reinforcement, and assertiveness training, (7) problem solving, and (8) the practice roles of coordination, monitoring, linkage, and advocacy.

# Chapter 4

# Chapter 4

# Interpersonal practice with the well-elderly

## INTRODUCTION

Butler points out that "we cannot prevent people from growing old and we cannot forestall death indefinitely" (1983, p. 16). Decline and death are inevitable for everyone. Decline, however, is often accelerated and death is often premature. Much can be done to retard decline and even at times to reverse a too rapid deterioration process.

As they relate to the elderly most preventive measures discussed in the literature focus on health promotion. Health promotion (as was previously discussed in Chapter 2) is aimed among other things at furthering health and well-being through such general measures as education, nutrition, and the provision of social services.

A variety of educational programs, particularly those that stress physical health, diet, nutrition, exercise, and accident and crime prevention, highlight the importance of prevention. Such programs are believed to be beneficial because of their strong emphasis on averting, discouraging, delaying, or controlling the development of specific health or social problems. These programs (where they are utilized) can help older people to achieve optimal levels of functioning.

One of the most frequently emphasized preventive programs for the elderly stresses the importance of an adequately controlled and balanced diet. Many people believe that an individual's rate of aging depends largely on diet and nutrition. Although scientists still have much to learn about the special nutritional needs of the elderly, a large number of nutrients that are essential to good health have been identified.

Most older people can get the nutrients they need by eating a wide range of nutritious foods each day. As a guide, a well balanced diet should include the following:[1] at least two servings of milk or dairy products such as cheese,

---

[1] These are general guidelines. Some people may have conditions that restrict their intake of certain foods.

cottage cheese, or yogurt; two servings of protein-rich foods such as lean meat, poultry, fish, eggs, beans, nuts, or peanut butter; four servings of fruits and vegetables, including a citrus fruit or juice and a dark-green leafy vegetable; and four servings of breads and cereal products (made with wholegrain or enriched flours), rice, or pasta. (U.S. Department of Health and Human Services, 1983 pp.1–2)

Such information is vital to social workers who are concerned about the "whole person" and whose goal is to maintain older people at their highest level of well-being.

In proper proportions exercise and rest are essential to good health. "Without exercise it is difficult to maintain muscle tone, and without rest one cannot have zest in living or recuperate from the strain of everyday life" (Gilbert, 1952, p. 318).

Periodic physical examinations are advisable at all ages, but for the elderly they are especially important. With periodic physical examinations an early diagnosis can be made of beginning difficulties. Another preventive measure relates to hearing and vision. The sense organs should be checked regularly, and any noted defect should be treated.

The habit of regular dental examinations should be practiced. The condition of teeth is important to good digestion and general health for everyone.

Older persons themselves can play a major role in warding off or perhaps forestalling the rate of decline. Significant others such as doctors, social workers, family, friends, and neighbors can aid and encourage older people, but in the final analysis it is up to the older person to decide whether it is worthwhile to make the effort to maintain peak efficiency.

Thus the future of the elderly, especially those who have aged successfully, lies to a large extent in their own hands. Much work has been done to prolong the life span, and the increasing numbers of older persons in the population testify to the success of this work. More needs to be done to make the advancing and advanced years worth living.

The focus of this chapter is on the health and wellness of the well-elderly, and on examining those measures that are useful for maintaining the elderly at optimal levels of well-being. The authors believe that such measures build strengths into individuals and systems as a way of avoiding problems and their inherent consequences.

The later years of life are characterized by progressive loss of vigor and gradual declines. However, the large majority of individuals withstand or endure such losses and declines with minimal difficulty and creatively adapt to them: The well-elderly aptly fit this description.

Well-elderly people are defined in this chapter as those individuals who may (or may not) have experienced a major social, economic, or psychological loss in their lives but have found ways to adapt to their loss(es) with minimal difficulty. Those older people who fit this definition can be located at the upper end of a continuum that ranges from the well-elderly to those who are chronically impaired.

The well-elderly category also includes those older persons who have experienced minimal physical declines as part of growing old, but who have adjusted readily to such declines and do not perceive themselves as unable to cope adequately. These "successful agers" will continue to face the normal problems and challenges of living that frequently require novel and creative coping skills. The well-elderly anticipate difficulties before they become manifest and engage in the kinds of preventive measures designed to maintain their well-being at optimal levels.

## HEALTH AND WELLNESS

If the reader is to become familiar with the category of persons identified as the well-elderly, then definitions of what constitutes health and wellness must be given.

This is necessary because such definitions are influenced by each person's particular background or orientation. For example, a psychologist views health from the perspective of behavior, development, adaptation, and mental capabilities. Thus the success of the individual to respond adaptively to environmental changes is important. A sociologist, however, views health in terms of the individual's ability to effectively carry out the roles and tasks associated with such institutions/activities as the family, job, community, and leisure.

The World Health Organization defines health as "a state of complete physical, mental, and social well-being and not merely the absence of disease or infirmity" (1946 p. 1268). This conceptualization represents an ideal because (1) people are rarely in perfect health, and (2) it can be interpreted in a number of different ways.

Nevertheless, the broad elements of health—physical, emotional, and social—are the framework in which one can begin to analyze what is going well and what is going wrong (see Butler & Lewis, 1977). For instance, as some persons age they experience little or no physiological pathology. But they may perceive their declining status as occurring in the social and sociological realms of their lives. As a result they may experience anger and resentment over the loss of certain family and occupational roles, and begin to withdraw and become isolated. Others may be plagued with chronic health problems but learn to live with their disabilities and adapt to the aches and pains that aging often brings. Therefore, the criteria for defining well-elderly must necessarily be broad and viewed from a variety of perspectives.

"The activity approach to successful aging holds that to age successfully one must maintain into old age the activity pattern and values typical of middle age" (Atchley, 1980, p. 239). The question is this: Can this pattern of behavior be appropriately applied to older people? Clearly some older people are more active than others and are therefore better able to adjust to aging. However, a number of factors must be considered, for instance, personal endowment including mental and physical capacities, environmental factors that may affect individual capacities and opportunities, and socioeconomic status, especially apparent if one compares the life-styles of middle-class people to those from minority groups. And age itself is a significant factor in activity limitation. Each of these factors affects the level of activity.

Health is a dynamic concept that changes with time, social circumstances, and social values. And each society defines for itself and in light of its values those conditions that should be viewed as healthy. Most older people, no matter how successfully they have aged, exhibit one or more signs of pathology associated with the aging process. While a broad definition of who the well-elderly are and what qualities make for successful aging is essential, this approach also creates problems. The research findings in this area are inconsistent because of the differential criteria used to define successful aging. But health and how it is perceived by the elderly has consistently been singled out as a major factor in successful aging.

## Health as a Factor in Aging

While no single factor can be attributed to successful aging, health is one factor that is frequently mentioned by those who have aged successfully. Quality of health appears to be related to degree of incapacity. For instance, according to Shanas and her associates "The highest proportion of people who say their health is good is found among those who can go outdoors without restrictions; the highest proportion of those who say their health is poor is found among the housebound" (1968, p. 215). Thus the more mobile the older person, the more likely that person is to say his or her health is good.

Health has its subjective as well as its objective aspects. Older people's self-evaluations of their health may be at variance with the physician's objective assessment. The Shanas study noted that "The self-evaluation that old people make of their health is highly correlated with their report of restrictions on mobility, their sensory impairments, and their overall incapacity scores" (1968, p. 215).

Thus if health interferes with the physical ability of the elderly to perform their major daily-living activities, it then becomes a problem. Otherwise, health is not perceived psychologically (or subjectively) as problematic, whatever the doctor's evaluation. It is reasonable to assume that when older people indicate their health is poor, they have some physical basis for making that self-judgment (see Shanas et al., 1968).

## Definitions of Health and Wellness

The dictionary defines health as "physical and mental well-being; freedom from disease, pain, or defect" (*Webster's*, 1970, p. 645). It is the ability of individuals to function well physically and mentally and to express the full range of their abilities.

The World Health Organization's definition of health as a state of "complete physical, mental, and social well-being" has the virtue of taking a holistic approach to the nature of health, but this definition lacks a broad understanding of the human condition. People, regardless of who they are, do not always feel in "tip-top" condition. Most people normally feel a bit tired, harassed, and slightly under the weather. These feeling states must be taken into consideration when examining the personal experience of older people.

Generally speaking, *health* is a limiting term because it does not take into consideration certain aspects of the human condition that are also considered essential to people's biopsychosocial functioning. Therefore, wellness or well-being should also be discussed.

## Wellness

Wellness is not given to a person; rather, it is a state of being and feeling that one strives to achieve. Education for wellness concerns the pursuit of the dimensions of self-responsibility, nutritional awareness, physical fitness, stress management, and sensitivity to the environment. All of these dimensions are crucial to one's well state.

*Well* is defined as being in a good, favorable, or satisfactory condition (see *Webster's,* 1970, p. 1613). It is more than the absence of illness. Wellness is an ongoing process that involves the individual's whole being; that is, the physical, mental, emotional, and spiritual—all of which are vital.

From this perspective, health can be viewed as *one* aspect in the achievement of wellness. The wellness approach suggests that every person has an optimal level of functioning for each position on the wellness continuum; and optimal functioning along the entire continuum allows for achievement of a good and satisfactory existence (well-being).

Successful aging, if it is to be understood at all, must be viewed from a broad perspective. The health-wellness concept provides such a perspective for understanding how some older people have been able to live their lives in such a way as to achieve a satisfying existence: They have maintained the kind of control over their lives that has enabled them to attain well-being.

More specifically, these older people can think and act rationally, can anticipate situations that may be stressful or problematic, can make decisions about their lives that are in their best interests, and can carry on the activities of daily living with little or no assistance. In essence, these older people are in relatively good states of physical functioning and cognitive ability.

Nevertheless, this success does not rule out the fact that most (if not all) of these well-adjusted older people have experienced some major losses in their lives. While such losses (or changes) may impose some amount of discomfort, well-adjusted older people are able to tolerate them with minimal stress: They can find effective ways of coping with and adapting to difficult circumstances.

For instance, the results of an eye examination may reveal the presence of cataracts. The older person, while distressed by the situation, agrees with the doctor that cataract surgery will be useful. This person is also confident that the surgery can be performed successfully. In addition, the older individual is looking forward to the resumption of normal activities when the recuperative period is over.

Cataract surgery can impose some amount of stress on older individuals. While some older persons tolerate such surgery with minimal stress and discomfort, others react with fear and alarm. Well-elderly people accept the surgery as a fact of life and are willing to take the necessary preventive measures following surgery such as wearing a contact lens or reading glasses for close work in order to maintain optimal vision for as long as possible.

## Admission of Illness

The elderly want to be productive and useful. Admission of illness or incapacity is, to older individuals, a sign of weakness (see Shanas & Maddox, 1976). In our society weakness is interpreted to mean that individuals are unable to carry their own weight or load. Those who are unable to carry their own weight are dependent and must look to society to carry it for them.

Dependency does not mesh well with our "youth-oriented work-oriented society" (Loether, 1975, p. 1). This is an unfortunate societal attitude. Nevertheless, it still exists. It is for this reason that older people strive to achieve and maintain optimal levels of health and wellness for as long as possible. Such functioning can be achieved either independently or with the assistance of significant others.

## SUCCESSFUL AGING

Against what standard do we measure success? Obviously, some people are more successful in coping with age-related changes than others. There is no one definition of successful aging. A lot depends on where the emphasis is placed.

The following is a discussion of several definitions of successful adjustment to old age that have been developed by various gerontologists. A sampling of definitions is included to provide the reader with an understanding of the factors that must be taken into account when defining successful adjustment to old age.

Huyck (1974) suggests that one definition of successful aging is survival. The survival of the fittest principle implies that those who die at a younger age are less fit than those who survive into old age. Biologically speaking, the latter group are often considered superior.

Another suggested definition of successful aging is maintenance of middle-aged activities. This definition assumes that those individuals who maintain very nearly the same level of activity that they maintained during their middle years have aged more successfully. According to this definition "seventy-year-olds who look like fifty-year-olds in terms of activity and involvement can be termed more successful at resisting or ignoring age" (Huyck, 1974, p. 152). This point of view has been termed the *activity theory*. There are those who believe that "this line of thought is ageism at its worst" (Kalish, 1982, p. 79).

Ward succinctly points out the following:

> It ignores qualitative changes accompanying retirement, declining health, or widowhood. Such age-linked events may shift both social and psychological orientations of individuals to different sources of satisfaction. Indeed, by suggesting that aged "ought" to remain active to age "successfully" it places people who are not, or cannot remain, active in an awkward position. (1979, pp. 104–105)

Another definition of successful aging relates to how older people feel about themselves and about their present status and activities. This definition presupposes that if older people are happy with themselves and if their morale is good, they will feel good about themselves. Obviously, this definition does not explain all of the phenomena of successful aging.

A fourth definition "assumes that a person who is aging successfully feels satisfaction with his present and past life" (Havighurst, 1961, p. 10). A number of studies in social gerontology have focused on the concept of life satisfaction. As a result this term has been defined and used in a wide variety of ways. Perhaps Neugarten has provided us with the most global (yet still somewhat imprecise) meaning. Neugarten perceives that life satisfaction for the elderly occurs to the extent that the individual:

1. "Takes pleasure from whatever round of activities constitutes his everyday life.
2. Regards his life as meaningful and accepts responsibility for what his life has been.
3. Feels he has succeeded in achieving his major life goals.
4. Holds a positive self-image and regards himself as a worthwhile person, no matter what his present weaknesses may be.
5. Maintains optimistic attitudes and moods." (1974, p. 13)

These five components of positive life satisfaction are indicative of how happy and satisfied people feel about their present and past lives. However, it should be pointed out that the life satisfaction approach is a subjective one since the older person "defines the success in terms of inner satisfaction rather than of external adjustment" (Atchley, 1980, p. 239).

## Personality

There are those who believe that personality is the most salient factor influencing life satisfaction in old age. In other words, personality is considered to be the crucial variable with respect to a psychologically healthy and successful old age.

Personality as a factor influencing life satisfaction can best be viewed in a study of men and women between the ages of 70 and 79 (see Havighurst, 1968). In this study each respondent was rated on the basis of the following three factors: personality, degree of role activity, and sense of life's satisfaction. An analysis based on the latter three factors led to the conclusion that there are at least eight patterns of aging, the first four of which represent successful aging; and that "successful aging" means different things to different people.

The eight categories of older people that were identified are:

1. **Reorganizers.** Life satisfaction to reorganizers means maintaining a high level of activity and substituting new roles for old ones.
2. **Focused.** Living a satisfying life is linked to medium role activity and to concentration on a limited number of cherished roles and interests.
3. **Disengaged.** Those who are successfully disengaged are passive and view life from a rocking-chair perspective. They welcome the chance to rest and be free of responsibility.
4. **Holding-on.** This category of older persons has a highly developed set of defenses to protect them against the anxieties of aging. These people enjoy a satisfied life as long as their middle-aged activities can be maintained.
5. **Constricted.** This personality type has a low level of life satisfaction and reduces its level of role activity in order to cope with life.
6. **Succorance-seekers.** These people maintain dependent relationships with others. As a result they have low levels of interaction and their gratification comes as a result of their dependence on others.
7. **Apathetic.** These people are immobilized, have limited interests and role activities, and are unable to structure their lives to satisfy their needs.
8. **Disorganized.** These peoples' lives are characterized by low role activity and medium to low life satisfaction.

As the reader can see, different personality types come to terms with the world in different ways. It appears that each of these personality types has its own unique ways of "coming to terms with life stresses and changing life circumstances" (Williamson, Munley, & Evans, 1980, p. 77).

## Defining Quality of Life

Quality of life has also been identified as an important component of successful aging. "The quality of one's life appears to encompass more than adequate material well-being. It also includes perceptions of self-worth" (George & Bearon, 1980, p. 2).

George and Bearon (1980) identified four underlying dimensions that they believed were essential in defining the quality of life. Although they did not believe these were the only components that defined the quality of life, they considered them to be the most crucial. They are:

1. Life satisfaction and related measures.
2. Self-esteem and related measures.
3. General health and functional status.
4. Socioeconomic status.

Each of these dimensions is briefly described below:

1. **The Dimension of Life Satisfaction.** A large number of studies have addressed the issue of the relationship between aging and life satisfaction. This relationship has already been discussed in regard to activity theory. However, a number of other pertinent areas must necessarily be examined with respect to successful aging and life satisfaction. Included among these are the following: Are older people satisfied with the way their lives have progressed? How do they feel about the situation in which they now find themselves? How do they feel about their future prospects, and so on?

2. **The Dimension of Self-Esteem.** Self-esteem is a self-evaluation. It is usually defined as a general sense of self-worth—a belief in oneself as a person of value, of considerable worth; an acknowledging of one's personal strengths and an accepting of one's personal weaknesses (see Wells & Marwell, 1976; Coopersmith, 1967). Self-esteem is an important component in a general assessment of life (see Andrews & Withey, 1976).

   George and Bearon point out that "self-esteem is developed and maintained through a successful process of personal interaction with environment" (1980, p. 9). They add: "Age-related events and stresses in late life may alter the individual's self-esteem" (1980, p. 9).

3. **General Health and Functional Status.** Disease and illness "represent the chief barriers to extended health and longevity" (Kart, 1981, p. 115). However, maintaining good health and being able to secure appropriate health care become especially problematic as a person grows old. Health is a major life concern to the elderly. Apparently, the most frequently reported concern of older persons is that health problems or disability will interfere with their capacity for independent living (see Louis Harris & Associates, 1975). Therefore, objective data concerning the older person's functional status must be obtained. Such information is generally collected by one of two basic methods. The first is to have a physician or other qualified health professional assess and evaluate the physical well-being of the individual. The second is to have the individuals report

their illnesses, activity limitations, and other specific health events to their doctors.

4. **Socioeconomic status.**   Socioeconomic status is a composite of such variables as income, occupation, and educational attainment. These are considered to be among the material conditions that influence the quality of one's life.

A careful examination of the various characteristics, personality dimensions, and patterns of life satisfaction that appear to be related to successful aging suggests that no single factor can adequately explain successful adaptation to old age. Thus it is reasonable to assume that these several factors, along with functional capacities and individual resources, must be viewed along a continuum. Obviously, some older people possess more functional capacities and for a longer period of time than others. In addition, these same people may have more social, economic, and psychological supports than others, and feel very good about themselves and life in general.

Those people who are this fortunate are located at the upper end of the continuum—a continuum ranging from the community-based well-elderly to those older people who are chronically impaired and in need of institutionalization. The category of the well-elderly is broad and may include those whose physical and/or psychological health ranges from moderate to excellent.

The well-elderly are people who have adjusted readily to economic, social, and psychological losses and who do not perceive themselves as experiencing definitive problems and needs for which outside help is required. People in the well-elderly category want to continue to maintain good physical and mental health and tend to engage in those activities aimed at prevention. They anticipate untoward problems and take action to prevent their occurrence.

Although the well-elderly continue to face the normal problems and challenges of living, they bring to the latter stage of life an intact self and a lifetime of successful coping and adaptation. It may be that their ability to deal with stressful situations is directly related to their ability to anticipate problems and needs, to how well informed they are about problematic situations, to the creative and resourceful means they apply to a situation, and to the support networks that are available to them.

Social gerontologists and other researchers continue to pursue the notion of successful aging as an ideal and to encourage others to open new doors of inquiry to explore alternative ways of understanding and preparing for old age. Clues to successful aging can be discovered in a careful evaluation of the middle years. For instance, a major developmental task during middle age is to develop an increased empathy for others, not only in one's own immediate family but in the community and in the world at large. As peoples' understanding grows, their sense of responsibility grows, and they acquire qualities of leadership and the ability to influence others. Their judgment, imaginative creativity, and intelligence are able to function at peak capacity during this phase of life (see Whipple, 1966).

Enriching the dialogue between the elderly and their middle-aged children is strongly recommended by gerontologists as a useful strategy for successful aging (see Schwartz & Peterson, 1979). According to Whipple:

> Each age has its tasks, its problems, its solutions. The individual who has, with reasonable success, met life head on, lived through periods of elation and despair, been the originator of ideas and children, destroyed as well as created, can finally accept himself as a member of the human race and feel a sense of oneness with other human beings, even those in distant cultures and distant times. (1966, p. 361)

## Old Age as a Satisfying Time of Life

It has been pointed out that old age can be an emotionally happy and satisfying time of life with a minimum of physical and mental impairment (see Butler & Lewis, 1977). Consider the following case example:

> Mrs. C., a 74-year-old retired schoolteacher, was lively, talkative, and alert. She was neatly and stylishly dressed, and the colors in her outfit were obviously selected with care. In standing and in sitting her posture was erect and there were no signs of psychomotor retardation. When interviewed she spoke in a calm and relaxed manner about her achievements and exhibited no sign of an appreciable intellectual decline. No memory impairments were found on the mental status examination. Some general forgetfulness was noted, however, on her history.
>
> Mrs. C. was born in Paris into a family of modest means. She was the third oldest of five children. Mrs. C. said that her parents got along reasonably well, although she sensed at times that her mother had ambitions to be other than a housewife. Her mother apparently had a strong influence on her life. As far back as Mrs. C. could remember her mother had stressed the idea of getting ahead through a good education. Mrs. C. finished college at age 20. She met her husband-to-be while in her junior year. At age 22 she married, and shortly afterward she and her husband emigrated to the United States.
>
> She still describes herself as being in love with her husband, whose health is reported as being very good. Mrs. C. went through menopause at age 49. She still has sexual relations with her husband on a regular basis.
>
> Mrs. C. enjoys talking about her three children, all of whom live away from home with their own families and are obviously doing well. Mrs. C. has five grandchildren and seems especially fond of them. She sees each of her children (who live in different states) at least once a year, and maintains frequent telephone contact with them throughout the year.
>
> Mrs. C. began teaching at the age of 32, two years after her last child was born. She and her husband especially enjoyed having the children at home during their late teenage years when their peers came to visit them. Somehow, they were re-

minded of their own teenage years and they realized how much they had changed since that time in their own lives.

Since she retired nine years ago, Mrs. C. and her husband have enjoyed a satisfying emotional and social life. They have managed their financial resources well and look forward to the future. Mrs. C. is aware that life cannot go on for them this way forever, despite the fact that she and her husband planned for and anticipated many of the changes they have experienced. Mrs. C. enjoys her present life, her participation in community and church affairs, and hopes these activities and interests will persist for some time. She and her husband have talked about death, but try not to actively dwell on it. They have made out a will and arranged for a burial site.

Mrs. C. is aware of certain changes in her functional capacity and has apparently accepted them. She knows she no longer walks as rapidly as she used to. She is also a bit more forgetful, but there is no evidence of psychopathology as she ages. She still has friends in, but entertains less frequently now that some of her old circle of friends have moved away or died. It is deemed likely that Mrs. C. will function well and adapt satisfactorily to further life changes as she continues to age.

Mrs. C. is obviously an example of an older person who has adapted to the latter stage of life with minimal stress, maximum adjustment, and a high level of morale. The fact that she has grown old with little or no pathology is suggestive of a normal, well-elderly person. It is apparent to Mrs. C. that she is experiencing gradual alterations in her psychomotor abilities, as well as a few behavioral changes—specifically, slight forgetfulness. Although Mrs. C. may not be in optimal health on all levels—physical, social, and psychological—she appears to be aging successfully. Any changes that have occurred are primarily on the physical level. For an older person described to be in optimal health, this kind of change is not unusual. Even in the absence of disease, there are important changes in physiological functioning with age (see Kimmel, 1974).

## NORMAL PROBLEMS OF THE WELL-ELDERLY

Mrs. C., like other successful agers, will continue to face normal problems and challenges of living that frequently require new and creative coping skills. At all stages of life certain demands, often referred to as developmental tasks, are made upon each of us (Lowy, 1979). Robert Havighurst states:

[A developmental task is] one which arises at or about a certain period of the life of the individual, successful achievement of which leads to his happiness and to success with later tasks, while failure leads to unhappiness in the individual, disapproval by the society, and difficulty with later tasks. (1972, p. 2)

When needs have been reasonably well met, people are more in tune with their feelings, actions, ideas, interests, and with their environments.

This state of being is essential because like all living systems, human beings—if they are to function effectively—must maintain a goodness-of-fit with their environment (see Germain & Gitterman, 1980).

Today's older people are constantly confronted with complex and continually changing environments that impose an overwhelming array of adaptive tasks upon them. Nevertheless, we must begin to think of old age as a time of potential health. For too long medicine and the behavioral sciences have mirrored society's negative attitudes by presenting old age as a time of a grim litany of physical and emotional ills. "Decline of the individual," according to Butler & Lewis, "has been the key concept and neglect the major treatment technique" (1977, p. 18). Thus efforts must be geared at pushing toward growth and change.

Old age is a unique stage of life with its own developmental tasks to accomplish.

> The elderly must teach themselves to conserve their strength and resources when necessary and to adjust in the best sense to those changes and losses that occur as part of the aging experience. The ability of the elderly person to adapt and thrive is contingent on his physical health, his personality, his earlier life experiences, and on the societal supports he receives: adequate finances, shelter, medical care, social roles, recreation, and the like. (Butler & Lewis, 1977, p. 20)

## LOSS AND CHANGE AND THE WELL-ELDERLY

Although there is considerable variation in the decrement of function of human organs over time, all older people exhibit to some degree evidence of changes that have accumulated during "normal aging" (see Andres, 1967). Even though there are no specific indicators for the beginning of the aging process, there are a number of changes that occur gradually and progressively.

In Chapter 2 the authors describe some of the physical and psychosocial losses that occur with the passage of time. We do not suggest that old age is synonymous with illness, even though morbidity does accelerate with age and the image of the elderly is that of a sick, isolated, and deprived group of people. According to Brody, "the majority do not fit that stereotype and age successfully (that is, they maintain good functional capacity intellectually, physically, and socially)" (1977, p. 59). Further, the elderly display widely varying modes of adaptation and competence in dealing with stress.

Generally speaking, certain changes in physical appearance—graying and thinning of hair, loss of elasticity of skin, decrease in fatty deposits underneath the outer layer of the skin, and so forth—are experienced by all older people including the well-elderly, despite variations in age at onset, sex, social status, and life history. It is conceivable that successful agers, people who have maintained themselves reasonably well throughout life as a result of diet, exercise, and meaningful sociocultural activities, perceive these gradual bodily changes less negatively than other older people who do little to anticipate the changes. These successful agers take their declining physical functions in stride and accept their physical limitations.

Some losses have a great deal of impact on the elderly and may severely tax their coping capacities. Such losses include: loss of assigned roles, economic loss, break-up of one's social network, loss of privacy, loss of options, and so forth.

It is reasonable to assume that these losses, while perhaps temporarily lowering self-competence and self-esteem, pose no permanent threat to those persons who have aged successfully. These individuals apparently bring to these situations an intact self (a mature and integrated personality) and a lifetime of successful coping and adaptation. Such people have the ability to enjoy life, to lead a full, creative, and serene existence, to give of themselves and to be warmly appreciated by others, to remain mentally alert, to maintain contact with family and friends, and to not overextend themselves.

Older people, if they are to continue to function successfully, need to learn more about the normal processes of aging, to know what losses to anticipate and how best to compensate for them, and to have available to them relevant resources for promoting an active state of positive health which, in turn, should promote optimal life conditions.

The fact that decrements in physiological functioning through adulthood into old age are gradual is hopeful because it gives most individuals time to reorder and deal with their lives in a more meaningful way. Weg points out that "to the extent that people can use, nourish, and extend their remaining capacities, the body and spirit will benefit and the whole person prosper" (1975, p. 253).

Even though the latter years are unquestionably characterized by progressive loss and gradual declines on a number of different levels, the large majority of older people withstand the losses and declines and creatively adapt to the changes they bring. It is reasonable to assume that any type of change, whether pleasant or unpleasant, will produce a certain amount of stress. But adaptation to loss is the single most important task facing the older person. This may not always be easy, especially if the stressful event involves the loss of a spouse, child, close relative, or friend.

Grieving such losses is normal and natural. However, if older persons experiencing such losses are to go on with their lives, they must begin to emancipate themselves from their bondage to the deceased, readjust to an environment in which the deceased is missing, and begin to form new relationships (see Lindemann, 1944).

Pfeiffer (1977) noted that adaptation to loss involved the following two tasks:

1. Replacing some of the losses that have occurred with new relationships (for example, new friends, remarriage); new roles (for example, second and third careers, volunteer work); or retraining of lost capacities (for example, speech and/or physical therapy after a stroke).
2. Making do with less. Older people who come to grips with these tasks and begin to deal with them effectively are taking direct charge of their lives. This gives them considerable power to control and manage their lives.

The following vignettes illustrate successful ways of coping for the well-elderly. In each case the person experiencing the trying and stressful event, adjusted to the situation with minimal difficulty.

### Case Example 1: Coping with a Health Problem

Mrs. Evans, a charming, attractive, and lively lady of 66 years, had worked for 31 years as a practical nurse. However, she retired from her job about a year ago, and has spent most of her time pursuing a leisurely life with her husband, her volunteer activities, and her friends. Mr. Evans retired from his job as an accountant two years ago. Since his retirement Mr. Evans has spent much of his time pursuing his hobby of woodworking—a hobby he dearly loves. Mr. Evans is 67 years old. Mr. and Mrs. Evans have two married daughters who live out of state with their families. The daughters keep in close contact with their parents.

Six months ago, the doctor informed Mr. Evans that he had coronary heart disease—a heart disease that could cause sudden death, or at least disability, unless an operation was performed. The doctor recommended open heart surgery.

Both Mr. and Mrs. Evans were initially afraid of the open heart surgery, but after discussing the positive results of this operation with their doctor, they decided to go ahead with it. Mrs. Evans's experience as a practical nurse confirmed for her husband the recovery rate of patients who had had open heart surgery. Mr. Evans felt relieved; so did their children and their friends. Mr. Evans did have open heart surgery and made a successful recovery.

Although Mr. and Mrs. Evans initially experienced the prospect of open heart surgery as a life-and-death trauma, they began to interpret the surgery differently as they learned more about its success. In fact, after Mrs. Evans became more relaxed, she drew on her years of experience as a practical nurse who had helped many patients through their period of recuperation. As a result Mrs. Evans saw the heart surgery as a reprieve from widowhood; her husband has an additional 20 years of life. The couple decided that they would set up a regimen that would include proper diet, exercise, and nutrition, as well as regular physical examinations.

### Case Example 2: Facing Retirement

Retirement from the labor force is usually viewed as a major event or transition in the life of the older person. Since work is central to the lives of most people, the transition from work to a period of relative leisure may be viewed with trepidation. To retire means to experience a role deficit. The older individual "loses the role of worker in the work arena and the role of breadwinner in the family arena" (Schlossberg, Troll, & Leibowitz, 1978, p. 104).

To people who have worked most of their lives, retirement will undoubtedly mean a major change in lifestyle. This may be very stressful for those people who feel quite comfortable with their current existence and wish to maintain what they have. Retirement also results in a reduction in income. Therefore, "the stress of retirement may be intensified by fear of poverty" (Schlossberg et al., 1978, p. 104). By planning ahead many people reduce the financial and psychological stress of retirement. Preretirement counseling and educational programs are very helpful in this regard.

Preretirement counseling and educational programs are a relatively new phenomenon. According to Glamser (1981) only about 15 percent of large companies have comprehensive preretirement programs. Most such programs are limited and provide the participants only with information regarding retirement options, social security, and pension benefits (see Ward, 1984). There is an obvious need for preretirement planning and preparation for those workers in lesser paying positions.

The focus of most programs is on information regarding finances and health. Information related to financial planning may include the increased tax advantages to which the elderly retiree is entitled. This would include such things as double tax exemptions, retirement income credit, special tax advantages on selling a home, medical tax deductions, energy savings, and many state personal and property tax exemptions. The older retiree is also made aware of the potential savings on clothes, transportation, gifts, business lunches, and entertainment.

Preretirement programs should ease the social and psychological transition from work to retirement. Ward believes that

> Preretirement programs, especially those involving group discussions, offer an excellent opportunity to explore the individual's attitudes toward work and retirement and to help people deal more effectively with situations encountered following retirement. (1984, p. 172)

Note the following case example.

> Mrs. Hubbard, age 66, worked as a buyer for a well-known department store for 35 years. Although she enjoyed her work and being with her co-workers, Mrs. Hubbard looked forward to the day when she could devote herself to some other leisurely pursuits such as volunteer work, travel, and attending fashion shows.
>
> At the age of 60, Mrs. Hubbard began attending, on a voluntary basis, the preretirement counseling and education program that the store made available to its workers. Mrs. Hubbard felt that the program was useful because it provided her with much-needed knowledge about retirement; that is, what to expect, what problems to anticipate, and how to prepare for them.

She learned that even though her income in retirement would be reduced, she would benefit from certain tax advantages once she reached the age of 65. The tax advantages from which she might benefit included: double tax exemptions, retirement, and so on.

At first Mrs. Hubbard was seen by a trained member of the personnel staff on an individual basis. These sessions gave her an opportunity to begin to deal realistically with some of her ambivalent feelings about leaving the job. They also enabled her to anticipate what she thought her retirement would be like, and gave her time to focus on the financial aspect of retirement and how to budget her income.

Mrs. Hubbard also attended the group sessions that were a part of the preretirement program. During these sessions she had an opportunity to exchange ideas and information about retirement with other employees and to discuss potential retirement problems with them. Each session lasted about two hours and usually focused on some major topic concerning retirement preparation. The topics generally included: health, finances, the social and psychological aspects of retirement, living arrangements and locale, the legal aspects of retirement, and the use of leisure time.

Mrs. Hubbard was given time off during working hours to attend the group sessions, which lasted a total of eight weeks. The meetings were held once a week.

It has been a year since Mrs. Hubbard retired, and she believes that she has made a successful adjustment, despite the fact that she misses her co-workers as well as her job.

The examples just cited are of older people who have obviously found successful ways of dealing with their situations and of meeting anticipated stress head-on.

## The Well-Elderly as Targets of Services

The well-elderly are not perceived as being victims of unrelenting needs that compel them toward dysfunctional behavior. They are not passive people living in a world of stimuli. Instead, they are master organizers who give their own unique meaning to life and its vicissitudes (see Rogers, 1951).

Those who have aged successfully are self-determining and assume responsibility for their own behavior. By acting maturely and responsibly the well-elderly (those who have aged successfully) are not only able to maintain themselves in a continually changing world, but are open to learning new, constructive ways of responding to that world.

As people age they may not be aware of or prepared for the declines in functional (emotional, physical, and social) capacity that occur with the passage of time. They also may be unaware of the alternatives available to them to enhance the quality of their lives. However, they may be open to meaningful educational experiences that will expand their knowledge and understanding of the aging process. If older people can learn to anticipate changes in their life patterns before these changes occur, they can take some kind of organized action before the situation or event becomes traumatic.

People are by nature free agents and have a right to participate actively in those choices and decisions that concern them. While not all people are capable of making their own decisions, it seems reasonable to assume that those who have aged successfully have taken responsibility for making these decisions. They have the capacity for self-direction.

Human beings are goal-oriented: They choose the kinds of lifestyles that will enable them to satisfy their immediate as well as their long-term goals. The well-elderly must necessarily be regarded in a positive light since they tend to strive for competence and a sense of completion.

Nevertheless, some successful agers may be shortsighted and at times impulsive. They may engage in pleasure-seeking acts such as making a costly move with little money to fall back on, investing in speculative stocks, and so on. Such impulsive behavior can interfere with or block the attainment of desired long-term goals.

In these cases successful agers need to alter their thinking by clarifying their notions of success and reviewing the goals they have established to achieve that success. Concrete measures might be offered to help the older person achieve this objective, and to teach him or her how to think more systematically.

### The Worker's Role in Relation to the Well-Elderly

Social workers who intervene in the lives of the well-elderly should be aware of their adaptive potential and of the "nutritive" qualities of their environments. Nevertheless, effective and efficient intervention in the environment of the well-elderly may be just as demanding as intervention that is required on a case-by-case basis. The type of intervention required in preventive intervention is generally aimed at individuals, families, and small groups, as well as social systems such as single institutions and communities (see Gilbert, Miller, & Specht, 1980).

The knowledge base that is necessary for the worker who intervenes in the older person's environment is the same as that required for the practitioner who works directly with clients. In this regard Turner states:

> [The worker] builds from an understanding of biopsychosocial development, interpersonal influence, the influence of significant others, and the influence of significant environments and systems as essential characteristics in the development and maintenance of healthy and fulfilling human living. (1979, p. 70)

Humans are rational, psychodynamic, and interacting beings; they are also physical entities. This means that social workers must necessarily have some understanding of a person's physical state. But causal-developmental knowledge is not enough. The worker must also be equipped with interventive knowledge "to prescribe principles and procedures for inducing change in behaviors and/or situations" (Fischer, 1978, p. 52). Interventive knowledge need not necessarily be limited to social workers. For instance, social workers functioning in the consultant-educator role can transmit knowledge to other mediators or caretakers such as teachers, nurses, parents, and volunteers about how to deal with a variety of situations in the environment. In this connection Turner states: "Knowledge of human behavior can be transmitted through cognitive methods; that is, other people can be taught to understand and influence human behavior" (1979, p. 71).

Acting in the consultant-educator role, social workers can also function to provide information (for example, information on safety and on avoiding criminal victimization) and to interpret agency rules and regulations. These kinds of activities are intended to enhance social functioning. This can be an invaluable approach to older people (or their families) seeking information related to a specific issue.

As the ranks of the elderly continue to increase, the consultant-educator role is bound to take on more importance. According to future estimates "Over the next fifty years, the Census Bureau projects that the number of Americans 65 and over will more than double from 26.8 million today to 65.8 million people in 2033. Clearly social work does not have the manpower to deal with the vast amount of personal and social problems many older people present. Thus:

> The importance of this role (consultant-educator) and of intervention at this level lies in the fact that a small amount of professional caseworkers can geometrically increase their potential for reaching clients by carrying out programs involving the training of people who have primary societal responsibility for care-giving. (Fischer, 1978, p. 19)

Social workers intervening at the preventive level must constantly increase their knowledge and understanding of older life, must be aware that human behavior can be influenced in a variety of ways, and must focus their attention on helping successful agers to find more productive and innovative ways to deal with impending situations.

Social work can readily adapt its diverse knowledge base and versatile methodologies to primary preventive interventions with the well-elderly. Social workers carrying out preventive activities can perform in a variety of roles as they seek to foster the highest levels of wellness in the elderly.

## THE IMPACT OF PREVENTION AND SERVICE DELIVERY

For more than a century public health in the United States was restricted, in the main, to environmental control of communicable diseases (see Rosen, 1978). However, over the years the epidemiological approach has been broadened from the study of the distribution of communicable diseases among the population to the ecological study (distribution in the population) of any disease or physical handicap (see Kark, 1974). In addition, interest in the control of chronic diseases has led to increased emphasis on the concept of multiple causation in disease. This means that biological factors are no longer considered to be the sole factors in the treatment of patients. In fact, it is reasonable to assume that such factors as past history, personal habits, family relationships, and type of housing may influence the outcome of treatment.

Multiple causation implies that prevention of disease involves not merely a few environmental controls, but long-range efforts in an attempt to protect all people—from the prenatal period to the grave. The task of prevention must of necessity rest on the shoulders of each individual, especially since it involves the participation of every citizen in educational programs that are conducive to their well-being. People must be motivated to do those things that will have long-term, positive effects on their lives.

However, the only way that people will begin to anticipate problems of older life and assume more responsibility for what lies ahead is when they know what to anticipate and are taught how to cope. Accomplishing the latter does not simply mean involving the youth of the mass media as teaching devices. An examination of the range of attitudes toward aging must be conducted as well: Some people are very fearful of and resistant to growing old.

Nevertheless, social workers who intervene at the preventive level must have a good understanding of how to help successful agers continue to develop their capacities and deal with their environments. Thus knowledge of behavior and the dynamics of interpersonal relationships are required when working in behalf of individuals. Since human beings have the capacity for self-direction and growth, the older person who has aged successfully can be taught about those aspects of his or her life that may need to be handled differently in the future.

Individuals should not wait until retirement to be presented with information on what to expect and how to plan for it. President Nixon's Task Force on Aging asserted that the elderly would be more adequately equipped to deal with old age if they were provided with opportunities to prepare for it during their middle years. This means that various thrusts in training must be undertaken. For instance, professionals (including preretirement and retirement counselors) capable of stimulating middle-aged adults and preparing them for retirement must be trained for this important undertaking. The type of training needed is that which is designed to "teach the middle-aged and aging about the developmental tasks they will face which will help countless individuals to enjoy greater fulfillment throughout their lives" (Woodruff & Birren, 1974, p. 261).

A social worker conducting a preretirement program for older people would probably never become as deeply involved with the individual participants as one providing clinical services, because that worker is not intervening with the idea of meeting needs directly. Instead, in the role of teacher-educator, social workers are imparting the kind of knowledge that can help older people develop insight and then act upon themselves. Hollis asserts that, "the caseworker's effort is then directed toward telling the client about possible opportunities, helping him decide whether he wants to use them and, if so, how to go about using them" (1972, p. 26). The role in this instance is clearly that of teacher-educator.

## Multipurpose Senior Centers

Generally speaking, multipurpose centers for senior adults emphasize the importance of the elderly helping themselves. As a result these centers act as a catalyst in raising community consciousness among the elderly and among agencies attempting to meet the needs of the elderly. Their overall goal is to enhance social interaction and to help relieve loneliness through voluntary participation in meaningful activities. Older persons are free to decide whether or not they wish to participate in the "center's" activities, and in what way they wish to become involved.

Multipurpose senior centers help many older people to achieve a high level of objective and subjective functioning since the centers aim at personal growth through the type of programs they offer. Participation in group activities is encouraged because it provides stimulation and offers a channel for the expression of the older person's interests and talents.

Multipurpose senior centers are characterized by varied recreational, social, and educational activities. For instance, some centers[2] have regularly scheduled classes on such topics as: ceramics, sewing, stained glass, music, drama, dance, creative writing, psychology of aging, weight control, exercise, boating, public speaking, preretirement, and many others.

Whatever preventive service is delivered to the well-elderly should be effective, efficient, and responsive. Human services have always played a key role in our society. For the most part prior to the Great Depression, the provision of human services rested simultaneously with the family and with the church. However, during the 1930s the role of the federal government in human services increased. According to Azarnoff and Seliger:

> The Federal government then began funding human services with the passage of the Social Security Act and other related legislation. The role of the government at all levels in human services has been increasing dramatically ever since. (1982, p. 1)

This was the case until the Reagan administration of the early 1980s. The theme of the Reagan administration has been limited federal involvement in social programs. However, individual initiative, volunteerism, and

---

[2] Vintage, a multipurpose center, provides comprehensive geriatric services for senior adults living in Allegheny County in western Pennsylvania. As a nonprofit corporation it is designed to meet multiple needs and to raise the quality of life for those persons 55 years of age and over by using and developing their potential. Vintage makes available a wide range of recreational, educational, and social activities.

the private sector have been encouraged to play a major role in the human services. All three of these aspects are important in preventive intervention.

The kinds of preventive services advocated here are those that will enable older persons to achieve or maintain their highest level of objective and subjective functioning. Life-enhancement services such as education would be instrumental in helping to achieve this objective.

### The Functions of Human Services

Human services are often categorized by functions. There are a number of different ways of looking at services, but the four categories of function identified here are the same as those used by Azarnoff and Seliger who state:

> In the first category are those programs whose function is providing access to other services. Programs to provide referral information, outreach, transportation, and escort services are examples. A second category, protective, includes programs such as child welfare, the guardianship of mentally incompetent adults, drug abuse prevention, and crime abatement. In the third category are those programs aimed at personal growth, or enhancement of the quality of life, such as recreation, education, and art as programs. The fourth category consists of programs providing basic services necessary for survival, including health care and housing. Programs whose function is to provide access to other services and those aimed at personal growth have functions that are closely allied to preventive intervention. (1982, p. 1)

## PREVENTIVE INTERVENTION THROUGH EDUCATIONAL PROGRAMS

One of the current trends in preventive intervention is aimed at making individuals aware that they are responsible for their own physical, social, and psychological well-being and at giving them the knowledge they need to bring about that well-being. Social workers are assuming leadership roles in the planning, development, and presentation of adult educational programs in a variety of settings. For instance, Knowles points out that:

> [Such settings include] living rooms, libraries, settlement houses, hospitals, church basements, military bases, grange halls, YMCAs, hotels and motels, and every other kind of facility used by adults, as well as in classrooms. (1977, p. 52)

To Knowles's list of adult education settings might also be added multipurpose senior centers. Social workers who have either taught courses in multipurpose senior centers, presented seminars or workshops, or developed training programs for volunteers and staff have no doubt learned that the concept of adult education is broad and "encompasses practically all experiences of mature men and women that produce new knowledge, understanding, skills, attitudes, interests, or values" (Knowles, 1977, p. 52). Because the term is broad and can encompass a variety of meanings, almost any adult educational effort or opportunity can be conceived of as adult education. Perhaps the most salient definition of adult education for our purposes is as follows:

> It is a process that is used by adults for their self-development, both alone and with others, and it is used by institutions of all kinds for the growth and development of their employees, members, and clients. It is the educational process—often used in combination with the productive process, political process, or service process. (Knowles, 1977, p. 52)

For those older people who are profoundly conscious of maintaining or raising their own wellness levels, and who want to and are able to continue to pursue an approach that will result in their staying healthy for as long as possible, adult educational opportunities are a most effective strategy. Consider the following educational effort.

### Leadership Training Course for 40 Successful Agers[3]

A 16-session course was funded by the Illinois State Department of Aging under Title IV-A of the Older Americans Act and offered to members of a number of senior citizen groups in the Chicago area in the spring of 1977. Three sites were chosen, and Ms. Schlesinger taught at two of them. The overall goals of the program were to teach students the basic concepts and issues related to the aging process, to develop positive attitudes toward the aging, to teach students about the services available for senior citizens, and to teach leadership skills that would enable participants to share what they learned with others.

The first eight sessions covered basic concepts and issues related to the aging process: It was, in fact, a gerontology course for senior citizens. The remaining eight sessions were addressed to the programs and services for older adults. A brief session on leadership for older Americans was also included.

Adult education principles were utilized. This meant that the life experiences and knowledge of the students would be an integral part of the educational content. The author identified a number of learning objectives eight of which follow:

1. To examine the student's personal perspective and understanding of what it means to grow old.
2. To increase student knowledge and understanding of the normal processes that accompany advancing age.

---

[3] The material for this section is based on a paper presented by Mary Ryan Schlesinger at the Annual Program Meeting of the Council on Social Work Education, New Orleans, Louisiana, Feb. 26–Mar. 1, 1978.

3. To examine some age-related mental and emotional changes of older life.
4. To discuss the results of these changes as they relate to the biopsychosocial processes of the elderly.
5. To identify some of the ways in which older people's social relationships change in later life.
6. To emphasize and discuss strategies that are useful for preventing, delaying, or controlling some of the consequences of older life.
7. To examine the role of the federal government in the provision of services to the elderly in the past and present, and to anticipate the federal response in the future.

Each session lasted for 50 minutes. The instructor adhered to a lecture-discussion format. The students looked forward to attending the classes, took part in the discussions, and drew on their own aging experiences. Of importance to the students was the distinction between senescence (normal biological aging) and senility (pathological aging). The students also actively participated in the discussions on psychological changes in later life. Feelings about oneself as an aging person and feelings about aging in general served as a basis for much discussion in some of the sessions. General information about social roles and social relationships in later life was presented with attention given to how these roles and relationships relate to life satisfaction. Events that produce a certain amount of stress and strain in the older person's life were also discussed including such stress-producing experiences as retirement, widowhood, institutionalization, and the "empty nest syndrome."

Other information was also covered in the first half of the course. For instance, four major topics were presented in an effort to help the students to learn how to negotiate the environment. They included: (1) the importance of understanding oneself, (2) the importance of understanding one's environment, (3) the importance of understanding stress and how it can be controlled, and (4) how loneliness impacts on the individual's life during the latter years. (Obviously, there was some overlap in the content covered in the class.)

The second part of the course focused on the provision of services to older people. The content included demographic data, historical information on service provision, a description of the U.S. Administration on Aging and the Department of Health and Human Services, the State Agency on Aging, and the local mayor's office for senior citizens and handicapped. Trends in the federal government's involvement in the welfare of the elderly were examined, and the White House Conferences on Aging were also discussed.

Toward the end of the class the instructor covered the topic of leadership training for older Americans. The session on leadership as a viable quality of older life was especially helpful for two reasons. Some of the characteristics associated with leadership qualities gave the students an opportunity to contribute examples from their own experiences. Assertiveness training was suggested as a useful tool in helping older people to exert their rights.

The course received an overall positive evaluation from the older participants. What was clearest was the value the students placed on this type of course as an educational opportunity that was made available to them. Many requested that a similar course be presented as soon as possible.

### Issues Raised by this Course

This course raises some questions that merit careful consideration. For instance, what should be the academic training for the social worker teaching such a course? Should personnel at the subprofessional level be recruited to teach a course such as this? What kind of training materials, that is, course syllabuses, textbook(s), films, case study materials, and teaching guides are needed in a course such as this? What kind of education about the life cycle should be included in such a course? Should there be follow-up courses for a similar age-based target population? Will the education and training presented in this type of course prevent or minimize suffering in later life? How much material should be covered in similar course offerings, and how long should the class last per session as well as per semester? What should be the age requirement, if any, for the class participants? No doubt there are many other questions that the reader can raise in conjunction with this and similar courses.

By this time the reader should have a higher level of awareness of the kind of preventive interventive strategies that are useful for those people who are identified as successful agers. The reader is challenged to think of other useful preventive interventive strategies.

The course described above was intended to teach healthy elderly persons about their own aging. There is no question that (given the growing number of older people in the population) more training and education is needed that is focused on the prevention of suffering in future elderly. One way to achieve this goal "would be to train a sufficient number of professionals and technicians in the field of aging to serve and attend the needs of the increasing population of elderly" (Woodruff & Birren, 1974, p. 260).

### OTHER PREVENTIVE INTERVENTION THRUSTS

The neighborhood family concept is built on the assumption that a major source of stress for the elderly is their sense of powerlessness to effect their own destiny. The neighborhood family is perhaps one of the best efforts at primary prevention. It brings together large numbers of elderly residents who live in close geographical proximity to each other.

The geographical areas in question are characterized by high concentrations of elderly, high crime rates, few agency services, limited recreational and educational facilities, and minimal social interactions for older people beyond shopping (see Ross, 1983). Staff gerontologists contacted residents of the area in which the neighborhood family concept was first tried on a door-to-door basis to broach the neighborhood family idea and elicit the resident's level of interest (see Ross, 1983). The "family" idea met with approval, and the survey designed by Ross and her associates not only identified the major concerns of the 110 elderly residents, but determined the degree of interest and possible participation in the program.

A deteriorated warehouse which was later refurbished was the meeting place of the 27 elderly residents first involved in the project. Initial meetings were devoted to the following five specific tasks: (1) giving feedback on the needs assessment, indicating the commonalities and priorities of issues that needed to be addressed; (2) establishing new alliances through recognition of shared concerns; (3) developing knowledge of resources that would match services with need; (4) teaching members how to establish linkages with agencies, utilize available resources, and develop organizational skills; and (5) involving the elderly members by making them a governing board.

Initially, the community mental health center gerontologists chose to work alone with no additional staff, especially since it was felt that this would reinforce the necessity for every member's participation. No other agencies were present to extend services to the elderly participants because it was important for the residents to see themselves as the major helping resources for each other. Ross (1983) points out that with the growth of membership and service needs three additional professional staff were added—a nurse, a social worker, and a part-time psychiatrist—as medical and mental resources. The participation of older people in this project has continued to grow. Despite the growth of the neighborhood family's clientele, the initial staff of four people has remained constant for several years. This is especially significant since it has allowed room for the older people to assume managerial roles and other responsible and meaningful positions as member volunteers. In essence, this model combines a kinlike supportive community, a multipurpose service and activities center, minimal staff, and indigenous decision making—particularly on the part of the elderly.

## A Group Approach for Working with Families of the Elderly

The idea that the family is an important source of support and help for older adults has been discussed in the literature on aging for some time. Families are a definite source of strength to the elderly and offer financial, emotional, and social support to older people living in the community as well as in institutional settings. This awareness of the importance of the family has led to the development of new family therapy models for working with the problems of the aging. One such interventionist strategy that centered primarily on the needs of the families of the elderly was developed by Cohen and staff (1983, p. 20).

The critical question raised by Cohen and her staff was "How can we provide services for the families of the elderly who have the grave responsibility of caretaking?" and "What kinds of services should we provide?" What evolved out of these concerns was a support group for families of the elderly. The Hartford and Parsons (1982) and Hausman (1979) supportive treatment groups served as significant sources of reference in developing the group discussed here. Cohen's primary objective in developing the group was to provide a helpful service to family members who were coping with the problems and concerns of caring for their older relatives. In essence, the specific goals were as follows:

1. To afford support for families of older people as well as a place where feelings could be shared and similarities as well as unique problems could be identified.
2. To provide information about three basic things including adult development, the process of aging, and readily obtainable community resources and services.
3. To provide assistance to those needing to make specific decisions.
4. To teach skills in the care of oneself including assertiveness, stress management, and communication skills.
5. To provide a facility in which group therapy could take place as it relates to issues such as sibling rivalry, guilt, role reversal, and unresolved childhood conflicts. (Cohen, 1983)

The group met weekly for two hours during a 10-week period. Early sessions included formal presentations by the group leader, films, and structured group exercises. As the group meetings progressed, it became less necessary for the leader to provide the structure. The result was that group members took more of the responsibility for actively sharing with and supporting one another.

The next several meetings included some didactic material on adult development, physical aspects of aging, death and dying, and psychosocial aspects of aging. A variety of films were shown: *Everybody Rides the Carousel, Part 3* (Pyramid Films), *Why Me?* (Pyramid Films), and *Growing Old* (McGraw-Hill).

The next sessions (five and six) were especially significant to the group participants because they allowed for more sharing with each other. The leader introduced a guided fantasy back into childhood. This enabled the group members to remember and share some of their childhood relationships with their parents as well as their current feelings of guilt, anger, love, hate, and responsibility that may have been rooted in these childhood relationships.

Assertiveness training and stress management were the focus of the next couple of meetings. The emphasis in these meetings was on skill building in both of these areas in order to strengthen the coping skills for dealing with various problems handled by people in the caretaking role.

Community resources were shared during the ninth group meeting. Information and referral personnel from the local agency on aging shared their materials, and group members shared their own special knowledge and tips with one another. The group ended by having a celebration for all of the members. During this time there was a quiet, reflective sharing of what had occurred during all of the sessions followed by evaluations and a potluck supper.

The participants in the group meetings were between 42 and 67 years of age, and six people were over 60. Thus a number of issues and role conflicts came to light during these sessions. Cohen (1983) and her staff report that responsibility for both parents and children was an issue for caretakers in their 40s. Dealing with their own aging and retirement issues, as well as coping with their resentment at having to take on new responsibilities precisely at the time when they thought they would feel free, concerned the older group members.

The group leader and her staff point out that the group was not intended to be a research group but primarily one that was therapeutic and supportive in nature. Participants frequently remarked to each other and to the leader about the value of the group. They were asked by Cohen and her staff to respond to a series of subjective evaluative questions at the conclusion of the group relating to the value of the experience, strengths and weaknesses of the group, quality of leadership, and possible improvement. According to Cohen (1983) most of the comments were extremely positive, and none were negative.

## Mutual Self-Help Groups

Mutual self-help groups are becoming increasingly prevalent in American society, and the need to continue such groups, particularly in this era of reduced federal funding for social programs, is continually being encouraged. Mutual self-help groups—especially those among black people—have a long history dating back to the 1700s when mutual aid societies began in the black church (see Frazier & Lincoln, 1974).

Mutual self-help groups among blacks, particularly those that were church related, served a recognized social need. The church was seen as an important agency for rendering group cohesion.

Haber has identified four major advantages that mutual self-help groups have over professional groups. They are:

1. The availability of various kinds of support over a long period of time without cost.
2. The sharing of personal experiences that bring about understanding, resource sharing, and depth of feeling that might not be reached with a professional worker.
3. Decentralize services that are more accessible than are centralized public service agencies and more reliable in a time of dwindling human services and resources.

4. The strengthening of networks in the community.

At the present time it is believed that the number of gerontological and intergenerational mutual self-help groups is growing. However, some of these groups are organized by professional workers and they terminate once those workers leave. This is unfortunate; it would appear that more professionals should encourage older people to initiate mutual self-help groups in the field of aging.

## SUMMARY

The focus of this chapter has been on the well-elderly and the preventive efforts they take to maintain themselves at the highest possible levels. Although social workers and other health professionals can aid and enhance their efforts, in the final analysis it is the well-elderly themselves who must assume ultimate responsibility for preventive maintenance. A variety of preventive measures such as exercise, diet, and educational programs were among those discussed, since they are frequently engaged in by the well-elderly.

Definitions of health and wellness must be viewed within a broad perspective because of the number of factors that must be taken into consideration. However, for those people who have aged successfully, health appears to be a major factor. People who are in poor health are often those who are housebound, whose activities are restricted, and who have little freedom to exercise a range of options that are frequently available to the well-elderly. The well-elderly have the fewest incapacities and are the least restricted in their daily activities.

Stress is generally considered to be a normal part of daily living. Health can be measured by an individual's ability to cope with stress.

A number of definitions of successful aging have been advanced. Neugarten's five components of positive life satisfaction is the most global of those included in this chapter. This definition reflects the individual's ego strengths as well as his or her capacity to deal with internal and external changes.

Personality, quality of life, and general health are all perceived of as important components of the concept of successful aging. Each of these elements is complex and must necessarily be analyzed separately for its ability to ward off the development of some of the problems of older life.

Primary prevention has taken on two basic directions in the past. One direction has been to develop methods of early detection, or the prediction of problems before they occur. The other has been to focus on the kinds of activities (specifically, diet, nutrition, exercise, and so on) that older persons can undertake for themselves. Assuming responsibility for one's behavior is important, especially since society regards dependency in a negative light. In addition, behavioral controls such as those discussed in this chapter are desirable in light of scarce professional resources.

From the early social work reformers to contemporary social policy planners, "the intent and goal have been the prevention of social dysfunction" (Wittman, 1977, p. 1050). In the past, social work intervened only after serious problems were already evident and social dysfunctioning was already occurring. However, over the past quarter of a century the social work profession has developed an increasing interest in the concept of prevention. Recently, there have been descriptions and elaborations of the objectives and methods of prevention. Also, in 1974 the National Association of Social Workers published a reprint series that brought together a number of articles dealing with the implications of preventive intervention for social-work practice. The articles also highlighted new forms of direct work with clients (see Kosberg, 1979). The goals of preventive intervention involve attempts to build strengths into individuals and systems as a means of avoiding problems.

There is no question that educating middle-aged and older persons to age-related changes and losses helps them to anticipate and perhaps cushion the impact of potentially harmful events when they do occur. In addition, the training of others such as professionals, paraprofessionals, and volunteers to work in the field of aging is a viable preventive strategy. These people can share with the aging and the aged knowledge about human development in its various complexities.

The types of educational activity discussed in this chapter were designed to help the aging and the aged to enhance the quality of life through the promotion of health. Programs such as these are helpful to the extent that they build strength into individuals and systems for the purpose of avoiding problems. Preventive programs and activities can be offered in a range of settings and situations.

Three other examples of primary intervention—the neighborhood family concept, a group approach for working with families of the elderly, and mutual self-help groups—were also discussed.

# Chapter 5

# Clinical social work with the elderly at the secondary level of practice

## INTRODUCTION

This chapter addresses clinical social work intervention at the secondary level of practice in the field of aging. The problems treated at this level are defined in terms of acute, specific, definitive, and presenting problems in physical-psychological-social functioning. The psychosocial systems approach to problem assessment/diagnosis and treatment planning is applied to cases at the secondary level of practice with the elderly. The various social work roles that come into play at this level of practice are also discussed.

The major emphasis in this chapter is on a presentation of the chief characteristics of a select number of functioning problems frequently experienced by the elderly. The problem dynamics are described, and suggested casework treatment interventions are identified and discussed. The problems selected for inclusion in this discussion are normal problems of stress associated with relocation, loneliness, sexuality and marriage/family, the psychological conditions of neurotic reaction to aging, depression, unresolved grief reaction and alcoholism, adaptational problems associated with widowhood and retirement, and the psychosocial problems associated with acute medical illness. The chapter concludes with a case that illustrates casework assessment and treatment planning with a depressed and suicidal widower. Some questions are provided for the use of this case in classroom discussion.

## THE SECONDARY LEVEL OF PRACTICE DEFINED

The major emphasis at the secondary level is on intervention with the elderly who already have problems in order to bring about a resolution of those problems, or at the least to prevent the development of serious states of functional impairment. The intervention offered is often referred to as clinical treatment, therapy, or counseling. In the social work profession, intervention at this level is called clinical social work or clinical casework. Medicine and psychiatry refer to problems at this level as acute illness, and they traditionally speak of curing the patient and preventing chronic illness.

Although casework intervention at this level is definitely oriented to the goal of patient recovery, the social worker speaks of problem resolution, problem solving, and problem amelioration. While those in medicine and psychiatry describe problems in terms of illness, caseworkers describe them in terms of physical-psychological-social dysfunctioning. The individual's state of wellness or well-being is disturbed: One or more aspects of human functioning is disrupted and dysfunctional.

Regardless of the different theoretical assumptions that underlie the etiological and diagnostic view of a problem, most professional practitioners and typical laypersons use a fairly common vocabulary to identify, describe, label, and categorize problems of human distress. For instance, a particular presenting problem is generally referred to as an illness, disease, pathology, disturbance, injury, condition, abnormality, malfunction, maladjustment, maladaptation, deviance, perversion, difficulty, and/or crisis. Any one of the preceding terms is usually modified by one or more of the following words: physical, mental, cognitive, thinking, psychological, sensory, perceptive, personality, behavioral, social, interpersonal, psychiatric, psychotic, neurotic, character, developmental, somatic, psychosomatic, mood, emotional, and/or affective. The individual's problem is further described in terms of its symptoms such as pain, stress, distress, nervousness, anxiety, apprehension, depression, sadness, confusion, disorientation, panic, fear, anger, conflict, compulsion, obsession, delusion, hallucination, agitation, tremors, and so on.

Almost anything that pertains to some kind of human difficulty in functioning can constitute a problem. The problem that presents itself may be simple or complex in composition. It may not be very serious or intense, or it may be critical. It may primarily involve only one of the three areas that constitute human makeup (physical, psychological, and social behavior), or it may manifest itself strongly in two or all three areas. Most people tend to classify a problem as either mental or physical. They generally speak of being mentally ill or physically ill, yet the two are often intrinsically linked.

The clinical social worker deals with a wide range of problems through a variety of medical settings, mental health settings, and community-based social service programs. In medical and psychiatric settings the geriatric caseworker usually works as a member of a multidisciplinary team and assists other team members in the diagnostic workup of the presenting problem. The worker also participates as a therapeutic agent. The caseworker's concern is with the overall effects of the patient's illness or problem. In the social service agency the caseworker functions as a primary counselor and service manager, and deals with a broad range of problems associated with the stresses of normal living.

## PROBLEM ASSESSMENT AND TREATMENT PLANNING

Casework intervention with all clients at the secondary level of practice is guided by the psychosocial systems process of problem assessment/diagnosis. In Chapter 3 the authors refer to this process as the generic casework process, because it is applicable to all cases of clinical social work intervention at all three levels of practice.

Casework intervention begins with the establishment of a trusting relationship and the identification and definition of the client's presenting problem. As the assessment/diagnostic process develops, the caseworker attends very closely to the particular interests and goals for which the client seeks help. The formulation of a definitive treatment plan is accomplished through a contracting process between the client and the worker. A contract is characterized by mutuality and clarity: The defined outcome goals must be acceptable to and understood by the client. The client must be informed of the interventive procedures to be employed, which must be acceptable to him or her. Contracting increases the client's motivation to engage in the helping experience. Pincus and Minahan (1973) point out that the parts of a contract upon which worker and client must agree are the major goals of the parties, the tasks to be performed by each in pursuit of these goals, and the operating procedures for guiding the process of change. There can be no secrets. When a contract is present in a case intervention, it is evident throughout every phase of the treatment process. At any given point the client should have a reasonably good idea of what is occurring, why it is happening, and how it is being done.

The caseworker's study and assessment of the presenting problem within a psychosocial systems perspective takes into account a broad overview of the client's total physical-psychological-social functioning without losing sight of his or her identified concerns. If a client carries a specific medical and/or psychiatric diagnosis, the caseworker must understand the nature of the clinical condition; however, the caseworker's assessment is not confined to the clinical entity. The casework assessment identifies and describes strengths and weaknesses in physical, psychological, and social functioning. The essential factors of physical functioning that need to be assessed include the client's ambulation, speaking, hearing, and visual capacities. The client's eating and sleeping habits need to be reviewed. The caseworker needs to find out if the client has breathing difficulties or complains of pain and physical illness. The caseworker's task is not to diagnose medical problems, but to determine if the client is in need of medical referral.

In the area of psychological functioning a general assessment should be made of the client's ability to perceive reality and reason logically. The client's emotional state and value orientation should be observed. The aspects of social functioning to be assessed are social-role performances, interpersonal relationships, economic situation, housing conditions, and informal social-network involvements.

This complex person-in-situation assessment attempts to locate causal sources for each dysfunctional element. The causes of dysfunction may be located within the client, the environment, or both. In most cases human dysfunction has multiple causes from several different sources.

Assessment-based treatment planning includes designated goals for change and identifies the causal factors that need to be modified if these goals are to be attained. At times the client must change from within; certain beliefs, values, and emotional and behavioral habits need to be modified. At times the way the client is treated by significant others may have to be modified. Components of the physical environment may have to be modified. (The absence of essential resources may be a cause of dysfunction.) At times the policies and procedures of health and social agencies create barriers for the client and thus contribute to the complex of factors that perpetuate the client's problem. Thus the various causes of human problems are the whos, whats, wheres, whens, and hows of the individual and his or her environment.

The symptom picture in two cases may be very similar, but the basic cause may be quite different. For example, mental confusion and irrational thinking in one client may be caused by an incurable neurological illness such as Alzheimer's disease, while in another client the same type of mental dysfunctioning may be caused by the external environment. In the following case example the major causation of an elderly woman's mental dysfunctioning is located in the environment.

Mrs. Miller, age 80, lived alone on the top floor of a two-story, age-integrated public housing apartment building. The building was located next to a busy highway and a railroad track. In addition to these sources of frequent noises, the roof of the building was used by the younger tenants for recreational purposes throughout the day and much of the night.

Mrs. Miller was confused most of the time and was quite disoriented in her own apartment. She was afraid to leave the apartment and she expressed paranoid ideas about the thumping noises and muffled voices that emanated from the roof. She believed that people were constantly attempting to break into her apartment. Her dimly lighted apartment created a rather eerie atmosphere, and her impaired vision made the environment appear all the darker and more dreary. She frequently perceived fuzzy shadows to be strangers lurking inside her apartment.

Mrs. Miller's symptoms of confusion, disorientation, illusions, and paranoid thinking were quite similar to those commonly displayed by patients who have some form of irreversible brain pathology or mental illness.

The caseworker's assessment concluded that Mrs. Miller's symptoms of mental dysfunctioning were causally related to her constant and long-standing exposure to a confusing and unpleasant environment. The noise from automobiles, trains, and people on the roof distorted Mrs. Miller's sensory and perceptual functions. The dimly lighted apartment, Mrs. Miller's poor vision, and the unexplained voices and footsteps on the roof promoted paranoid thinking, sensory illusions, and the related fears. Because Mrs. Miller lived alone, there was no one available on a daily basis to provide her with consistent, correct explanations of the noises from the roof, to reassure her that she was safe from intruders, and to provide her with orderly, concise conversational stimuli to compete with the bombardment of confusing stimuli from the external environment.

A caseworker's assessment-based treatment plan must include specified goals and a selection of interventive procedures to be applied to the various elements of causation.

In the case of Mrs. Miller the primary goals are to promote socialization, restore rational cognition, and minimize anxiety. The indicated environmental changes are: (1) relocating Mrs. Miller to a well-lighted apartment in a neighborhood accessible to socialization resources; and (2) linking her to formal and informal socialization networks.

Because the client's emotional and mental difficulties have existed for a prolonged period of time, casework intervention to promote some change in Mrs. Miller is indicated. The caseworker needs to help Mrs. Miller develop a positive attitude toward her new home and assist her in overcoming her anxiety about making friends in the new neighborhood and participating in socialization programs at a senior center. As an eclectic practitioner the worker may utilize treatment procedures from a number of different approaches. For instance, the following combination of procedures might be utilized to ease Mrs. Miller's anxiety about social interaction: (1) role rehearsal (behavioral approach), (2) reflective discussion (psychosocial approach), (3) empathy (client-centered approach), and (4) cognitive restructuring (cognitive approach).

## NORMAL AGING AND PROBLEMS OF STRESS

Many of the elderly cope successfully with a variety of losses associated with the aging process. They feel pain and disappointment, but they manage to avoid excessive stress and dysfunction. Many others are not as fortunate. According to Germain and Gitterman upsets in the adaptive transactions between people and environments create stress. They define problems in terms of stress and its sources.

> In our conception of the life model, we treat stress as a psychosocial condition generated by discrepancies between needs and capacities, on the one hand, and environmental qualities on the other. It arises in three interrelated areas of living: life transactions, environmental pressures, and interpersonal processes. (1980, p. 7)

Retirement is a life transition that precipitates stress for some older people, particularly when a person has to retire against his or her wishes. (Some people have a strong psychological need to continue working while others perceive a financial need to remain employed.) Widowhood is another life transition that precipitates stress for many older people.

Environmental pressures refer to conditions of the social and physical environments wherein need-meeting resources and supports are not available, are insufficient, and/or have a negative effect on the elderly. For instance, stress may be precipitated as a result of obstacles presented by complex social organizations such as health care and social service agencies. Interpersonal processes as sources of stress include maladaptive personal relationships in marriage or family. Faulty communication is most frequently the cause of stress between husband and wife or between parent and child.

The Germain and Gitterman model rests on the psychosocial systems perspective. It emphasizes the need to intervene with the individual and the environment at the points at which they converge. Casework is viewed as a multirole endeavor involving counseling, education, advocacy, linkage, and brokerage. The caseworker intervenes with the individual client, couples, family units, natural groups, and formed groups. This model of casework draws upon treatment techniques from a wide variety of approaches.

The task-centered casework model conceptualized by Reid and Epstein (1972) is also a transactional approach to problem solving that addresses the numerous sources of stress associated with normal living. This brief-oriented casework approach is discussed by Cornican (1977) in reference to the elderly client. Cornican believes that many elderly clients want to and can make their own decisions when faced with problems.

In this model the caseworker assists the client in defining major outcome goals and the specific tasks the client must perform in order to attain each of these goals. The client carries out the tasks with only minimal guidance from the worker.

A stress-related problem in daily living is uniquely defined for each elderly client. There is no problem typology for difficulties of this nature; that is, such problems are not conceptualized in terms of physical and or mental illness. They are, nevertheless, real problems in human functioning that can frequently be resolved through casework intervention.

The major portion of problems addressed at the secondary level of casework intervention derives from stress-related difficulties in daily living and experiences with life transition. Timely intervention with these kinds of problems can prevent for many the development of serious physical and mental illness and dysfunction. The following discussion focuses on six problem areas. The problem dimensions for each are described and the casework interventions are discussed.

## Relocation

Many older people are forced to change their place of residence due to health and financial reasons. Forced or unwanted relocations are usually perceived as major losses. The sense of loss is especially strong when one must leave a home one has occupied for a long period of time. Many of the elderly who own their homes have to give them up after retirement because they are unable to pay real estate taxes and they cannot finance home maintenance on their limited and fixed retirement incomes. Further, because their incomes are low, new living arrangement choices are limited. Thus the new arrangements and the surrounding environment are often of poor quality.

A small number of old people who are forced to move out of their homes are fortunate because they have access to new, low-cost housing that is subsidized by the government. The greater the contrast between the old and new living arrangements, the greater the experience of distress. For instance, it is very difficult to adapt to apartment living if one has always lived in a house, or to adapt to a tenement district when one has always lived in a residential neighborhood. Additional discomfort is often associated with the loss of easy access to stores, church, and community service centers. Another sense of loss results from the absence of casual, daily contact with friends in the old neighborhood.

Older people usually feel uneasy about living in an unfamiliar environment. The process of making new friends in a new environment is no easier for an older person than it is for a young one. The impact of an unwanted move can be greatly minimized if the individual or couple has an opportunity to carefully plan and prepare for the relocation. Casework counseling can contribute to this process of planning and preparation by helping the client see that he or she has some choices, however small and few in number. For instance, often the timing and pace of the move can be controlled by the client. The client also can decide what personal belongings will be retained. With the caseworker's assistance a number of possible living arrangements, types of dwellings, and geographical locations can be identified; and from this pool of alternatives a choice can be made.

The following case illustrates secondary preventive intervention with a distressed elderly woman who is in danger of losing her home.

Mrs. Jones is unmarried, 75 years old, and lives alone. She draws a small pension and has a low-paying, part-time job in a local bakery. She has lived by herself in the family home for the last 10 years—since her mother passed away. It has become more and more difficult for her to bear the ever-increasing cost of home maintenance. If it were not for her part-time job she would have lost the house some years ago.

Although Mrs. Jones is in relatively good health (considering her advanced age and hard work), she has recently been more and more troubled with arthritic pains in her legs, chronic tiredness, and depressed moods. Her doctor has urged her over the last year to give up her employment. The house is in need of repair, but she cannot afford to have the work done. Over the last year she has found it increasingly difficult to keep up with the minor repairs and daily routines of home management. It greatly taxes her to do such chores as mow the grass, put up storm windows, clean the furnace and shovel snow. She cannot afford to pay someone to do these things without taking money away from other pressing areas. Her greatest fear at this time is that she will not be able to pay the real estate taxes, which were increased again this year, while her income remained the same.

Mrs. Jones is aware that the cost is constantly rising for almost everything she needs—medicine, food, clothing, transportation, household supplies, and so on. She has pared the budget to the bone, cannot cut expenditures any further, and sees no new financial resources that might be available to her. Over the last six months she has become more and more worried and apprehensive about her future in general. For the first time in her life she finds herself feeling depressed and agitated most of the time. More and more often she feels like staying in bed instead of going to work.

Being a rational and intelligent person, Mrs. Jones has frequently thought about the possibility of giving up the house and moving to smaller and cheaper quarters. This would mean moving to a small apartment, a prospect that is quite distressing to her given the fact that Mrs. Jones has lived for 75 years in a spacious house in a quiet, residential neighborhood. She knows, however, that she has to do something soon about her difficult situation, but she continues to put off making a decision. Very recently she has come to realize that her nervousness and depression may cause her to lose her job, and that the income reduction would make her situation critical. Mrs. Jones was persuaded by a co-worker to talk to a social caseworker at the local senior citizen center. After a few days of resistance, Mrs. Jones "got up her nerve" and made an appointment at the center.

It took several sessions for the caseworker to hear Mrs. Jones's complete story and to arrive at a general assessment of her psychosocial situation. Although the caseworker recognized the client's depression and anxiety, she viewed the distress as a reaction to Mrs. Jones's perceived inability to resolve a problem situation that was rapidly approaching a critical state. Because Mrs. Jones had many psychological strengths, including a strong motivation to help herself, the worker decided to use a problem-solving and task-oriented treatment strategy.

The worker began by teaching the client the sequential steps of a problem-solving approach. This was acceptable to Mrs. Jones and they contracted for brief, task-oriented counseling in which approximately eight weeks would be devoted to searching for a possible solution to the client's problem. They agreed to terminate counseling when Mrs. Jones had in hand a definite plan of action including the specified problem-solving tasks she had contracted to complete.

During counseling at least six different possible and feasible problem-solving alternatives were identified, designed, evaluated, and analyzed. The alternative selected for Mrs. Jones was to look for a live-in companion of similar age with a similar lifestyle and interests; and one who could pay enough room and board allowance to permit Mrs. Jones to hold onto her home. The plan also included Mrs. Jones's securing a position as a paid volunteer with a senior companion program. The money she would earn from such a job would allow her to give up the taxing job at the bakery. The worker informed Mrs. Jones of several income-augmenting programs for which she was eligible. Mrs. Jones took the responsibility for applying for food stamps, fuel supplement payments, and real estate tax rebates.

Mrs. Jones was successful in resolving her problem. The caseworker's timely and structured brief intervention helped to prevent a psychosocial crisis that could have resulted in chronic depression and an overall decline in functioning.

## Social Isolation and Loneliness

Many of the elderly become socially isolated. Most of those who are isolated live alone, but some reside with others in boarding houses, foster homes, or with their relatives. The socially isolated person (living alone or in midst of others) is deprived of regular and meaningful interpersonal interaction. The most serious consequence of social isolation is loneliness. An old person does not feel lonely just because he or she is alone. Loneliness is related to the absence of socially stimulating activity and mutually fulfilling interpersonal relationships. The lonely person needs ongoing, warm interaction with significant others. According to Lowy (1979) loneliness is also related to boredom and apathy. Some lonely people feel isolated from others because they have no outlets for interaction and no direction and status in a world of busy people. Clark and Anderson (1967) observe that women are more often lonely than men, and that isolation and loneliness are also prevalent among those elderly who have had long-standing personality difficulties characterized by seeking solitude to avoid others. Many well-adjusted people are lonely because the relationships they lost through the death of a spouse and/or friends have not been replaced. Burnside (1973) believes that many of the lonely elderly have little ego energy left to invest in new relationships, and that many who live alone have limited opportunity to pursue new friendships.

MacMillan (1969) warns us of the dire consequences of prolonged social and emotional isolation. For instance, in some cases senile breakdown with symptoms very similar to organic brain disease (confusion, disorientation, and depression) is due to prolonged loneliness.

In general, casework intervention with the lonely client constitutes promoting resocialization and creating a socially stimulating environment. Each lonely client needs to be carefully assessed so the factors that are maintaining social isolation and loneliness can be targeted for intervention. In cases of long-standing isolation and loneliness, the client-worker relationship becomes a "stepping stone" to the client's involvement with others. When the client is able to trust the worker and engage comfortably in social and emotional exchange, he or she will be more open to interaction with others. In some cases counseling may have to focus initially on modifying a client's antisocial attitudes and irrational negative beliefs about the social world. Some clients may need social assertiveness training in order to increase their capacity to successfully relate to others (see Chapter 3).

When the client is emotionally ready, the caseworker needs to link him or her to opportunities for interpersonal interaction. Such opportunities are generally available through the social/recreational programs of senior centers and other social agencies that have programs designed to meet the socialization needs of the elderly. Most centers conduct socialization groups.

Reminiscing is encouraged through group discussions to help individuals recall those past socializing experiences that were personally fulfilling. These pleasurable memories often serve to motivate the withdrawn client to redevelop interpersonal social skills and relationships.

Much has been written about the phenomenon of reminiscence. Elderly people seem to frequently and regularly reminisce. Only those who are depressed do not reminisce, or if they do they keep their thoughts to themselves (see Mc Mahan and Rhudick, 1964). The reminiscences of depressed people frequently reflect themes of guilt, unrealized goals, and wished-for opportunities to make up for past failures. In Robert Butler's theory of life review, reminiscing is asserted to be the way in which the elderly person conducts a mental review of life. Butler asserts that all elderly throughout the world engage in a life review process brought on by the realization of their inevitable and approaching mortality.

Life review through reminiscence is characterized by the progressive return to consciousness of past experiences, particularly those associated with unresolved conflicts and disappointments. This critical, self-analytical quality of the life review process helps the individual work through unresolved conflicts and promotes a sense of integration and satisfaction with oneself during the remaining years of life (see Butler, 1963; Butler & Lewis, 1977).

The fairly common activity of reminiscing among the elderly serves important intrapersonal and interpersonal functions beyond and in addition to the life review process. Reminiscence in general helps the individual cope with the aging process, maintain self-esteem, and reinforce a sense of social attachment, belongingness, and continuity. Cornican (1977) stresses the adaptational qualities of typical reminiscence. She sees reminiscence as a method for releasing and rekindling personal strengths and a positive self-image.

Older people who are not depressed and bitter about their lives like to share their memories of past good times with others. This kind of conversational sharing through group interaction is found to be very enjoyable by many older adults. Inclusion of the socially and emotionally isolated client in a reminiscence group may help this person to gradually develop a sense of belongingness with other older people and therefore facilitate the client's desire to develop meaningful, new friendships.

As the isolated client makes progress in social interaction, membership in a variety of recreational groups should be encouraged. In the interest of expanding the client's social network, the caseworker can look toward the extended family, church, and neighborhood and community clubs and associations for opportunities for meaningful social involvement. If not available transportation services need to be arranged so that such social contacts can be realized.

For the lonely and isolated person who is physically confined to the home, efforts must be made to bring significant others into the home on a regular basis. The caseworker can attempt to locate and generate interest from the client's long-lost relatives, promote the development of neighborhood friendships, and encourage visits from church and social club members. Many cities have a number of formalized, friendly visiting services.

One such program, which has been highly successful in providing ongoing friendly visitors to the shut-in elderly, is the Senior Companion Program, funded and administered by the Federal Volunteer Agency. This program trains and supervises senior citizen volunteers who, on a regular and continuing basis, visit other elderly people who are confined to their homes. The senior companion provides a close and friendly supportive relationship to the home-bound person. In Pittsburgh, Pennsylvania, a volunteer program known as Generations Together has been very effective in using adolescent volunteers who provide friendly visiting and emotional support services to the shut-in elderly (see Newman, 1982). Both the adolescent and the elderly person benefit from their close, warm relationship.

In those cases of social and emotional isolation where the elderly person resides with family members, casework counseling with the family as a unit may be indicated in order to help the family resolve the interpersonal conflicts that distance the elderly client from the emotional life of the family. In some of these cases the relatives may not be aware of how to deal with the older person's tendency to withdraw socially and emotionally, and casework can be focused on educating relatives to provide a socially stimulating daily environment for the withdrawn client.

**Sexual Problems**

A significant number of older people experience distress in relation to sex and sex-related problems. Gochros and Gochros (1977) identify the elderly as one of the sexually oppressed groups in our society. Various aspects of sexual expression and function are denied the elderly because many Americans, including older people, hold negative attitudes and inaccurate beliefs about sexuality and aging (see Rubin, 1978). For instance, it is popularly believed that due to the nature of old age people lose the ability to become sexually aroused and achieve orgasm. When this belief is held by an older person it serves to inhibit or prevent sexual response. In other words, many older people are sexually dysfunctional because they believe it is impossible to be functional.

Moreover, those older people who know that sex is possible in old age may lose the ability to perform because they have the attitude that old people should not be interested in sex. This attitude produces shame, guilt, and anxiety, which in turn psychologically block sexual functioning.

Problems of sexual dysfunction that have no physical basis (those caused by inhibiting anxiety associated with negative attitudes and/or inaccurate knowledge about sexual capacity) can often be successfully treated through casework counseling that modifies negative attitudes and provides accurate information about sexual functioning capacities in old age. Those with complaints of sexual performance problems should be referred to a physician so a determination can be made about whether the problems are due to physical illness and/or the side effects of medication. When sexual dysfunctioning is caused by psychological factors, such as performance anxiety, a client should be referred to a professionally trained sex therapist.

Some unmarried older women are interested in sexual involvement but have difficulty finding appropriate male partners who have similar interests due to the shortage of available unmarried older men. A caseworker can help this kind of client by linking her to informal social networks and directing her to social recreational settings where there are increased opportunities to meet men who are interested in similar relationships.

Many older, homosexually oriented individuals need supportive casework therapy. They are depressed and anxiety ridden because they are victims of severe negative stereotyping. According to James Kelley (1977) this seems to be particularly true for the elderly homosexual male. Kelley's study of older gay men in the Los Angeles area revealed that the gay subculture itself negatively stereotypes the older, male homosexual. He is viewed as a lonely, unattractive, effeminate, unhappy, and silly person who craves physical sexual relations with young men and is unable to maintain a stable, lasting relationship with an age-appropriate partner.

Kelley's subjects did not fit this stereotype, but because of it they felt rejected by and were isolated from the mainstream of the gay community. Many of the study's subjects were quite fearful of the potential for job and housing discrimination and therefore were extremely careful to hide their homosexuality from both the homosexual and heterosexual communities. Supportive casework can help these individuals locate supportive social networks and advocate for them when they are victims of discrimination.

Many older people need and request accurate information about the numerous and different aspects of human sexuality and the later years of life. In recent years more and more professional authorities have been writing about aging and sexuality. For a sampling of this multisubject professional literature the reader is referred to the following publications: Weg (1978), Long (1976), Christenson and Gagnon (1965), Birren and Moore (1975), Rubin (1969), Wasow and Loeb (1977), and Butler (1975).

## Marital and Family Problems

Older couples, like those of any age group, can develop conflicts around many aspects of marital life. Some couples carry their long-standing relationship problems into their retirement years, while others experience their first conflict as a consequence of stress deriving from retirement.

The newly retired couple has more time to devote exclusively to their relationship than they ever had before. Thus tensions may develop between them about how to use that extra time. One or both partners may have expectations or make demands that create conflict and/or resentment. For example, a husband in search of meaningful and constructive use of his leisure time may interfere with his wife's household activities. Or a couple may have recurring disagreements about how to budget their reduced income. Many couples are able to work out compromises and within a short period of time develop a fulfilling companionship and lifestyle (see Medley, 1977).

Unfortunately, some spouses are unable to talk openly to each other about their disagreements, disappointments, dissatisfactions, and hurt feelings. Instead of communicating in a direct and clear fashion, they try to get what they want through manipulation, coercion, and/or pouting. This kind of dysfunctional communication can be successfully treated with conjoint relationship counseling.

The caseworker who sees both partners together teaches them how to effectively express their needs and interests to each other. The couple's new or restored communication skills in turn facilitate their ability to develop a compatible and satisfying relationship. The caseworker might employ guided reminiscing to help the couple recall the compatible aspects of their relationship in their early years of marriage. Reminiscing may also help the couple to remember the good thoughts they had when they were younger about what they would do together when they retired.

Peterson (1973) promotes the use of couples groups to treat marital conflict among the elderly. Couples can gain a sense of relief in learning that others in their age group have similar difficulties. They can share ideas with each other about how they go about the task of building marital compatibility in old age. A secondary gain from this kind of group experience may be the development of new and lasting friendships.

Some older people experience intergenerational family conflict. This often occurs when an elderly parent lives with the family of an adult child. Conflicts usually arise over issues of parenting, home management, divisions of labor, family authority, privacy, and interference. For example, Grandma may upset the family by usurping one or more of the roles that previously belonged to the parents. Or she may cause stress for her daughter and son-in-law by encroaching upon their marital companionship and privacy. She may undermine or criticize the parents' disciplining of their children, criticize her daughter's housekeeping, or try to make family members feel guilty because they do not pay enough attention to her. Sometimes these kinds of intrusions cause serious marital conflict and/or parent-child conflict.

Cases of this nature call for direct intervention with the entire family unit. Family roles must be clarified and defined along generational lines. The elderly member needs to be provided with the opportunity to perform the appropriate grandparenting role, as well as the opportunity to perform a parental role with his or her adult children.

Relationships between elderly parents and their children can become strained because the children disapprove of their parents' lifestyle. For instance, an adult child may try to prevent a widowed parent from living with a lover or getting remarried. Unless the older person is the victim of a charlatan, the caseworker should support his or her acts of independence and right to self-determination. The caseworker can offer to talk to the adult children on the client's behalf and/or to help the client find effective ways to diminish the children's worries and stop their interfering.

Recognizing the fact that in our society the family has a strong tendency to hold together across generations and that adult children and other relatives can often be resourceful to the elderly in times of distress, the caseworker should in every instance give careful consideration to the appropriate involvement of the family network. Kirschner (1979) stresses the importance of family intervention in the case of the older person who is in a state of crisis. She instructs the worker to include all available relatives in both the assessment and treatment phases of intervention.

## Problems of Widowhood

Widowhood is prevalent in the elderly population. A majority of those who are widowed are women. (In 1980, 77 percent of elderly men were married while 52 percent of elderly women were widowed.) This disparity is caused primarily by the shorter life expectancy for men, the fact that most men marry women younger than themselves, and the fact that the remarriage rate is several times higher for men than it is for women. (Most women outlive their husbands by many years.) On the basis of current mortality rates a widow in her 60s can expect to live another 15 to 20 years. Widows constitute 41 percent of women in the 65 to 74 age range and 70 percent of the female population over the age of 75.

The Federal Council on Aging (1981) reports that many widows suffer from the multiple hazards of low income, failing health, and social isolation. Schaie and Geiwitz (1982) discuss the statistical dimensions of widowhood in terms of a growing social problem. As each year passes an increasing number of the very old widows become dependent upon society for all aspects of care.

Widowhood does not cause a serious psychosocial problem for all elderly who experience it. All who lose a spouse through death feel an intense emotional loss and experience personal distress associated with the adaptational demands necessitated by the social transition from the status of marriage to that of widowhood. A large percentage of elderly widows makes a successful adjustment within one year of the death of a spouse. The process of adaptation is facilitated when the elderly widow or widower has access to an informal, social-support system.

Some widowed men and women, however, are not successful in working through the grief brought on by the loss of a spouse. Unresolved grief may linger for a long period of time and require special therapeutic attention. The symptoms of abnormal grief reaction and the treatment for this condition are discussed later in this chapter.

Some elderly women find widowhood quite stressful because they lack the internal and/or external resources that are needed to cope with the new demands of single life. Some are unable to financially and/or physically maintain their homes and are stressed by the experience of an unwanted relocation. Most widows live alone, and many find that they lack many of the skills that are needed to cope with the many normal tasks of daily living such as transporting themselves to the grocery store, church, and other routine destinations. (Frequently these women depended entirely upon their husbands for transportation.) Unless the widow can afford to pay others to perform such tasks, daily living can become quite stressful.

Many low-income widows who need some assistance with various tasks of daily living are fortunate in that they have access to a network of friends, neighbors, and relatives who are willing to provide assistance. Some of these women, however, are reluctant to request or accept help on a regular and continuing basis because they perceive themselves as burdens and are afraid that they may become too dependent on others. Those who have limited incomes and are in need of assistance with daily-living tasks should be referred to social service agencies that provide a range of concrete services such as home repairs, heavy household chores, and transportation to those places that cannot be reached by public transportation.

Some widows, despite having sufficient resources to comfortably maintain their previous lifestyle, experience an initial period of overwhelming stress due to their husband's deaths. Their new social position and the unfamiliar experience of managing daily life on their own create confusion, disorganization, and a sense of identity loss. Brief-oriented casework can help these individuals take an orderly, problem-solving approach to their new life situation. Reflective discussions can help them to identify emotional and social needs and outline an appropriate plan of action for the attainment of ongoing personal need fulfillment.

According to Lopata (1970) the elderly widow identifies loneliness more often than not as the major distress in her life. The most common cause of loneliness is the absence of meaningful, close, interpersonal relationships. Those who are widowed at a very old age and those who reach advanced old age as widows are most vulnerable to severe loneliness and social isolation. Most widows in the old-old age group have outlived many of their friends and relatives. Many are impaired by chronic illness to the extent that they cannot leave their homes. Social agencies must reach out to these individuals and provide them with human contacts on a regular basis.

Although the problems experienced in widowhood are fairly similar from one case to the next, casework intervention should be highly individualized. Each case needs to be assessed to determine the person's unique complex of needs and to develop an appropriate, individualized treatment plan. For instance, in two cases with similar degrees of emotional distress, one individual may require only brief supportive casework to ease the initial pains of widowhood, while the other may require intensive casework therapy to help her work through acute, unresolved grief.

## Problems of Retirement

A long-standing popular belief contends that retirement from gainful employment is a psychosocial crisis experience for most people. This myth has been soundly exploded by a host of studies over the last two decades. For most people retirement is welcomed and proves to be a stable and satisfactory phase of life. Baum and Baum (1980) present a thorough summary and analysis of retirement research. They point to the substantial evidence that a majority of the elderly make a good adjustment to retirement. The Baum text cites the impressive research findings reported by Shanas et al. (1968), Havighurst et al. (1969), Atchley (1971), Rose and Magey (1972), Harris (1975), Miller (1965), Ash (1966), Katona et al. (1969), and Orbach et al. (1969).

Some older people do not make a successful adaptation to retirement. Those who are forced to retire on a small pension experience a very drastic reduction in their standard of living. Some may experience a state of poverty for the first time in their lives. Many actively seek new jobs, but few are successful because of the general shortage of jobs in today's economy and because many employers are reluctant to hire the elderly. Human service workers in the field of aging should advocate for those in search of gainful employment and serve as their brokers in the employment market.

The life transition of retirement involves the loss of a major role. However, most people successfully replace the work role with a number of meaningful leisure activities within the home and the community. Those people who never developed self-satisfying leisure or nonwork interests during their preretirement years usually do not make a satisfactory adaptation to retirement. Often this type of individual based his or her self-worth and identity on the status of work and the virtue of productivity. According to Manney (1975) these individuals find it difficult to justify a life of leisure activities. Atchley (1976) reports that they tend to have a very strong negative attitude about the meaning of retirement in general. Depression, apathy, and social withdrawal are frequently experienced by this group of poorly adapted retirees.

Keller and Hughston (1981) suggest the use of a cognitive restructuring approach to modify the rigid, negative attitudes about retirement. Rational therapy procedures outlined by Ellis and Harper (1976) have been used effectively to modify rigid, irrational attitudes such as those held by some retired people. The primary goal of treatment is to get the client to replace irrational assumptions about retirement with rational ones. The caseworker first confronts the client with the specific irrationalities. Through careful discussion the caseworker presents the client with obvious evidence that the negative perceptions and attitudes about retirement life are inaccurate and therefore irrational.

Through this analytic process clients are helped to arrive at the rational assumption that retirement in and of itself is not an emotionally unbearable condition. They discover that holding the negative attitude is producing the emotional distress and preventing them from pursuing meaningful and satisfying activities. The clients are challenged to supply proof that to be retired is to be useless and unworthy, and are presented with evidence of personal strengths and skills that can be used in a variety of meaningful activities in the home and in the community.

Some people are unhappy and restless after they retire, not because they are negativistic about retirement, but because they are simply bored and don't know what to do with much of the time available to them. These individuals need to be provided with structured opportunities for meaningful social participation.

In addition to involvement in social and recreational activities in community centers, engagement in structured, volunteer-work positions in a wide range of community services provides many retired individuals with meaningful experiences. Many retired elderly are currently involved in formal volunteer work programs designed to provide energetic and motivated senior citizens with productive service roles. Three such federally funded programs that have been overwhelmingly successful are The Senior Companion Program, Foster Grandparents, and Retired Seniors Volunteer Program.

Some married couples experience a period of interpersonal conflict immediately following retirement because prior to retirement they did not spend a great deal of time with each other on a daily basis. In some cases the retired husband's attempts to keep busy interfere with his wife's long-standing household routines. A caseworker can help a couple experiencing this sort of conflict to define a mutually agreed upon, complementary division of labor, and to develop interest in both individual and joint recreational and social activities that can be pursued at home and in the community.

The educational and counseling formats and procedures which are widely used today to help the middle-aged person prepare and plan for a successful psychosocial adaptation to retirement can also be effectively used with currently retired people who find retirement a stressful life transition. Postretirement counseling can be done very effectively through group intervention. Group members can assist each other in finding satisfactory solutions to their problems. Caseworkers can assist a variety of community organizations to set up self-help group programs for newly retired people in need of mutual support and guidance that will help them to cope with the stresses associated with their new way of life.

## MENTAL ILLNESS

The elderly are not immune to any of the clinical categories of mental illness. Some carry chronic states of mental disturbance into old age, while others experience mental illness for the first time during old age. The limited space in this text does not permit a description and discussion of all of the known conditions of mental and emotional disturbance. Thus in this chapter only four mental problems have been selected for discussion. These include neurosis of aging, depression, abnormal grief, and alcoholism. Although these problems are often chronic in nature, they can also present themselves as acute illness. In the latter instances timely and intense casework intervention may be effective in achieving recovery at a relatively good level of mental and emotional functioning.

Other serious mental dysfunctions such as senile dementia are discussed in the next two chapters where the text focuses on casework intervention with the chronically impaired elderly who constitute the clientele of the tertiary level of practice.

In mental hospitals, mental health clinics, and community mental health centers, the caseworker functions as part of a multidisciplinary team. In this capacity the caseworker participates in the clinical diagnostic process by providing a psychosocial history secured from the patient and family. In the hospital setting the caseworker assists with admission procedures, financial arrangements, and discharge planning. Often the caseworker is called upon to carry out various aspects of the inpatient treatment plan. In both in- and outpatient settings the caseworker often functions as a primary therapist. As such, the caseworker develops an assessment/diagnosis that carefully takes into consideration the patient's formal clinical diagnosis. The caseworker's assessment goes beyond the clinical diagnosis and serves as a foundation for a treatment plan whose purpose is to promote the best possible level of physical-psychological-social functioning.

Many cases of mental breakdown among the elderly are acute crises wherein timely, brief, and intense crisis intervention may prevent the need for hospitalization. When hospitalization is necessary a crisis interventive approach increases the likelihood of an early discharge and decreases the likelihood of chronic, permanent impairment.

### Neurosis of Aging

Some elderly people have a neurotic reaction to the realization that they have reached old age. Kral (1983) believes that neurosis of aging is quite prevalent among the elderly today and that geriatric psychiatry ignores the significance of this condition. Kral describes the symptom picture of aging neurosis as follows: a flat depression, tiredness, weakness, feelings of being unappreciated, expressions of resentment, somatic complaints, and hypochondriacal fears. The person with this condition is fearful of getting older, of losing independence, of declining physical ability, and of the loss of loved ones.

This condition is also referred to as neurotic depression. Dr. Kral identifies the following aims of therapy: (1) the relief of anxiety, (2) the relief of loneliness, and (3) the restoration of self-confidence. The therapist is instructed to repeatedly point out to the client and family that old age is not a disease. Client and family must be informed of the numerous typical characteristics of decline and loss associated with advanced age.

Rechtschaffen (1969) reviewed the literature on psychotherapy with the elderly and concluded that elderly neurotics profit the most from supportive therapy in which the therapist is action oriented rather than passively reflective. Rechtschaffen refers to a treatment focus that is very similar to eclectic casework. Treatment interventions set forth by both Dr. Rechtschaffen and Dr. Kral address the patient's internal and external worlds.

The patient should be encouraged and helped to reminisce freely about the "good and bad" of his or her past. Discussions about being old should focus on the advantages and disadvantages. The worker must help the client perceive some positive aspects of his or her current existence. The patient needs to be linked to a social network of peers who are actively involved in life and who are accepting of their old age. Self-help groups and socialization/recreational/educational group programs are helpful to these clients.

Positive reinforcement, assertiveness training, values clarification, and cognitive restructuring are procedures that can be considered for use in one-to-one or group counseling with the neurotic client. These techniques serve to build self-confidence, self-esteem, and feelings of usefulness. Peer group involvement provides well adapted models for the poorly adapted neurotic. The neurotic client should not be pampered, and excessive expressions of distress should be ignored by the caseworker. The client's significant others should be advised to do likewise. All adaptive and positive statements by the client should be rewarded with praise.

## Depression

Depression is the most common psychopathological syndrome among the elderly. It is estimated that between 30 and 60 percent of Americans 65 or older will experience at least one episode of depression severe enough to interfere with daily functioning (see Solomon, 1981). Freedman (1982) contends that this high rate of depression not only constitutes a serious clinical concern for individuals, but also a grave social problem for the community.

Although depression is a common psychiatric disorder among the elderly, it frequently goes undetected. It is estimated that only 25 percent of the cases of depression among elderly, ambulatory medical patients are detected by their physicians (see Kitchell, 1982). Even more alarming is Solomon's (1981) observation that many patients with depression have symptoms similar to those of senile dementia and are frequently misdiagnosed. In the latter situations the depression goes untreated and early and/or unnecessary institutionalization often takes place.

Psychological depression is difficult to diagnose because many of its symptoms are also prevalent in a number of medical conditions. For instance, depression is present in the symptom picture of brain tumors, anemia, minor strokes, early Parkinson's disease, cancer, cardiovascular illness, and other serious diseases. Furthermore, many people do not recognize that they are depressed: They believe their discomforts are a result of being old. Salzman (1978) points out that some depressed individuals mask their depression through a variety of defense mechanisms including denial, reaction formation, and hypochondriasis.

Depression frequently accompanies episodes of serious physical illness and/or injury. Medical caseworkers must be alert to this fact and be prepared to intervene before the patient's depression becomes chronic. Caseworkers who are employed in community-based agencies need to be alert to the possible presence of depression in their clients. They should not hesitate to refer a client to the appropriate medical or psychiatric personnel for diagnostic confirmation of a suspected depression. It is imperative that the caseworker recognize the symptoms of depression.

Because many people deny that they are depressed, the caseworker may have to work especially hard to persuade an individual to seek medical and/or psychiatric attention. Since we know that many physicians do not look hard enough for an underlying depressive disorder, the worker must be prepared to advocate for the client to receive thorough medical attention.

In addition to the features of depression noted above, the following symptoms are characteristic: general insomnia, early morning awakening, constipation, anorexia, weight loss, memory loss, decreased libido, poor appetite, psychomotor agitation, sleepiness, indecisiveness, and loss of energy.

The caseworker must base the treatment plan on a diagnostic understanding of each client's unique symptom picture. A treatment outcome goal for each major feature of a client's depression needs to be defined. For example, guilt-ridden clients must overcome their guilty feelings. Clients who perceive themselves as useless and unworthy must achieve an adequate level of self-esteem, and socially inactive clients must develop the motivation to interact with others. In all cases the first treatment goal and the one requisite to attaining other goals is for the caseworker to establish a solid, trusting relationship with the client.

In pursuit of each goal the worker should utilize all relevant resources: those within the client, those within the client's informal social network, and those within the formal care system. Treatment procedures from many different therapeutic approaches may prove useful, as well as the caseworker's own unique techniques (as long as they are based on scientifically established treatment principles). Reminiscence is widely used as a procedure to treat depression in the elderly (see Butler, 1963; Pincus, 1970; Lewis & Butler, 1974; and McMahan & Rhudick, 1964).

Assertiveness training is an effective way to promote self-esteem in the depressed client (see Chapter 3 for a discussion of this treatment technique). Task-centered casework, a technique discussed earlier in the text, is useful in helping the depressed client develop feelings of usefulness: Accomplishing some daily-living tasks proves to be self-reinforcing for the client. All expressions of interest and behavioral accomplishments on the part of the client should be immediately reinforced.

Mental health workers usually differentiate between two basic types of depression. Major depression (also referred to as psychotic and organic depression) requires both chemotherapy (medication) and psychotherapy, while minor depression (also referred to as neurotic or reactive depression) can be effectively treated with psychotherapy alone.

Minor depression is a condition that is usually brought on by an external cause such as a loss, a rejection, or some other unpleasant event or experience. This condition can often be ameliorated by changing the situation that is causing the depression and/or by modifying the individual's reactions to the precipitating causes. (Some cases of major depression are caused by an external factor and therefore respond to psychotherapy.) It is not always possible to distinguish between the two categories of depression. As pointed out earlier individuals can mask depressive symptoms. In some cases of major, organic depression the symptoms may not appear until some external event causes them to become manifest. Regardless of the assumptions held about the underlying cause and type of depression and the type and severity of symptoms presented, depression should be viewed as a serious condition that requires expert attention.

### Suicide

People who make serious suicide attempts are depressed. This is not to say that most depressions end in suicide or that depression causes suicide. However, using a broad definition of depression, Stenback (1980) estimates that almost 100 percent of elderly suicides are preceded by symptoms of depression. Suicide is more prevalent among white males over the age of 60 than in any other segment of the population. By age 85 the suicide rate for this group is triple that of all others. Single, white males (widowed, divorced, or never married) commit suicide at an even higher rate.

Miller (1979) suggests that elderly women may attempt suicide as frequently as men but do not succeed with the same frequency. Suicide among the elderly population in general may be higher than the statistics indicate, since the statistics account only for successful suicides. There are no data available on the frequency of attempted suicide.

Some theorists speculate that men are more successful suicides than women because they customarily use violent methods such as shooting and jumping, while women tend to use less violent methods such as pills and gas: The violent methods don't miss their mark as often as the more passive ones. Belsky (1984) suggests that the passive methods used by women are sometimes construed as accidents rather than legitimate suicide attempts. Weeks (1984) speculates that elderly white men have a higher suicide rate than elderly black men because white men do not experience as much adversity during their lives as black men and thus are not as well equipped to cope with the losses experienced in old age.

Miller (1979) observes that events such as the death of a loved one and a diagnosis of terminal illness may trigger the elderly person's decision to commit suicide. Experts in geriatric mental health point out that those elderly who are socially isolated, ill, and/or depressed are most likely to consider suicide. The elderly do not have a tendency to make suicide gestures in order to manipulate others or to get attention; therefore, suicide threats should be taken very seriously.

Lowy (1979) believes that the most preventable suicides are those related to depression and are situations in which suicide represents a passive giving up. He believes that the provision of skilled treatment early in the course of the depression is the best method for reducing suicide. Involvement in a social network of close relatives and friends also decreases the likelihood of suicide among the elderly.

The case presentation at the end of this chapter involves a potential suicide on the part of an elderly widower who is depressed over the loss of his wife and who passively gives up.

## Abnormal Grief

A frequent and painful task of old age is the grieving over a major loss, particularly the loss of a loved one. Patterson (1969) defines grieving as the gradual process of eradicating the intense emotional ties to the dead person and making restitution for the loss. As painful as this task may be, many elderly people successfully complete each stage of the grieving process. It may take up to a year or longer for a person to successfully grieve when he or she has lost someone as close as a spouse.

Many people fail at doing their grief work, remain depressed indefinitely, and become more and more socially isolated. According to Gramlich (1969) inhibited or chronic grief is common among the elderly, and unresolved grief is the root of numerous psychological and social symptoms. He identifies three forms of abnormal grief: (1) delayed grief due to denial, (2) inhibited grief due to repressed mourning behavior, and (3) chronic grief, a prolonging of the normal process. Gramlich believes that when an elderly person denies a loss but is doing well psychosocially, the denial should be permitted. But those clients who are distressed because of unsuccessful grieving need treatment that will take them through the grieving process.

With warm and gentle confrontation the worker encourages the client to think and talk about the deceased loved one. Intense anger, sadness, and guilt must be ventilated. Reminiscing about life with the loved one should focus on both the positives and the negatives of the past. It has frequently been observed that the client must reminisce repeatedly about the loved one until the memories lose their painfulness. Photographs and personal belongings of the deceased help to break through the client's wall of repression. The client must also be encouraged to talk freely about the actual death episode and the funeral. Reflective discussion is a useful technique in helping the client to gain an understanding of why he or she was unable to successfully grieve. The insight gleaned from this therapeutic experience may prepare the client to cope successfully with future losses.

Flannery (1974) reports the successful application of a behavior modification approach treating the unresolved grief of a 77-year-old man who was suffering from agitated depression over the death of his sister. In this case behavioral contracting was used to eliminate dysfunctional behavior in five specific areas of the client's life.

### Alcoholism

Alcoholism has only recently been recognized as a serious problem among the elderly. Older, problem drinkers—including those who have survived into old age—are much less visible than their younger counterparts. For instance, alcoholics are most often detected through the workplace, automobile accidents, and family crises. Many elderly problem drinkers go unnoticed because they do not work or drive and they live alone.

The two types of elderly alcoholics are the early- and the late-onset drinkers. The former carry a serious drinking problem into old age while the latter develop a drinking problem for the first time when they become old.

Rosin and Glatt (1974) point out that psychopathology is characteristic of the long-standing drinker while social pathology best explains the drinking problem of the late starter. The late-onset alcoholic can be thought of as an elderly, reactive, problem drinker. This type of drinker resorts to the use of alcohol when former coping mechanisms are unsuccessful in the face of the stresses of old age. Rathbone-McCuan and Trugard (1978) believe that elderly alcoholics drink primarily to alleviate depression associated with poor health and family difficulties. They know that the elderly drinker is more socially isolated and alienated than the younger alcoholic.

Many doctors fail to associate symptoms such as frailty, weight problems, unsteadiness, disorientation, and irrationality with a possible condition of alcoholism, and therefore they misdiagnose the patient. The older person's relatives and friends are often reluctant or unable to acknowledge alcoholism due to protectiveness, shame, tolerance, or even encouragement. Like their younger counterparts, most older alcoholics deny having a drinking problem. Some older drinkers who admit their alcoholism to themselves may not want to stop drinking in spite of the serious consequences because alcohol numbs their many pains. And some deny—to themselves and others—out of a strong moral prohibition about the use of alcohol.

Before definitive treatment procedures can be applied the client must have the motivation to stop drinking and express a commitment to sobriety. According to Zimberg (1974) the confrontation allegedly required to secure an admission of alcoholism from a young client is not necessary and may in fact be counterproductive with the elderly alcoholic. When a strong, trusting relationship is offered by the worker, the elderly alcoholic is likely to admit his or her problem.

Gomberg (1976) stresses the importance of social therapy with the elderly alcoholic. Gomberg holds that the client needs to be resocialized without the use of alcohol as a support. Because elderly problem drinkers are basically a lonely people, attempts need to be made to mobilize members of their social network who will provide them with opportunities to socialize outside of a drinking atmosphere.

Because of the social stigma attached to alcoholism, the elderly are very reluctant to participate in agency-based special programs for alcoholics. Mishara and Kastenbaum (1980) found that the elderly patient shies away from mental health, outpatient facilities. Special group programs and individual counseling services for the elderly alcoholic seem to be more readily accepted when they are offered through settings such as a neighborhood-based senior citizen center.

Since alcoholism is often combined with serious physical illness and/or depression, the direct, successful treatment of these conditions may indirectly cure the drinking problem. In such cases alcohol is "medicine" for the suffering patient. Zimberg (1974) reports the successful treatment of geriatric alcoholism with a combination of antidepressant medication and socialization therapy. Many chronic alcoholics need to be detoxified before resocialization therapy can be initiated. After detoxification every attempt should be made to meet the client's basic daily-functioning needs, physical health needs, and emotional needs. Whenever feasible relatives and other members of the client's informal network can be taught how to provide relevant and consistent positive reinforcement of the client's sobriety, and how to withhold positive reinforcement of the client's drinking behavior. Duckworth and Rosenblatt (1976) describe treating difficult binge drinkers with the use of very strong verbal confrontation. They do not hesitate to order the client to get "dried out" and to express their disgust with his or her irresponsible drinking behavior.

When working with the "late start" alcoholic, a careful psychosocial systems assessment should be conducted in order to distinguish between those transitional, related factors that precipitated this relatively new problem and those that are helping to maintain it. Factors within the client such as self defeating attitudes and irrational assumptions about being old may have to be changed through the application of cognitive procedures and insight development. Care must be taken to intervene with all factors external to the client that reinforce the drinking problem.

A rich professional literature exists on the treatment of alcoholism in general. This body of knowledge should be carefully scrutinized for procedures that can be modified for use with the elderly alcoholic.

## PHYSICAL ILLNESS

Many social workers are employed in health and health-related settings where they play a major part in the treatment of those elderly who are suffering from acute episodes of physical illness or injury. In settings such as medical hospitals, clinics, health-care centers, and home-care programs, the social worker's role is a combination of medical team member and medical casework counselor. The social worker also plays a significant and important role in the physical health of the elderly in all settings of practice by being constantly on the alert for indications of ill ness.

Many elderly people have health problems for which they are not receiving medical care. In some cases the older person is not aware of a health problem, but the alert and observant caseworker can detect early symptoms and make an immediate referral for medical diagnosis. Thus those older people who do not feel well but cannot, for whatever reason, seek medical attention are reassured that it is safe to do so. Some do not know how to secure the appropriate medical help and need assistance from the caseworker to negotiate the confusing health-care arena.

As a member of a multidisciplinary health-care team the caseworker assists other team members with the clinical diagnostic process and helps with the technical arrangements of service admission and discharge planning. The caseworker as counselor addresses the overall physical, psychological, and social consequences of the patient's illness.

Frequently, the caseworker has the primary responsibility for interpreting and explaining to the patient and his or her family the doctor's diagnosis, prognosis, prescriptions, and treatments. During the hospital stay and the convalescence period at home the caseworker helps the client and family deal with their emotional reactions to the illness. Psychosocial therapy and client-centered techniques are useful in helping the patient deal with illness-related depression and anxiety.

When working with the hospitalized client, the caseworker should engage that client's participation in planning and preparing for the necessary convalescence arrangements. Such arrangements might include nursing-home care, home-health care, a visiting nurse's service, or scheduled, periodic visits to a clinic. Where the required services are not available or readily accessible due to the client's limited income, the caseworker must become involved in personal advocacy and brokerage activities in order to help the client secure the best possible care.

For many elderly people an acute illness or injury becomes a psychosocial crisis. Often the crisis breakdown does not become manifest until the point of discharge from the hospital. The traditional crisis intervention model (which is outlined in Chapter 3) should be applied. It is often the caseworker's job to coordinate the health team's crisis interventive efforts. Acute medical episodes or illnesses such as hip fractures, heart attacks, strokes, and cancer are frequent among the elderly population, and more often than not they precipitate a psychosocial crisis.

The caseworker, more than any other professional, pays attention to and assists the elderly with the subjective and objective psychosocial consequences of physical illness. Caseworkers view the ill person as a whole individual and are alert to the dynamic interplay between physiological, psychological, and social forces. Physical illness can have negative effects on cognitive, emotional, and social behavior, which can in turn negatively effect the patient's physical condition.

Berkman and Rehr (1972) and Berkman (1972) stress the importance of early case finding for the medically hospitalized patient, and they identify a host of social and psychological needs that require attention throughout the patient's confinement. Early casework involvement can help to prevent serious psychosocial regression, which occurs regularly among the hospitalized elderly.

Hip fractures and other broken bones are traumatic for the elderly. Lipner and Sherman (1975) believe that many cases of hip fracture are preceded by some change in the individual's emotional and social situation, which causes uneasiness about daily living and makes a person accident prone. These patients are likely to regress psychologically and withdraw socially upon hospital discharge, and if the regression process is not halted they are likely to have future accidents. Lipner and Sherman recommend that casework therapy with these types of patients should focus on insight development. The patient needs to deal with past unresolved conflicts, which may underlie the regression and withdrawal tendencies. Insight can be promoted through the use of reflective discussion techniques, interpretation, confrontation, empathic responding, and warm reassurance.

The recovery period at home following major surgery and/or acute physical illness is usually long and gradual. Those who are involved in monitoring the patient's convalescence must give the patient continuing encouragement during this difficult time.

The convalescing client who lives alone or with a spouse who is also in poor health may become discouraged and despondent. Consideration should be given to involving the client in an appropriate health-recovery group. Interaction with others who are recovering from a similar condition can be greatly reassuring to the client, and the interpersonal involvement helps to prevent social isolation. For instance, stroke recovery groups have become quite popular in recent years and have played an important part in the patients' recovery.

## Case Illustration

This case illustration deals with a problem at the secondary level of clinical social work practice. In this case the client presents a specific psychological problem that can be defined as severe depression with suicidal intentions.

Mr. B.'s overall functioning does not constitute a condition of chronic, irreversible impairment. The caseworker has reason to believe that intensive casework treatment can be successful in resolving Mr. B.'s problem.

This case illustration includes a client profile, a description of the presenting problem, a case assessment/diagnosis, and a treatment plan. The treatment plan provides a detailed outline of proposed session-by-session casework activities and client homework assignments. Discussion questions are provided for classroom use. Students are encouraged to speculate about various treatment procedures that could be applied in the implementation of the caseworker's proposed treatment plan. This kind of discussion should help the student to understand the meaning of eclectic treatment.

**Client Profile.**  Mr. B. is a 70-year-old, white, upper middle-class, retired jewelry maker and shopowner. He retired at age 62. His wife of 48 years died 18 months ago from a massive stroke. His 45-year-old, unmarried son has been living at home with Mr. B. since Mrs. B.'s death. Mr. B. has owned and lived in the same house for the last 40 years. It is a large, expensive house located in a well-to-do neighborhood in a midwestern city. Mr. B.'s retirement income is quite lucrative. His son is self-supporting with a handsome income. Mr. B. has a married daughter and two adolescent grandsons. They live about 1,500 miles away, and he visits with them about every 6 months.

Mr. B. has a younger brother and sister, a number of nieces and nephews, and some distant relatives who live within the metropolitan area. He has a lot of old friends who are accessible to him, and he knows all of his immediate neighbors quite well. Mr. B. is a member of a Presbyterian church, is a Mason, a country club member, and belongs to a number of other organizations. Since his wife's death he has not gone to church or been involved with any of the organizations in which he holds membership. He drives his car, does most of the shopping, and cooks most of his own meals. He has a part-time housekeeper who takes care of the other areas of housekeeping.

After Mr. B.'s retirement Mr. and Mrs. B. were practically inseparable. They enjoyed a busy social/recreational lifestyle. They spent three months in Florida every winter, traveled, frequently went to the theater and movies, attended sporting events, were involved with country club activities, were active in numerous organizations, worked in their garden, and played bridge quite frequently.

**Presenting Problem.**  Mr. B. was discovered by his son in an unconscious state with an empty pill bottle on the bedside table. He would have succeeded in killing himself if his son had not returned home unexpectedly and discovered his father in time to save Mr. B.'s life. Mr. B. was hospitalized for two weeks. An extensive diagnostic work-up revealed Mr. B. to be physically well, free of psychosis, and without neurological pathology. He was severely psychologically depressed. The depression was a reaction to the death of his wife 18 months earlier. There was no doubt among the hospital staff that Mr. B. had clearly intended to commit suicide.

After two weeks of hospital care that included antidepressant medication and supportive psychiatric therapy, Mr. B. was discharged with the understanding that he would accept outpatient, psychosocial therapy.

*First Casework Session.*    Mr. B. politely but firmly informed the caseworker at the outset of the interview that he was in therapy only to please and calm his son. The caseworker found it easy to relate to Mr. B., who was intelligent, honest, and willing to express his feelings and thoughts readily. The caseworker informed Mr. B. that the primary purposes of counseling were to help him overcome depression and abandon his suicide plans. Mr. B. said he did not want to try any longer to overcome his depression because he was now absolutely sure that he did not want to live without his wife. He wanted to join her in death. He felt that it was his right to die as he saw fit. He could understand the good intentions of those who were trying to help him, and he felt guilty about causing them distress. Primarily for the sake of his son, with whom he has a very good relationship, Mr. B. indicated that he wanted to mask his depression as well as he could and refrain from any hint of suicidal intentions. Then, in about three or four months, he would go on a trip and while gone quietly do away with himself.

The caseworker told Mr. B. that she could neither professionally nor personally condone or sanction his plan, but at the same time she highly valued his right to self-determination and confidentiality. The caseworker assured Mr. B. that the confidence would not be violated. She asked Mr. B. if he would give her the opportunity to try to effect some change in his determination to remain depressed and commit suicide. The caseworker explained the nature of structured, short-term, contractual, task-centered casework. She pointed out that they could develop a contract wherein counseling would be terminated in three months and therefore would not interfere with Mr. B.'s current plans, which he had said were to appear less depressed and not to consider suicide for at least three or four months. The caseworker stated that if counseling was unsuccessful she would not attempt to alter his plans. Mr. B. accepted this approach and the caseworker detected a hint of enthusiasm. Mr. B. said that the structured involvement of counseling would at least keep him busy and therefore help him to hide his depression from his son. An appointment was made for one week later, at which time a specific contract would be formulated.

**Treatment Contract.**    The second contact between the caseworker and Mr. B. produced the following treatment contract.

1. Weekly one-hour counseling sessions for 12 consecutive weeks. Every other session to be held in Mr. B.'s home starting next week. The other sessions would be held in the counselor's office.
2. The worker would try to maintain the agreed upon focus of treatment sessions. The client would try his best to involve himself genuinely in the treatment process.
3. Outcome goals: Lessen Mr. B.'s depression, and eliminate his suicide intentions.
4. Worker will refrain from using moralistic and persuasive tactics.
5. Mr. B. will carry out all feasible homework assignments.
6. The 12th and final session will be devoted to treatment evaluation and, if indicated, consideration of another contract.
7. The weekly sessions will focus on discussion about the pros and cons of life

and the pros and cons of death, giving homework assignments and discussing Mr. B.'s homework experiences, and a historical review of Mr. B.'s life.

8. The worker will make arrangements for those homework assignments that will put the client in contact with formal settings (child day-care center, nursing home, and senior center), and Mr. B. will be responsible for arranging all other assigned activities.

**Diagnostic Impression.**

1. Mr. B. is deeply depressed over the death (loss) of his wife. Depression is psychologically based. There is no evidence of organic depression, psychosis, or neurological disease.
2. Mr. B. is relatively well physically. He complains of tiredness and poor appetite.
3. He keeps himself socially isolated most of the time.
4. Mr. B.'s long and hard grief work did not succeed in lifting his deep depression.
5. A brief period of psychotherapy, antidepressive medication, and forced social involvement had not been successful in lifting the depression.
6. Although he is resigned to and looking forward to death, Mr. B. seems willing to sincerely involve himself in 12 weeks of therapy. He is convinced, however, that the therapy will not change matters.
7. The worker believes that Mr. B. will hold up his end of the contract because of Mr. B.'s deep integrity and his wish to please his son for a few months.
8. Although deeply depressed, Mr. B. makes a good overall appearance. He seems in many ways to be younger than 70.
9. His intellectual functioning is sound. His sensory capacities are strong, and his conceptual abilities are good.
10. Mr. B.'s quality of functioning is very high in spite of his deep depression and loss of desire to live. He is totally independent and able to care for himself.
11. The caseworker believes that Mr. B. has the ability to understand and perform the numerous homework assignments that are outlined in the proposed treatment plan.
12. The essence of the following treatment plan is the caseworker's uniquely designed course for grief work and stresses active, intense exposure to a complex set of stimuli that may succeed in providing Mr. B. with a challenge and the desire to live.

**Treatment Plan.**

1. One-half hour of each session for the first eight weeks will be devoted to Mr. B.'s "Life Review." The caseworker will guide Mr. B.'s reminiscence through the years, focusing special attention on marriage, family, and work history. The good and bad memories will be attended to. Life review sessions to be held in Mr. B.'s home will utilize family picture albums, home movies, and personal items. This time slot during sessions 9, 10, and 11 will be used for open discussion.
2. Ten minutes each week will be devoted to talking about living and dying. Lists will be made of all possible pros and cons of living and of dying—for Mr. B. specifically and for people in general.

3. Twenty minutes each week will be devoted to giving Mr. B. his homework assignments and discussing his homework experiences of the previous week.
4. Homework Assignments.
   a. First Week.
      (1) Attend a film on death and dying and a follow-up group discussion at a senior center.
      (2) Eat out at an expensive restaurant one time.
      (3) Go to a movie of your choice.
      (4) Go to church.
      (5) Look at family albums and home movies with your son.
      (6) Read your will. Consider possible changes.
      (7) Visit a neighbor for at least 30 minutes.
      (8) Visit your wife's grave for one hour.
      (9) Stay up very late one night.
      (10) Sleep in very late one morning.
   b. Second Week.
      (1) Observe for one hour a preschool, day-care program.
      (2) Buy a gift for someone.
      (3) Take your son out to dinner.
      (4) Visit your wife's grave four times.
      (5) Visit a friend who is not a neighbor.
      (6) Go to your country club.
      (7) Go to a sporting event.
      (8) Read a novel.
      (9) Telephone your daughter.
      (10) Write a letter to someone.
   c. Third Week.
      (1) Visit your wife's grave five times.
      (2) Sit in the waiting room of an emergency unit in a hospital for three hours.
      (3) Go to a bar and have a drink.
      (4) Visit your best friend.
      (5) Call your best friend three times.
      (6) Cook a nice meal for your son.
      (7) Read your will.
      (8) Work in the garden.
      (9) Ask your son for a favor.
      (10) Listen to the radio for five hours.
   d. Fourth Week.
      (1) Talk with the Presbyterian minister.
      (2) Go window shopping for three hours.
      (3) Go into three different jewelry stores and look at the merchandise.
      (4) Buy at least one item.
      (5) Read the newspaper every day.
      (6) Go to a poor section of the city and walk the streets for two hours.
      (7) Go away with your son for the weekend.

e. Fifth Week.
  (1) Stay at home all week. Do not do anything special. Eat all meals at home.
f. Sixth Week.
  (1) Eat all of your meals in restaurants.
  (2) Go to a movie.
  (3) Go to a club that has live entertainment.
  (4) Visit the country club.
  (5) Make it a point to watch television.
  (6) Make it a point to listen to the radio.
  (7) Spend an hour each day listening to your favorite records.
  (8) Visit a friend.
  (9) Visit your wife's grave at least once.
  (10) Read your will.
g. Seventh Week.
  (1) Stay at home most of the time.
  (2) Look around in the cellar, attic, garage, and storage spaces.
  (3) Fix something in the house.
  (4) Throw something away.
  (5) Reminisce about your childhood and share your memories of your grandparents and parents with your son.
  (6) Do something that the doctor says is not good for you.
  (7) Write out instructions for your funeral and burial arrangements.
  (8) Visit the cemetery plot where you are to be buried.
h. Eighth Week.
  (1) Tour a nursing home.
  (2) Sit in the waiting room at Children's Hospital for two hours.
  (3) Visit a shut-in or hospitalized member of your church.
  (4) Make a special donation to the church.
  (5) Give some of your old clothing to a charitable organization.
  (6) Buy some new clothing.
i. Ninth Week.
  (1) Attend a congregate meal at a senior citizen center.
  (2) Ask a favor of your son.
  (3) Ask a favor of a friend.
  (4) Buy yourself a gift.
  (5) Do not do any chores around the house.
  (6) Ask a friend to stop by for a visit.
j. Tenth Week.
  (1) Go to the country club for dinner.
  (2) Go out with a friend.
  (3) Go out to some special event with your son.
  (4) Talk on the phone with your daughter, son-in-law, and grandchildren.
  (5) Talk with a fellow Mason.
  (6) Watch something on TV that you really enjoy.

(7) Look at your wedding pictures, pictures of your children when they were young, and vacation pictures.

(8) Put flowers on your wife's grave.

(9) Go to church.

(10) Talk to your son about his work and his social life.

   *k.* Eleventh Week.

      (1) From the list of all previous assignments, select any 10 and complete them during the coming week.

**Final Session of the Treatment Contract.**   The final treatment session was devoted to the evaluation of the treatment experience. Mr. B. was no longer depressed, and he expressed a strong desire to continue living. He spoke with the worker about many future plans. He was genuinely enthusiastic about expanding and enriching his lifestyle. Additional treatment was not indicated and the case was closed.

The caseworker made a six month follow-up contact with Mr. B. at which time he was found to be free of depression and very much involved in an active and rewarding lifestyle.

**Discussion Questions**

1. Are you satisfied with the caseworker's diagnostic conclusions? Based on the case facts (as provided in the client profile and presenting problem), does the caseworker overlook any plausible diagnostic hypotheses?

2. What treatment outcome goals other than the ones defined by the caseworker (lessen depression and abandon suicide plan) might be appropriate?

3. The caseworker proposes a treatment approach that involves a task-centered model. How is this model related to any of the five approaches discussed in Chapter 3?

4. Keeping in mind the meaning of eclectic treatment, what procedures drawn from the five broad approaches might be appropriately used in this case?

5. Identify some treatment procedures for use in this case that are not discussed in this text.

6. List the client's strengths and weaknesses. What client strengths do the caseworker's proposed treatment procedures use?

7. What case facts and diagnostic impressions support the caseworker's planned treatment procedures? In other words, what do you think the caseworker's rationale is for each of the specified procedures for the interviewing sessions and the client's homework task assignments?

8. What casework roles in addition to counseling might be useful in this case?

9. On the basis of the case profile, presenting problem, and the first casework session, how might you modify the contract outlined in this illustration?

10. What value dilemmas and ethical conflicts might arise for both the case-worker and the client?

## SUMMARY

Social work intervention at the secondary level of practice is commonly known as clinical casework. In the field of aging clinical casework at the secondary level deals with acute problems in physical-psychological-social functioning. A great variety of problems is encountered by caseworkers who work in medical, psychiatric, and social-service settings.

Regardless of problem type and work setting, casework is guided by the generic, psychosocial, systems process of problem assessment/diagnosis combined with definitive treatment that utilizes the eclectic perspective.

Each problem is seen as unique and casework treatment is highly individualized. Many problems experienced by the elderly involve the symptoms of stress associated with the normal process of aging, as well as pressures from environmental forces. Loss of home with limited relocation options is a common cause of stress for many elderly people. Timely casework intervention can help the relocating client hold onto some decision-making power and effect the best possible plan of action and relocation outcome.

Loneliness and social isolation are distressing conditions for many older people. Timely casework intervention can be effective in halting the process of social isolation. The distress of loneliness can be combatted through linking the client to opportunities for social interaction and helping him or her to develop new friendships. Many elderly, due to prevalent sexual taboos, experience problems in sexual functioning and sexual expression. Casework can play a significant role in removing sexual stress by exploding myths and modifying self-defeating sexual attitudes.

Much of the stress experienced by older people is related to problems rooted in marital relationships and family units. Many of these problems can be successfully resolved through the use of conjoint marital or family therapy.

Although widowhood is not a problem state in and of itself, many widows experience long-term distress due to poverty, social disengagement, and social isolation. Casework intervention here focuses on the provision of concrete social services and socialization opportunities.

Although most people adjust quite well to retirement, many find it distressing because of a reduced living standard, boredom, and/or the lack of meaningful social attachments. Postretirement counseling can be effective in reversing these conditions.

The elderly can develop serious psychological problems. The most prevalent are the problems of aging neurosis, depression, abnormal grief reaction, and alcoholism. These conditions can often be successfully resolved through intensive casework counseling. If full recovery cannot be achieved, the intervention often prevents the development of total functional impairment.

Physical illness and injury of an acute and specific nature escape very few of the elderly. Serious psychosocial consequences of acute illness can often be prevented or at least minimized through early casework intervention.

# Chapter 6

# Clinical social work practice with the functionally impaired elderly who live in the community

## INTRODUCTION

This chapter and the one that follows focus on clinical social work practice with and on behalf of the functionally impaired elderly. The authors refer to clinical practice at this level as tertiary intervention. Tertiary intervention involves the provision of long-term care. We are particularly concerned in this chapter with long-term care intervention for the functionally impaired elderly who reside in the community.

We begin the chapter with a description and discussion of the functionally impaired elderly population who are not institutionalized. The dimensions and causes of physical, psychological, and social impairment of functioning are discussed in terms of chronic conditions of medical and mental illness. A major illness—Alzheimer's disease—which is a leading cause of functional disability among the elderly, is discussed in detail.

The next section defines the field of long-term care in general and is followed by a discussion of clinical social work in long-term care practice with the community-based, impaired elderly. Special attention is given to the service case management function of social work practice and to social work intervention with informal caretakers of those impaired elderly who live outside of institutions.

The chapter concludes with a case presentation that describes various dimensions of functional impairment in an elderly couple and illustrates numerous aspects of clinical social work intervention at the tertiary level of practice.

## THE FUNCTIONALLY IMPAIRED ELDERLY

The prevalence of chronic health conditions increases with age. According to Cohen (1980) nearly 86 percent of the elderly have all types of chronic health conditions. Thus it is not uncommon for one older person to have several chronic health problems which limit the capacity to function independently on a day-to-day basis. One is considered to be functionally impaired when he or she needs assistance in one or more areas of daily functioning. For instance, assistance may be needed in carrying out tasks of daily living such as bathing, dressing, toileting, eating, household cleaning, and/or shopping. The functional consequences of chronic conditions vary considerably from one person to the next. The accumulation of chronic health conditions makes the older person more vulnerable and increasingly dependent upon others for carrying out many functions and activities of daily living (see Brody, 1979). An impairment may involve physical, mental, and/or social functioning capacities.

Anderson (1978) estimates that about 14 percent of the noninstitutionalized elderly population are impaired to the extent that they require the help of others on a daily basis. Lowy (1979) estimates that chronic illness prevents nearly 1 older person in 5 from carrying out some of the basic activities of daily living, and that by age 75 the prevalence of disability rises to 60 percent.

Many of the physically and mentally impaired elderly live alone. Some are completely socially isolated. The physically impaired among this group are home-bound in settings such as single rooms, boarding homes, public housing units, or their own homes. Also prevalent among the elderly population are the mentally impaired who are socially isolated. Although physically able to leave a place of residence, many seclude themselves on a regular basis. And many of those who regularly venture out roam aimlessly through the streets and through public facilities. They are frequently victimized by the "criminal element." Some elderly, vulnerable "street people" are mugged, beaten, or unmercifully taunted.

The actual size of the socially isolated impaired population is unknown but estimates run high. This group is the most underserved segment of the functionally impaired elderly population, and it greatly needs expanded, outreach, protective services.

Although many of the socially isolated impaired are poor, many are not. Some of the well-to-do live under deplorable and hazardous conditions because they are without social support and cannot make rational decisions about self-care. Social work must reach out to this hidden population and link it to protective care. Many of these people need financial guardianship services.

A large number of the functionally impaired elderly live in boarding homes where they receive no care other than "bed and board." Many boarding homes are substandard dwellings with fire hazards and unsanitary conditions. Most boarding-home proprietors totally ignore the psychosocial needs of their residents. Many are overcharged for the meager services they receive. Some mentally impaired and emotionally disturbed boarding-home residents never leave the facility. They are virtually prisoners who exist in total social isolation.

## Mental Disorders

Some elderly are functionally disabled due to chronic mental illness. Many of these people can live in the community for an indefinite period of time but need daily supervision from others. Illnesses called functional mental disorders are those conditions for which no established organic (physiological) cause has been found. Two such illnesses that severely impair psychosocial functioning are schizophrenia and manic depressive psychosis. Although these illnesses do not often develop for the first time in old age, they are carried into old age by a number of individuals who have a history of chronic cognitive impairment and emotional instability. For example, many "burned out" schizophrenics live to advanced age and continue to need ongoing supervision in the community to the same degree that was required when they were in their late 40s.

Chronic depression is one of the prevalent causes of mental impairment among the elderly. (The symptoms, causes, and treatment of depression are discussed in Chapter 5.) Those who suffer from chronic depression—which impairs functioning—are able to stay in the community if they receive close daily care and supervision. The chronically depressed person has considerable difficulty making rational judgments and decisions related to daily living. A prolonged state of depression can physically immobilize an individual and make it impossible for that person to care for him- or herself on a daily basis.

Organic brain diseases are the major causes of psychological impairment among the elderly. These diseases (Chronic Organic Brain Syndrome—COBS) are estimated by researches to affect 10 to 15 percent of the over 65 population (see Tift, 1981).

Dementia is a major cause of mental impairment among the elderly. The term *dementia* actually refers to a group of chronic brain diseases. These diseases have basically the same symptoms. All intellectual functions progressively decline. The ability to remember very recent events is the first problem to develop. As time passes this problem gets worse and all other aspects of thinking become involved. A person can no longer make accurate judgments or think through options when making decisions about even the most routine tasks of daily living. Language becomes faulty, and the ability to communicate ideas is limited or lost. Behavior may become reckless as the individual loses awareness of the dangers to health or life.

The two most common types of dementia are senile dementia (Alzheimer's disease) and multi-infarct dementia. These two conditions account for almost all dementia cases among the elderly. Both of these illnesses are classified as organic diseases because they involve brain damage. Brain diseases other than the dementias that are found among the impaired elderly are Huntington's Chorea, Progressive Supernuclear Palsy, Multiple Sclerosis, and Parkinson's disease.

Of the two types of dementia, multi-infarct is the least common. Although it was once believed that this type of dementia, popularly termed *hardening of the arteries* (arteriosclerosis), was the most common type of dementia, it is now believed to constitute only about 15 to 20 percent dementia cases (see Terry & Wisniewski, 1977). This type of dementia is caused by the death of a significant number of brain cells due to many small strokes (infarcts). High blood pressure is a major cause of strokes. The strokes tend to accumulate and progressively affect larger segments of the brain; thus, the condition of dementia progressively worsens.

### Alzheimer's Disease

The Institute of Medicine (1977) estimates that 60 percent of all the functionally dependent elderly are suffering from dementia of the Alzheimer's type. Up to 1.2 million adults over age 45 are believed to have this disease. The National Center for Health Statistics (1979) estimates that 63 percent of those elderly persons institutionalized in all public and private mental hospitals, nursing homes, and personal care homes have Alzheimer's disease: It is the primary cause of intellectual deterioration in this country.

The onset of symptomology related to Alzheimer's disease occurs between ages 50 and 60, while the average age at which Alzheimer's is diagnosed appears to be 70 (see Heston, Mastri, Anderson, & White, 1981). Symptoms begin in an insidious fashion, which makes early detection difficult.

Alzheimer's disease is characterized by a reduction of spontaneity, progressive intellectual deterioration, and changes in personality and behavior. One of the early signs of the disorder is periodic disorientation due to recent memory loss. (Remote memory loss occurs much later.) The second loss to occur is disorientation to place. There are often problems with general information processing and mathematical ability. The ability to think concretely declines, and speech disorders are common.

Although the behavioral forms of Alzheimer's disease vary, intellectual dysfunctioning is prevalent and severe. The memory loss is quite disabling; for example, a person may forget what he or she is doing in the middle of completing a simple task such as making a sandwich, shopping, paying bills, eating, and so on. Some people take to wandering around—especially at night—and get lost. Many people with this disease remain fairly socially appropriate despite their impaired cognitive functioning.

As the disease progresses the individual may experience speech difficulties to the extent of not being able to speak in sentence form, and using instead incoherent jargon or a "word salad." Some patients become severely depressed and/or agitated. There may be impairment of the ability to correctly use the senses. This can include the inability to use a concrete object, respond to someone's spoken words, or respond to other stimuli from the immediate environment. Some with Alzheimer's disease may experience temporary hemiplegia (weakness on one side of the body) or paraplegia (weakness of the legs or lower portion of the body). Control of bowel and bladder may be lost. Other physical manifestations observed in some patients are facial paralysis, muscle tension, shuffling gait, and stooped posture. In some cases the patient in the final stages of the illness is completely physically helpless. For a more detailed discussion of the symptoms and disabling features of this disease, the reader is referred to Heston et al. (1981), Kolb (1977), and Miller and Cohen (1981).

## Physical Illness

Chronic physical illness makes it difficult, if not impossible, for many older people to function independently on a day-to-day basis in the community. Medical problems such as arthritis, heart disease, hypertension, cancer, diabetes, and respiratory diseases are the major causes of impaired physical functioning among the elderly. Even when an illness is arrested or gains a remission, permanent physical impairment may occur. For example, diabetes may be brought under control at some point in time, but not before blindness has occurred or a leg has been amputated. Cancer may be checked with radical surgery at the expense of one or more bodily functions. Due to illness and/or the results of surgery, a patient may, for the remainder of life, be confined to bed or a wheelchair.

Cardiovascular diseases and conditions are often severe enough to drastically limit physical mobility. To minimize the chance of heart attack, stroke, or congestive heart failure, some elderly people have to restrict their daily activities to such an extent that they can do little for themselves. Severe sensory impairment caused by disease and injury also limits the ability to function independently on a daily basis. For many, severe physical pain, depressed mood, and anxiety associated with the medical condition have a negative effect on their cognitive functioning. Suffering preoccupies the mind in some cases to the extent that the individual has little if any mental energy to use for making those decisions, judgments, and plans that are necessary for successful management of routine daily living.

Some elderly people become physically disabled as a result of broken bones. Hip fracture is fairly common among the elderly, and in numerous cases some degree of permanent disability results.

## Dimensions and Degrees of Functional Impairment

Some elderly people are impaired in physical functioning, some are impaired in mental functioning, and some are impaired in both areas. Many who have serious cognitive disabilities are in good physical health. From the standpoint of physical abilities, they have no trouble walking, feeding themselves, and performing a variety of motor behaviors; however, impaired cognition often prevents the successful accomplishment of physical tasks. For instance, the ability to ambulate freely doesn't help people to function independently if they forget where they were going. Or the physical ability to control bladder and bowels doesn't help much if people have forgotten where the toilet is located. In such cases daily assistance with physical tasks is needed.

Many of the physically disabled elderly are free of mental impairment associated with brain disease or injury, but nevertheless have problems in mental functioning because of chronic depression and/or anxiety.

On the other hand, many physically impaired home-bound elderly are well adapted mentally and emotionally. Their intellectual functioning is sound and they are emotionally stable. They have a positive outlook on life and are motivated to do as much as possible for themselves within the limitations of their physical disability. Although they may need considerable concrete help with numerous tasks of daily living, they play an extensive and responsible role in overseeing the care that is provided by others. Some make the arrangements for the required formal services such as meals on wheels, homemaking, and errand services. They also take the initiative to secure assistance from their informal network. They successfully fulfill their own interpersonal relationship needs. They maintain old friendships and family relations. When physical disability precludes their ability to maintain their former social/recreational lifestyle, they develop new interests.

The term *frail elderly* is widely used today to refer to a large segment of the community-based elderly population in need of some sort of attention from both the formal and informal long-term care systems. The Federal Council on Aging, the appointed advisory committee of the Federal Administration on Aging (AOA), is a major advocate for this heterogeneous population of functionally vulnerable elderly. According to the council "frailty is defined as reduction of physical and emotional capacities and loss of a social support system to the extent that the individual becomes immobilized and unable to maintain a household or social contacts without continuing assistance from others" (Federal Council on Aging, 1976, p. 2).

Many who promote policy to benefit the frail elderly include within this target population those who are currently functional but at high risk of functional disability. Since 1976 the Federal Council on Aging has been proposing the legislative enactment of some form of entitlement to long-term care for those who are over the age of 74. The council contends that statistical data reveal that the great majority of the relatively well-elderly in the 75 and older age group are at great risk. The proposed legislation would provide for a cost free, annual, functional needs assessment for every member of the 75 and over age group. This assessment would be conducted by a master's level, trained, clinical worker (the term social worker is not used in the council's documents).

In addition to providing a physical-psychological-social functional assessment, the program would provide the individual with a "significant other" if such a person was not available in the existing informal social network. In essence, this attempt to provide formal services to the well, frail elderly represents a primary preventive intervention component in the rapidly growing field of long-term care.

## THE FIELD OF LONG-TERM CARE

Traditionally, the field of long-term care for the elderly was confined to the institutional care of the chronically ill, disabled, and functionally impaired. In recent years this field of professional practice has been redefined to include the care of the functionally impaired who live in the community. According to Brody "Long-term care refers to one or more services provided on a sustained basis to enable individuals whose functional capacities are chronically impaired to be maintained at their maximum levels of health and well-being" (1977, p. 14).

The multiple concerns of this field are identified by English. "Long-term care includes not only therapeutic rehabilitative efforts to improve levels of functioning, but also efforts aimed at maintaining current levels of functioning, slowing down deterioration, and providing protective care during the terminal stage of life" (1981, p. 275).

Long-term care practitioners strive to provide the impaired elderly who live in the community with the right services at the right times for as long as they are needed. A major goal of long-term care is to keep the elderly out of institutions for as long as possible. Advocates for the improvement of long-term care for the impaired elderly stress the need for a range of alternatives to institutionalization. To keep the impaired elderly in the community for as long as possible, society must provide a variety of services and living arrangements to match the impaired client's unique need constellation (see Kahana and Coe, 1975).

The range and variety of services and special living arrangements are generally referred to as the continuum of long-term care. English points out that "The assessment and placement of the functionally impaired individual along a continuum of long-term care means matching an individual's strengths and needs to three different dimensions: type of service, amount (intensity) of service, and living situation" (1981, p. 276).

Some of the formal, long-term care services that aid the community-based, impaired elderly are delivered to the client's home, while others are provided at agency sites. The important services provided in the home are medical treatment, nursing care, social casework, nutrition services, homemaking services, friendly visiting, personal care assistance, home repair services, errand services, telephone reassurance, and transportation. The long-term care services provided at agency sites are medical clinics, psychiatric and medical day care, individual and group counseling, legal aid, congregate meals, recreation and socialization, and respite care.

A major portion of the overall long-term care received by the impaired elderly who live in the community consists of informal care provided by the family and other members of the social network. The formal caregivers do what they can to assist, supplement, and augment the informal care systems.

## SOCIAL WORK PRACTICE IN LONG-TERM CARE

Traditionally, social workers have been involved in the provision of long-term care to the impaired elderly who reside in the community. Today, both baccalaureate- and Master's-of-Social-Work (MSW)-level workers perform clinical social work jobs in a variety of community-based agencies that serve the long-term care needs of the elderly. The number of MSW personnel employed by these agencies is usually limited due to a shortage of funds. Thus most direct clinical intervention is conducted by baccalaureate-level social workers under the supervision of MSW-level practitioners.

Service case management is a major function of clinical social work practice in the field of long-term care for the community-based elderly. This multirole function constitutes a major portion of the social worker's job and may be performed by both baccalaureate- and MSW-level personnel in settings such as public protective service agencies, neighborhood-based, multipurpose programs, and home health-care programs. Agencies of this kind provide the bulk of long-term care services funded by Title XX of the Social Security Act and the Older Americans Act.

Service case management refers to a process of intervention that consists of the following sequence of activities: (1) conducting a physical-psychological-social functional needs assessment; (2) developing a service plan to meet the identified needs; (3) arranging for the delivery of services; and (4) conducting an ongoing follow-up with the client to monitor, coordinate, and evaluate the service provision. When indicated by the needs assessment, the service case manager provides counseling for the client and significant others.

The needs assessment and service planning steps of the case management process correspond to the assessment/diagnosis and treatment-planning steps of the generic, psychosocial, systems process of case intervention (which is discussed in Chapters 3 and 5). The service case manager must establish a trusting and respectful relationship with the client.

The social work practice roles (see Chapter 2) of advocacy and brokerage are often performed in carrying out the service case management function. For instance, needed services are often not readily available to the client, and the social worker must aggressively advocate for the client's well-being and work as a service broker within the public and private service arenas to acquire the needed elements of quality care. The following case example illustrates various aspects of the service case management function.

Mrs. Smith was confined to a skilled nursing home for six months following a stroke that affected her speech and the right side of her body. Upon discharge to her married daughter's home, Mrs. Smith was able to ambulate very slowly, had the use of her right hand, and was able to speak in a slurred manner. It was believed that with the proper daily exercise, good nutrition, continued medication, and outpatient speech therapy, Mrs. Smith (barring unforeseen complications) could regain much of her prestroke level of functioning.

Her daughter and son-in-law were confident that they could provide her with the prescribed home care needed to restore her functional capacities to a level that would allow her to live by herself in her own home. Upon discharge, formal arrangements were made for Mrs. Smith to receive speech therapy at a local agency. The other areas of prescribed care were, by plan, to be provided by Mrs. Smith's children.

Although the daughter had a part-time job (four hours a day), she believed that she would be able to care for her mother without giving up her job. Six months after Mrs. Smith's discharge from the nursing home the situation in the daughter's home was quite distressful. The speech therapist referred the family to a local multipurpose program for older adults. A service case manager visited the home to conduct a functional needs assessment.

Mrs. Smith's condition had not improved at the anticipated rate, and her daughter had underestimated her own ability and the time required to provide adequate care for her mother. In addition to these problems Mrs. Smith had become despondent, agitated, and demanding of her daughter and son-in-law. The daughter and her husband were beginning to feel some strain in their marital relationship and some economic pressures associated with Mrs. Smith's care.

The caseworker's assessment revealed that Mrs. Smith was psychologically depressed about her poor health. Her daughter had found it necessary to miss some work because of the time and effort she had had to devote to encouraging and assisting her mother with her exercises and daily care. Because of her depression, Mrs. Smith had not progressed in her physical rehabilitation. She was acting helpless and did not want to be alone at any time. She refused to use her walker unless her daughter was at her side every second. Mrs. Smith's daughter and son-in-law had been arguing more frequently about Mrs. Smith's apparent helplessness and demanding attitude.

The caseworker determined that Mrs. Smith was eligible for a number of social and health-related services, and she outlined an interventive plan that included the following:

1. Mrs. Smith would attend a day-care program three days a week where she would receive physical therapy and speech therapy. With Mrs. Smith in day care her daughter would have more time for her employment responsibilities and some general relief from her mother's demanding behavior at home.
2. On two different evenings each week Mrs. Smith would be taken to the local senior center to participate in group activities. One activity would consist of a stroke recovery discussion group and the other a general socialization/recreational group. Mrs. Smith was also eligible for transportation by van to and from the day-care facility and the senior center.
3. On the two days each week when Mrs. Smith was home alone because her daughter was at work, low cost meals would be provided by Meals on Wheels.
4. The caseworker would see Mrs. Smith alone once each week for individual counseling that would focus on her depression and on planning for her return to independent living in her own apartment.

5. The caseworker would meet with Mrs. Smith's daughter and son-in-law to support their efforts to help Mrs. Smith and to advise them about how best to deal with her depressive state and physical rehabilitation in the home. The worker would also help the daughter and her husband talk about their marital tensions.

Over a six-month period of time the caseworker as service manager monitored the services provided by others (day care, Meals on Wheels, center group activities, and transportation). Casework therapy with Mrs. Smith had been successful. Her depression had lifted and she was making strides in her physical and social rehabilitation. The daughter and her husband had become much more effective in their care of Mrs. Smith, and they were no longer in conflict with each other.

At this point Mrs. Smith was functioning well enough to be able to return to her own apartment. It was determined that with continuing daily Meals on Wheels service, continuing involvement in group activities at the senior center, and continuing regular medical follow-up, Mrs. Smith could live by herself. She was functional to the point that she could manage her own personal care and small, daily, routine chores. Her daughter was more than willing to check in on her daily, as well as do basic housecleaning once each week. The caseworker would continue to monitor the ongoing provision of concrete services, and through this follow-up she would be in a position to know when new problems or difficulties might develop.

The service case management function is an essential component of the professional intervention provided by a home health care agency. Medical treatment and nursing care are more effective when they are provided in conjunction with services that address the client's psychosocial needs. The social worker as service case manager must make certain that the medical, psychological, and social components of care are carefully integrated to meet the client's complex constellation of physical, psychological, and social needs.

The professionally trained social worker, more so than the doctor and nurse, assesses the impaired client from a "holistic" (systems) perspective, and is therefore the most qualified member of the health care team to be in charge of case management. Unfortunately, most of those who direct and define the policy for home health care programs are not social workers and, more often than not, they exclude social work from the service management function.

In many long-term home health care cases there is a considerable need for social work counseling. Many home care patients need psychosocial supportive therapy to help them accept the prescribed medical treatment. Counseling can also help to alleviate the psychological depression and anxiety that often exacerbate the client's medical problems.

The impaired individual who lives alone and who does not have contact with an informal social network needs continuing, close, casework attention. The caseworker provides the client with the close, warm, personal relationship that is necessary for the client's psychological well-being. A major casework goal for the socially isolated client is to locate a significant other with whom the client can form an ongoing, close, personal relationship.

Without assistance in daily living from friends or relatives, the isolated, functionally impaired client is dependent upon numerous home care services. The caseworker must make regular home contacts to be sure that the services being received by the client are adequately meeting the client's needs. As time passes the needs of the chronically impaired client invariably change. Close service monitoring by the caseworker determines when modifications in home services are indicated.

Those cases of severe physical and/or mental impairment that involve a high degree of vulnerability are often called *protective service cases*. Most county governments or area agencies on aging directly or indirectly provide protective services programs targeted toward older individuals who are at-risk. Such programs attempt to protect those who are dysfunctional to the extent that they may be harmful to themselves and/or abused by others.

A primary goal of protective services is to avoid institutionalization for the frail elderly. If individuals are unable to live alone, attempts are made to place them in a protective living arrangement such as a foster home, a supervised boarding home, a group home, or a personal care home.

Some mentally impaired elderly are unable to make rational judgments and decisions concerning their well-being. They may not be able to protect themselves from neglect and/or hazardous situations, and they become victims of abuse, exploitation, serious injury, or situations that result in their death. In some cases legal interventions are necessary to protect these individuals against self-neglect or abuse from others. Legal interventions to protect an individual's assets or person may be voluntary or involuntary. Because of the high regard for the individual's right to self-determination, involuntary legal interventions are used as a last resort. All voluntary and private means are usually exhausted before court action is taken to appoint a legal personal guardian, a legal financial guardian, or to force someone out of his or her home and into a protective living environment or institution.

In some protective service agencies caseworkers are appointed guardians of persons and their estates. For the worker who is burdened with a heavy caseload and who does not have special skills in financial management, guardianship responsibilities can prove to be overwhelming. It would seem advisable to have the technical guardianship functions handled by a full-time, administrative-level person who would work closely with the protective services caseworkers conducting direct counseling with the clients.

Social workers can play a major counseling role in day-care centers for the functionally impaired elderly. Both individual and group counseling are useful formats for helping patients with emotional problems and cognitive impairment. Group reminiscence procedures (see Chapter 5), reality orientation classes, group validation therapy, and remotivation group therapy (see

Chapter 7) are all useful approaches with those mentally impaired who are served at day-care centers. Casework service should be extended to the day-care patient's family to help them coordinate and integrate the care efforts at the center with those provided in the home.

The medical caseworker who practices in a general hospital setting is not considered a part of the long-term care field. However, many patients who are served by social work in the acute-care medical hospital are suffering from chronic illness and functional impairment. The hospital social worker is often the person responsible for initiating arrangements for their long-term care, postdischarge provisions—either in the community or in a nursing home. These tasks require a knowledge of long-term care resources and the skills associated with making effective referrals.

When an elderly patient goes from the hospital into a nursing home for a period of convalescence, the hospital caseworker must work closely with the patient's family and the caseworker at the nursing home so continuity of care and planning can be assured. Entering a nursing home is usually a traumatic experience, even when the stay is expected to be brief. The patient should be given a great deal of emotional support and should be encouraged to actively engage in the process of choosing a nursing home. Family and patient should be informed of the goals of nursing home convalescense care, and they should be involved in planning for the patient's eventual release from the nursing home to the most appropriate community living arrangement.

### Impaired Clients and Their Caretakers

Most noninstitutionalized, chronically impaired elderly are cared for in the community by a spouse, adult child, or sibling. In a small percentage of cases the informal caretaker is a close friend, distant relative, or neighbor. Some patients are so impaired that they cannot survive outside of an institution without a live-in caretaker.

The social worker plays a major part in helping to maintain the impaired person in the community for as long as possible. Both the impaired individual and the caretaker benefit from social work intervention. The social worker links the client and caretaker to the needed social and health supportive services, directly counsels both people, and attempts to mobilize all available resources in the client's informal social network.

Although illness and related dysfunction in the chronically impaired elderly are usually irreversible (as in cases of dementia), a primary goal is to promote the best possible state of health and psychosocial functioning. The quality of the caretaker's work with and supervision of the impaired patient may improve the patient's health.

First and foremost the caseworker must see to it that the patient is receiving the best possible medical and/or psychiatric care. It is imperative that the illness has been accurately diagnosed and that all known medical treatments are being applied. The caseworker helps the caretaker to understand the patient's illness and its prognosis. The family can be referred to the appropriate literature, community lectures, workshops, and other sources that provide caretaking knowledge and skills.

Safford (1980) describes an educational and support program for families of the mentally impaired elderly which was conducted over a three-year period at the Isabella Geriatric Center in New York City. Caretakers received intensive training for two hours a week over a six-week period. Participants received practical knowledge about the nature of mental impairment and learned how to supervise and care for the patient in the home. The family members also had the opportunity to discuss their individual problems. This three-year project demonstrated that intensive, short-term training of caretakers was quite effective.

Beaulieu and Karpinski (1981) describe a group treatment program for well-elderly with ill spouses. The group treatment process focuses on the personal needs of the caretakers, and the group experience helps spouses adapt positively to the changes in their lives that result from the incapacity of their partners. In this kind of therapy group members can learn how to share their hopes, fears, depression, anxieties, and frustrations with others who understand these feelings. Such groups can help to prevent the emotional deterioration of the caretaker.

The major thrust of the daily care of the mentally impaired involves supervision and guidance of the patient's behavior. In some of the more severe cases of mental illness and dementia, supervision needs to be provided 24 hours a day. Without it some patients will roam around at night and get lost or injured.

The caseworker can help the caretaker learn how to guide the patient's daily behaviors by giving him or her careful, clear instructions about such matters as how to supervise the patient's eating, bathing, dressing, and performing of tasks around the house. When the patient requires some physical assistance with these tasks, it is important for the caseworker to help the family provide the kind of care that will maximize the patient's functioning and minimize his or her dependency. This involves providing the *minimal* level of direct assistance to the patient. Bayne (1978) stresses that the initial step in treatment should be to mobilize the patient's own control mechanisms.

Eisdorfer, Cohen, and Preston (1981) state that operant reinforcement procedures can be effective in changing or modifying some of the patient's problems with verbalization, motor behaviors, and self-care. The caseworker can teach the family how to select and apply the most effective positive reinforcers on a day-to-day basis. Attempts can also be made to arrange elements of the physical environment, the timing of family routines, and social interactions in such a way that the cues for specific functional behaviors are as clear to the patient as possible. A modified version of the reality orientation approach can be used in the patient's home (see Chapter 7).

Providing the patient with factual information about her- or himself and the environment helps to minimize confusion.

Caring for the severely mentally impaired person in the home can be physically and emotionally taxing. The psychological impact on the caretaker can be profound. The patient's change in personality is usually the most upsetting factor for the caretaker. This personality deterioration is more destructive of the quality of family life than the patient's physical disability (see Coni, Davison, & Webster, 1980).

The caseworker must give the caretaker a continuing opportunity to ventilate feelings of distress about the patient's misfortune as well as his or her own. Some professional helpers believe that the most valuable service the caseworker can provide to a caretaker is empathic listening. Many caretakers say they just need an understanding person to talk to on a regular basis.

Caring for the functionally dependent elderly, particularly those who are mentally impaired, can result in physical and mental burden for the caretaker (see Sanford, 1975; Eggert, Granger, Morris, & Pendleton, 1977). A decision to institutionalize the impaired, home-bound client is most likely when the caretaker feels overly burdened.

Richard Morycz's (1982) excellent doctoral dissertation reveals that a major element in caretaker strain is role overload/contraction and subsequent role exhaustion. In this study it was found that strain precipitated the desire to institutionalize for white, female, and daughter caretaking groups, but not for black or male caregivers. The Morycz study offers a detailed discussion of the intervention that must be developed to relieve strain and burden on the caretaker.

> In clinical work with families of Alzheimer's patients, three phases have been noticed in professional counseling: (1) an education phase where families need to know about and understand the disease; (2) a problem-solving stage where they learn various ways to manage patient's inappropriate behaviors and fully capitalize on their remaining abilities (minimize unrealistic expectations and maximize patient functioning); and (3) an affective stage where families begin to recognize and come to terms with how they feel about the changes in their elderly family member and their caretaking role. In addition, such counseling and support (individually or in groups) may help not only in alleviating problem severity, but in identifying additional social support and encouraging the utilization of the support. (1982, p. 218)

Home care is recognized as an effective means of preventing or postponing costly and unwanted institutionalization. Home health care visits from the doctor, nurse, and health care aid help to sustain the burdened caretaker.

In many cases of severe physical disability and/or terminal illness, the caretaker often becomes physically and emotionally exhausted. The social worker can make arrangements for the family to get periodic relief from their caretaking burden by having the patient attend day care and/or spend an occassional weekend in a partial hospital program. Robertson, Griffiths and Cosin (1977) report that the impaired patient's periodic readmissions to a hospital for short durations provide significant relief for the burdened family caretaker.

Both the terminally ill and their caretakers need special psychosocial attention. The patient and the family need the opportunity to deal openly with their feelings about impending death. The caseworker can help the patient and family make plans and decisions related to the fact of approaching death. The patient who is approaching death should have the opportunity to choose where he or she wants to die—at home or in a hospital.

The caseworker should attempt to link the patient to hospice care, which provides the dying patient with special, personalized attention during the final weeks or months of life. A hospice service provides professional care with as much family involvement as possible (see Stoddard, 1978). Control of pain is a primary hospice objective, as is the prevention of the patient's emotional isolation.

Hospice care is a team service. The doctor, nurse, aids, social worker, and even the cleaning personnel work together to provide a comfortable, home-like atmosphere. They attempt to make the experience of dying as comfortable and as peaceful as possible. A hospice is a place, but it is also a program of care. In some programs the dying patient may move back and forth between home and the hospice facility. Hospice workers make home visits as frequently as needed. In some communities hospice services are offered exclusively as a service—without a special physical facility. In this kind of program the designated hospice team works with the patient and the family within the home and/or the medical hospital.

The clinical social worker can play a significant role in the provision of hospice care. The caseworker's capacity to be empathic, genuine, and respectful facilitates the patient's and family's coming to terms with the reality of death. The caseworker may be called upon to assist the patient in making a decision about where and when to die. For example, some patients give explicit instructions to the medical staff and their relatives about how the final period of care should be handled in the event they are not coherent or conscious and thus are unable to make decisions. Many people say they prefer not to be kept alive for a prolonged period of time by artificial means when there is no hope for recovery. Some people put their written wishes in the form of a document called "A Living Will."

The caseworker can help the family and the patient with practical matters such as financial planning and funeral and burial arrangements. The caseworker may work closely with individual family members and/or meet with them as a group to help them with the painful grieving experience. They need an opportunity to ventilate the feelings of anger, sorrow, and fear associated with the anticipated loss of a loved one (see Pilseker, 1975).

In some cases the caseworker may be very helpful by assisting the dying patient with the life review. Encouraging and facilitating reminiscing gives the patient an opportunity to resolve old as well as recent conflicts.

### Case Illustration

This case illustration of long-term care practice features the social work function of service case management.

**Case Profile.**    Mr. and Mrs. Walker have been married for 60 years: He is 90 years old and she is 85. They have lived in the same small town since birth. They have outlived their siblings and most of their long-time friends. Their three married sons and grandchildren live a considerable distance away. One son lives two hours away, and the other two have a five-hour drive to get to their parents' home. All three children frequently telephone their parents and visit them fairly regularly on weekends.

Mr. and Mrs. Walker are both suffering from chronic hypertension. They have been taking medication for many years. Over the last five years their conditions have worsened, and more and more medication has been prescribed in an attempt to control the illness. In recent years the illness has slowed them down. Both must avoid heavy work, physical exertion, and emotional excitement in order to minimize the chance of stroke and heart failure. On several occasions during the past five years, each has blacked out from physical exertion.

Although their physical functioning has been quite limited for a number of years and has continued to decline gradually, they have been able to live on their own. Mrs. Walker is very hard of hearing. This condition has gradually worsened over a seven-year period. They both take medicine for mild diabetic conditions.

They live in a mobile home that requires only minimal maintenance. Mrs. Walker has been preparing meals and doing the house cleaning. For two years neighbors and relatives have been doing the shopping. When the weather permits, Mr. and Mrs. Walker sit on the porch swing and take short walks in the yard. When medical attention is needed, a neighbor or one of their sons drives them to the doctor's office. Mr. Walker has been very contented for years watching television. Mrs. Walker watches some television and reads a little. She enjoys company better than anything.

Mrs. Walker greatly misses the things she used to be able to do outside of the house before the reduction in her mobility. She has been discontented with the home-bound situation but has not become depressed or agitated. Both Mr. and Mrs. Walker have been able, over the years of declining physical mobility, to maintain a positive attitude.

Mr. and Mrs. Walker's retirement income is limited but sufficient to finance their rather simple lifestyle. They own their home and are free of debts. They have savings sufficient to cover their funeral expenses. Their home is comfortable, and when new furnishings or appliances are needed, they can afford to make the purchases.

A catastrophic illness requiring extended hospitalization and/or nursing home care would, in a short period of time, wipe out their savings and make them eligible for SSI and medicaid benefits.

**A Presenting Need for Long-Term Care.**   Over a two-week period, neighbors and relatives became aware of a change in Mrs. Walker's mental functioning. During telephone and face-to-face conversations Mrs. Walker revealed very marked short-term memory loss and time disorientation. Her mood seemed to be mildly depressed and her affect was somewhat flat. Her hearing capacity seemed to be worse, but she was not wearing her hearing aid.

Close inspection revealed some disorder in the customarily very tidy home. Mr. Walker, when pressed by his children, admitted that he was worried about his wife. He said she was very forgetful lately and confused about the days of the month and the month of the year. He said she was able to prepare the meals and clean up a little each day, but that she seemed weak and was spending a lot of time in bed. He was worried that her blood pressure was out of control and that she might have a stroke.

Upon further questioning Mr. Walker reluctantly told one of his sons that several weeks ago Mrs. Walker had been too weak to get out of the bathtub. When he tried to help her, *he* passed out. He said it took him four hours to get up enough strength to eventually drag her out of the tub. On that occasion they had both crawled to bed.

Upon learning these facts and observing Mrs. Walker's obvious mental confusion and forgetfulness, the son took her to the family doctor, the only physician who had cared for the Walkers during the last 20 years. The physician confirmed an elevation in blood pressure. When asked if Mrs. Walker had experienced a small stroke, the physician was very evasive. He preferred to believe that Mrs. Walker's mental symptoms were caused by her failure to take all prescribed medication.

The doctor believed that Mrs. Walker should continue on the same medication. Mrs. Walker was on five different medicines, each taken three or four times a day. No one could be certain that Mrs. Walker was taking the medicine properly. Even Mr. Walker could not be sure because he was not in the habit of watching her closely. Mrs. Walker appeared confused about the medicine but said she did not need any help. She was not aware of the extent of her confusion and memory loss.

The children could visit only on weekends. They coordinated their visiting, so that thereafter one of them would be with their parents each weekend. Whoever was home for the weekend prepared Mrs. Walker's weekly medication. Each separate dosage was placed in an envelope properly labeled for day and time of day.

Over a three-week period Mrs. Walker's condition neither worsened nor improved. The family became increasingly concerned about Mrs. Walker. They realized that their parents needed some sort of assistance if they were to remain in their home and sought advice from the adult services agency, which was located in a neighboring town—the county seat.

## Long-Term Care Intervention with Mr. and Mrs. Walker

A service case manager (caseworker) responded to the Walker family's request for help.

*Functional Needs Assessment.* The social worker made two home visits to complete the initial assessment. The first interview was conducted with Mr. and Mrs. Walker and their oldest son. The second interview was held with Mr. and Mrs. Walker one week later. The caseworker secured a general social history and a detailed description of past and current functioning. Special attention was given to a discussion of health problems. The caseworker closely observed the couple's mental and physical behavior.

Mr. and Mrs. Walker were asked what kinds of assistance they felt were needed. The caseworker informed them about the different kinds of services that were available to assist people who were not able to do everything for themselves. The caseworker secured detailed information about the informal resources currently available to the Walkers.

## Caseworker's Recommendations

1. A diagnostic work-up for Mrs. Walker at a geriatric medical center. (Special attention to memory loss, confusion, weakness, hearing loss, and elevated blood pressure).
2. Home-bound meal service for Mr. and Mrs. Walker (hot midday meal Monday through Friday).
3. Several hours of service from a personal care aid every Wednesday to help Mrs. Walker take a bath and groom her hair.
4. Several hours of house cleaning service every Wednesday (to clean floors, kitchen appliances, bathroom fixtures, and dust furniture).
5. A weekly visit from the caseworker for supportive counseling, ongoing needs assessment coordination, and evaluation of in-home services.
6. Mrs. Walker seemed well enough to do the following routine living tasks since they required minimal physical exertion.
   a. Preparing breakfast and a light evening meal.
   b. Washing the dishes.
   c. Doing the laundry with automatic washer/dryer.
   d. Daily, routine, personal care (excluding the use of the bathtub).
7. Mr. Walker could assist his wife with the light housekeeping chores, but he should avoid all heavy work. He should continue with his current medical treatment (take prescribed medication and see the family doctor once a month).
8. The Walker children would take turns visiting their parents, assuring that a son and daughter-in-law were present every weekend. The daughter-in-law would assist Mrs. Walker with her weekend bath. The children would do the required heavy house cleaning and grocery shopping.
9. Neighbors and friends who had been helping out in recent years would continue to make casual, social visits on a regular basis and do the light grocery shopping during the week. Close neighbors could be expected to respond to emergencies.

10. Each weekend an adult child would prepare Mrs. Walker's medication for the upcoming week. Mr. Walker was to remind her at each meal to take her medicine and see to it that she opened the right envelope of pills.

**Subsequent Modifications in the Long-Term Care Service Plan.** Six weeks later the extensive diagnostic work-up was completed with a fairly certain conclusion that Mrs. Walker's recent cognitive impairment had been caused by a small or several small strokes. Because of the continuing hypertension, additional strokes could occur. It was highly probable that Mrs. Walker was in the early stages of dementia (multi-infarct type). Because Mrs. Walker had been taking fairly high dosages of three different antihypertensive drugs, which often have side effects of mental confusion, there was a possibility that some of her impairment was caused by overmedication.

Mrs. Walker's medication was adjusted, and she was required to have her blood pressure regularly and frequently monitored. It was also recommended that extra care be taken to keep Mrs. Walker on a salt-free, low-fat, low-cholesterol diet.

Proper diet, medication, and the avoidance of physical and emotional stress on a permanent basis might slow down the process of accumulating strokes.

### Revised Service Plan

1. A visiting nurse every Wednesday to monitor blood pressure and observe for negative side effects of medication.
2. Nurse and caseworker will teach relatives and friends how to observe for medication side effects.
3. With consultation from a nutritionist the caseworker will teach the family how to provide the proper diet.
4. The caseworker will use reality orientation procedures to minimize Mrs. Walker's confusion.
5. Mrs. Walker will be fitted with a new and more effective hearing aid.

### Discussion Questions

1. Considering the poor prognosis for Mrs. Walker's illness (dementia, multi-infarct type), speculate about future modifications in long-term care interventions.
2. Identify and discuss the interventions in this case which may have the potential to prevent, minimize, and/or delay further dysfunction for Mrs. and Mr. Walker.
3. Identify and discuss the areas in which the caseworker might expand the counseling (psychosocial treatment) role in this case. Drawing upon material covered in Chapters 3 and 5, what treatment procedures might be appropriate for application in this case?
4. Identify and discuss the eclectic nature of the intervention in this case. Identify the different treatment approaches which were drawn upon by the caseworker.

## SUMMARY

Chronic conditions of physical and mental illness are prevalent among the elderly. Serious impairment in physical and/or mental functioning requires assistance in daily living. Without some assistance a large number of the impaired would not be able to live in the community. The demography of this group is heterogeneous. Some live alone, some with relatives, and others in a variety of group living arrangements such as boarding homes, personal care homes, and foster care homes.

Cancer, heart disease, arthritis, and diabetes are major medical causes of functional impairment. These chronic conditions are responsible for decline in both physical and psychological functioning. Severe mental impairment for a sizable number of the elderly is caused by dementia. Dementia refers to a group of organic brain diseases. Senile Dementia (Alzheimer's disease) is the most prevalent brain disease among the elderly. Up to 1.2 million adults over the age of 45 are believed to have this incurable, debilitating illness.

The field of practice known as long-term care has traditionally served the institutionalized elderly. In recent years this field has been redefined to include the provision of health and social services to the functionally impaired elderly who reside in the community. The bulk of long-term care for the elderly consists of the help in daily living provided by relatives, friends, neighbors, and other people who are a part of the elderly person's informal social network. A major goal of long-term care practice is to support, supplement, and augment the informal caretaking system.

Social work plays a significant and central role in long-term care practice. A recently emerged interventive function provided by the trained social worker in long-term care is that of service case management. This multirole function incorporates the basic steps of the generic process of psychosocial systems intervention used for all cases at all levels of intervention—primary, secondary, and tertiary.

Service case management including the casework counseling component is applied in a variety of different agencies that serve the functionally impaired elderly in the community. Protective service agencies, home-health agencies, and day-care programs comprise a major portion of the community-based, long-term care field.

The long-term care social worker makes a valuable contribution to the informal caretakers of the functionally impaired elderly. They train family caretakers to be more effective in their caregiving. They serve as advocates and brokers for needed, quality services from the formal systems of care. The social worker uses supportive therapy to help ease the psychological burden experienced by many caretakers. Direct treatment of the impaired client in the home is frequently provided to promote the best possible level of psychosocial functioning.

# Chapter 7

# Clinical social work practice with the institutionalized elderly

## INTRODUCTION

The focus of this chapter is on clinical social work practice with and on behalf of the elderly who are confined to mental hospitals and nursing care facilities. Social work practice in these settings falls into the tertiary level of intervention category, because almost the entire patient population is in need of long-term care. The primary goal of intervention with this population is to promote the best possible level of personal functioning while preventing further decline.

Approximately 5 percent of the population over the age of 65 currently resides in institutions. While this is a rather small portion of the total elderly population, the provision of institutional care for the elderly is an important segment of the field of long-term care and will continue to be so in the years ahead. For instance, it is estimated that 20 percent of all people alive today who are over the age of 65 will spend some time in an institution. The risk of institutionalization increases with age: 10 percent of those over the age of 75 and 20 percent of those over the age of 80 are institutionalized (see Cohen, 1980).

Clinical social work practice with the elderly who are in mental hospitals and nursing homes is provided by professional social workers who received training at the baccalaureate or MSW level. Social workers play a major role in the patient's admission process and the patient's discharge planning. They also conduct psychosocial treatment with patients on both a one-to-one and a group basis.

## CLINICAL SOCIAL WORK IN THE MENTAL HOSPITAL

Almost 1 percent of all persons aged 65 and over are confined to public and private mental institutions (see Lowy, 1979). Approximately half of the elderly who reside in mental hospitals are patients who grew old in the institution. The rest were hospitalized due to a breakdown in mental functioning that occurred in their old age. Many of the latter group are suffering from irreversible organic brain syndrome and are so severely functionally impaired that they cannot be maintained in the community.

Many of the patients who grew old in a mental hospital are no longer actively ill. However, their psychosocial functioning capacities are severly limited as a result of long-term confinement in a nonstimulating environment. Resocialization and remotivation treatment programs can restore many of these patients to a level of functioning that enables them to live in the community with minimal supervision. The hospital must provide a daily environment that stimulates and reinforces appropriate cognitive and social behavior. Group treatment can be used to help patients learn how to socialize with others and to help them develop the basic coping skills required for daily living in the community.

Gottesman (1967) reports the short-term success of a milieu treatment program for long-term patients. The therapeutic milieu was continued around the clock. The hospital staff placed more difficult expectations, demands, and challenges on the patients in order to encourage the use of ego skills and afford them the opportunity to develop new skills. This program had almost immediate results: Within a few days most patients had abandoned the sedentary and empty behavior that is characteristic of long-term patients in mental hospitals.

Some long-term patients are so functionally impaired that they will never be able to be discharged from the hospital. Because of staff shortages these patients receive little if any psychosocial intervention; however, they do receive adequate custodial care. For these patients the hospital is a permanant home. The social worker is encouraged to advocate for a more humane social environment within the hospital community for these patients. They should be actively involved on a daily basis in recreational and socializing programs where there is ample opportunity for regular personal contact with significant others.

Although the attention given to psychiatric, inpatient, geriatric treatment is meager throughout the country, the professional literature reveals that some progress is being made. For instance, Oberleder (1970) reports the successful treatment of "senile" symptoms during a six-month, intensive treatment program based on crisis therapy. The patients carried a diagnosis of organic brain syndrome or psychosis.

Upon admission to the hospital the subjects of this study were described as disoriented, irrational, rambling, and unable to care for themselves. Their deterioration in functioning had started about five years before hospitalization.

The immediate therapeutic goal was to help these patients deal with their feelings regarding past unresolved crises and current distress. Treatment was based on the assumption that the patients' dysfunctional symptoms were not due to brain damage, but were the consequences of rigid ego defenses against unresolved psychic conflicts. Patients received both one-to-one and group psychotherapy. Throughout the period of psychotherapy, progress and planning conferences were regularly held with all the patients. Plans and preparations were made for their eventual discharge to a community living arrangement. They were prepared for independent living in a "hotel" ward. All 12 patients in this study recovered to the degree that discharge from the hospital was a possibility.

In recent years a considerable effort has been in progress to deinstitutionalize the long-term, hospitalized, chronic population. Numerous authorities believe that many of these chronic patients can function outside of the institution if they are placed in protective, supervised, community living arrangements such as boarding homes, personal care homes, group homes, or foster homes. (Rarely does the elderly patient have relatives available who can provide home care.) Special care must be taken in selecting a community living site for the discharged patient, because some boarding homes and personal care homes offer little more than custodial care. When patients are moved to these kinds of community placements, where social and recreational programs are not provided, they become emotionally and socially isolated, and their psychosocial functioning capacities deteriorate.

Many elderly patients who have been continuously hospitalized for a long period of time are not motivated to leave the institution. They are obviously fearful about going into the community—a place where they have not been for a long time. The social worker can prepare the patient for relocation through group programming. Group discussions can focus on fears about returning to the community, and group members can participate in role-playing exercises designed to teach them how to deal successfully with the unfamiliar demands and expectations of daily living in the community.

Gottesman (1965) stresses the value of a stimulating milieu in the resocialization of psychiatric patients who become ill for the first time in old age. According to Gottesman a therapeutic milieu should be provided on a 24-hour basis, and treatment should rest on the assumption that a patient's coping ability or ego functioning is enhanced when he or she is given an opportunity to confront meaningful life crises. In this particular project, as described by Gottesman, patients were involved in a sheltered workshop that paid them for their work. This therapeutic approach was based on the belief that work ordinarily requires and teaches elementary social skills in a relatively nonthreatening context.

Token economy programs have been widely used in mental hospitals to promote patient socialization and appropriate behavior. Mishara and Kastenbaum (1973) report the positive impact of a token economy program on 80 patients with an average age of 68 years. More desirable social behavior was produced by rewarding positive, social behaviors with tokens that the patients were able to use as money. The patients were given many choices about how they could spend their money.

The active treatment of both the acutely and chronically mentally ill should be approached from an eclectic perspective. Many of the treatment procedures discussed in the following sections of this chapter on nursing home care are highly appropriate for use with the elderly population in mental hospitals.

## NURSING HOMES AND THEIR RESIDENTS

The term *nursing home* is generally applied to residential facilities in which 50 percent or more of the residents receive nursing services. Homes that receive medicare and medicaid reimbursement are certified by the federal government as skilled nursing facilities (SNFs) and intermediate care facilities (ICFs). According to the 1977 national survey of nursing homes (National Center for Health Statistics, 1979), 75 percent of all nursing homes had federal certification. Among this group of homes 53 percent were certified as either an SNF or both an SNF and an ICF, while 45 percent were certified as only ICFs.

The services defined as skilled nursing care are those that are provided to patients by professional or technical personnel through medical prescription. The personnel providing such services are registered nurses, licensed practical nurses, physical therapists, and occupational therapists. The patient receiving skilled nursing care is considered to be seriously ill. Intermediate nursing care entails the provision of health-related services to patients who do not require the degree of treatment that is needed at the level of skilled nursing care, but who *do* require service and care beyond room and board (see Vladeck, 1980).

There are three categories of nursing home sponsorship: proprietary (for profit), voluntary, and government. Most voluntary homes are run by non-profit religious organizations and have been traditionally called "homes for the aged." Government sponsored homes are run by municipalities, counties, states, and the federal government. (Nursing facilities provided by the Veterans Administration are examples of federally funded homes.)

Nursing homes have approximately 66 employees per 100 residents. About half of all nursing home personnel are nurses' aides (also called orderlies or nursing assistants). Only 1 in 10 employees is a registered nurse or a licensed practical nurse. About 5 percent of nursing home employees fall into other professional categories such as administrator, social worker, activity director, physical therapist, and occupational therapist (see Vladeck, 1980).

The services provided in most nursing homes are prescribed by detailed federal regulations. Reference is made to Vladeck (1980) for a summarization of the 17 federally mandated "conditions of participation" which include over 85 standards that specify the requirements for nursing home participation in medicare and medicaid reimbursement. It is important to note that certified nursing homes are required to provide medical supervision, nursing services, rehabilitation services, and patient activities, but they are not required to provide social services.

The federal government requires that all certified nursing homes obtain a state license. The licensing requirements vary considerably from state to state; however, in recent years more and more states have moved in the direction of requiring social services in nursing homes. For example, in Pennsylvania, licensing requirements stipulate social service provision by graduates of accredited social work programs. Most private facilities meet this requirement by employing a full-time baccalaureate-level social worker or a part-time MSW consultant. Most large public nursing homes around the country tend to employ a number of professionally trained social workers at both the baccalaureate and MSW levels.

There are approximately 1.3 million people residing in nursing homes, and most of these are functionally impaired, elderly individuals (see Eustis, Greenberg and Patten, 1984). According to the Federal Council on Aging (1981) the typical nursing home patient is an 81-year-old widow who requires some assistance with numerous daily functions, is poor, and has little if any family support.

According to Hing (1981) the most common reasons for nursing home confinement are those disabilities associated with heart disease and circulatory problems. In many cases these conditions cause severe mental impairment. Hing also reports that only 7 percent of all nursing home patients are able to perform daily-living activities independently (bathing, dressing, going to the toilet, moving about, maintaining continence, and eating). Hing believes that it is reasonable to assume that many of these independently functioning patients suffer from mental disorders that may lead to disorientation.

Among the most disabled patients in nursing homes are those who are in an advanced stage of chronic brain disease such as Alzheimer's disease or infarct dementia. These patients require total and constant care. The majority of people who enter nursing homes are quite ill and they stay for a long time. The average length of confinement is 2.6 years; and more than 25 percent stay for more than 3 years. Thirty percent of all nursing home discharges are due to death. This figure would be greater, but many terminally ill patients are transfered to general hospitals where they die shortly afterward. A small portion of nursing home residents are rehabilitated to a degree of functioning that permits their return home or to some form of supervised community living arrangement such as a foster home or a personal care home.

Brody (1977) states that nursing home patients are a disadvantaged population in our society. The nursing home industry has been widely and dramatically criticized. For example, nursing homes have been referred to as "last way stations," "elderly repositories," "dumping grounds," and "custodial warehouses." One critic has made the harsh accusation that the long-term care system for the aged is a branch of organized crime (see Comfort, 1976).

Nader (1971) describes the nursing home population as poor, sick, lonely, forgotten, and powerless.

## CLINICAL SOCIAL WORK IN THE NURSING HOME

According to Linstrom (1975) and Brody and Brody (1974), the greatest and most common area of neglect in our nation's nursing homes is the psychosocial aspect of care. Kosberg (1973) also points out that the patient's social needs are usually ignored, with the result that social and psychological capabilities deteriorate.

A study by Halbfinger (1976) concludes that frustration, helplessness, hopelessness, and powerlessness prevail among nursing home patients because they are not provided with social supports. Mercer and Kane (1979) report that helpless and hopeless feelings can be minimized when patients are given the opportunity to make some choices and exercise some control over their daily lives. This is the area in which the social worker can make a valuable contribution to the patient's quality of life.

Jorgensen and Kane (1976) point out that much knowledge exists in the social work profession that can be used to help fulfill the human needs of nursing home patients. They describe a demonstration project that shows the effectiveness of a range of social work roles in the nursing home setting. The social worker can play a major role in training nursing and recreational personnel to provide a daily atmosphere that addresses the residents' psychosocial needs.

### Social Work Functions and Roles

When budgetary resources are adequate, the functions of the social worker within the long-term care facility include the following: preadmission planning and preparation with the applicant and his or her family, admission procedures, patient's introduction to the home, patient assessment, development of an individualized patient care/treatment plan, one-to-one counseling, group work, family and community intervention, staff training, psychosocial program development, patient linkage to concrete social services and resources, patient advocacy, discharge planning, and community placement.

The social worker views the elderly patient as a whole person and upon the patient's admission conducts a systems-based functional needs assessment. On the basis of this individualized assessment the caseworker devises a comprehensive psychosocial treatment plan. Such a plan includes goals related to the patient's physical problems, emotional needs, cognitive functioning, and interpersonal social needs. Feasible goals are set, and treatment procedures are designed and/or selected to bring about an improvement in any and all areas of the patient's functioning.

In a small percentage of cases the elderly patient may be functionally rehabilitated and returned home. The latter situation requires intensive casework intervention with the patient and his or her significant others in the community. When the prognosis for functional restoration or recovery is good, assessment, treatment, and discharge planning should ideally begin during the nursing home admission process.

For those patients who are permanently impaired and highly unlikely to ever return home for good, psychosocial intervention is highly justified if the value of humane treatment is to be honored. For these patients the long-term care facility is "home." It is their total daily environment. The institution is a person's social and physical living environment on a day-to-day basis for the remainder of life. In a sense it is the individual's family, neighborhood, and community.

Medical, nursing, and social service care are the patient's formal resources; yet, these caregivers are simultaneously part of the patient's informal social network. From this perspective, all personnel have the potential to be informally resourceful to the residents. Moreover, the patients represent potential informal resources for each other.

The overriding social work objective for the permanent resident is the enhancement of the quality of life in the institution. Quality of life is associated with a best possible level of human functioning. All direct casework interventions with the patient and with others on behalf of the patient should focus on the improvement of functioning. In the role of educator/consultant, the caseworker can share with other staff members the knowledge and skills associated with psychosocial treatment.

The worker can develop various psychosocial programs that promote better functioning and enhanced quality of life. For instance, group therapy, socialization groups, recreational programs, milieu treatment, and reality orientation programs are some of the ways to promote quality of functioning and of life. Many of these activities require the involvement of nursing service personnel, other nonsocial work staff members, and volunteers. It is the social worker's responsibility to train these individuals and to monitor their participation in psychosocial treatment programs.

The social worker as therapist or counselor must be alert to the patient's need (at any given time) for intensive treatment associated with a personal problem. For example, a patient may never be able to live outside of a nursing home because functional impairment is so extensive and irreversible, but that patient's depression can be reduced through the use of intensive therapy. Many brain damaged patients who are extremely confused and disoriented can be effectively helped through counseling.

In the process of providing the best possible warm, humane, friendly, meaningful, and socially stimulating patient environment, the worker should make efforts to link the patient to the community. This includes contact with members of the informal social network, as well as with the community-based providers of concrete social services and other formal resources.

The worker must be ready to serve as a personal advocate for a client when there is evidence of neglect, abuse, and/or poor quality of care. Federal nursing home regulations include a resident's "Bill of Rights" (see Messinger, 1981). The following is a condensed statement of that Bill of Rights.

1. The patient is fully informed of his or her rights.
2. The patient is informed of all available services and any related charges.
3. The patient is fully informed of his or her medical condition and can participate in treatment planning.
4. The patient is transferred or discharged only for medical reasons or nonpayment of bill. The patient is given reasonable advance notice of any planned relocation.
5. The patient is encouraged to exercise his or her rights as a patient and as a citizen. The patient may lodge grievances and recommend changes.
6. The patient may manage his or her own personal financial affairs.
7. The patient is free from mental and physical abuse and from chemical and (except in emergencies) physical restraints.
8. The patient is assured confidential treatment of personal and medical records.
9. The patient is treated with consideration, respect, dignity, individuality, and privacy.
10. The patient is not required to perform services for the facility.
11. The patient may associate and communicate privately with persons of his or her choice.
12. The patient may meet with and participate in activities of social, religious, and community groups.
13. The patient may retain and use personal clothing and possessions as space permits.
14. If married, privacy is assured the patient for visits with a spouse. If both spouses are patients, they are permitted to share a room.

In a number of the above provisions, the patient's right is dependent upon the attending physician's judgment.

The term *medically contraindicated* is used to establish the conditions of the patient's rights. For instance, a patient can be denied visitors if the doctor believes that the experience would be bad for the patient's health. Or, for example, the doctor can decide that the patient needs—for safety and health reasons—to be chemically or physically restrained. It is believed by many that the medical contraindication exception is manipulated and loosely interpreted in many facilities for the convenience of the staff.

The existence of the federal "Bill of Rights" for nursing home residents and similar regulations set forth by a number of states definitely provide the social worker with the necessary sanctions to openly and aggressively advocate to guarantee patients' rights.

### Concepts to Promote Quality of Life Care

In a discussion of the humane treatment of old people in institutions, Kahana (1973) stresses that long-term care facilities must operate from a care perspective that goes beyond the pathology model (which views the patient in a "sick role") and that staff must refrain from stereotyping the patient and thereby reducing him or her to a diagnostic entity.

Many nursing home patients become confused and disoriented because the nursing home environment is socially sterile, nonstimulating, and disordered. This kind of environment reinforces tendencies toward emotional and social isolation. Some patients are bored with the environment. Confusion, boredom, disorientation, and emotional isolation can cause psychological depression, the most prevalent emotional problem among nursing home residents. The nursing home must strive to provide a stimulating living environment. A variety of opportunities for active emotional and social involvement must be made available to the patient.

Bourestrom (1976) discusses the social role component of an enriched environment. He points out that the patient loses the normal roles of worker, consumer, homemaker, friend, and citizen. A positive living environment may be promoted by devising strategies to reintroduce these roles into the lives of nursing home patients. The patient care and psychosocial treatment plan should include opportunities and procedures for the patient to function in as many of these roles as possible. Role carrying adds meaningfulness and purpose to the patient's life. Through meaningful roles, patients can feel that they have some choices in life and a degree of control over their existence.

A conceptual model that can help to promote a humane environment for the elderly in long-term care institutions is offered by Cook (1981). This model reflects Maslow's (1954) theory of human motivation and his hierarchy of human needs. From the lowest level to the highest level the human needs are: (1) physiological needs, (2) safety and security needs, (3) love and belongingness, (4) self-esteem, and (5) self-actualization. Needs at the lower level of the hierarchy must be satisfied for the individual to direct his or her resources toward satisfying needs at higher levels. The patient's physiological needs are for the most part satisfied by the medical and nursing care staff, while the social worker has primary responsibility for addressing the patient's higher level needs.

Maslow's model can be applied to the caseworker's assessment and interventive planning for each patient. All treatment goals can be viewed in terms of the patient's safety and security needs, love and belongingness, self-esteem, and self-actualization. The worker's goal-directed interventions with the patient and others should attempt to fulfill these needs. The worker can address these needs through counseling, linkage, staff education, advocacy, and brokerage.

For instance, nursing home patients will feel more safe and secure when they perceive evidence that they have not been abandoned and forgotten by the outside world. The social worker can provide linkages between the patient and the community. The worker may increase the patient's sense of safety when she or he advocates for safer conditions and for an improved quality of basic care. To help satisfy the patient's love and belonging needs, the caseworker can help the patient to maintain meaningful personal attachments through group interaction, the casework relationship, and contact with friends and family in the community. Most nursing home patients have very low self-esteem due to loss of independence, control, and choice in life. Residents may come to feel better about themselves if given the opportunity to participate in directing their lives within the nursing home. Patients need to be seen as competent and useful: They need to be respected and appreciated.

### Entering the Nursing Home

Entering a nursing home is a threatening and stressful experience. Higher mortality rates and further health deteriorations are reported during the first year of confinement. Sorensen (1981) believes that the following actions help to lessen the negative consequences of institutionalization: (1) allow the patient to be involved in the decision-making process around the choice of facility and timing of admission; (2) guide the patient and family slowly and smoothly through the preadmission planning and preparation process; (3) allow the patient to bring along as many personal possessions as possible; and (4) upon admission develop an open communication system between the patient, staff, and family.

Whenever feasible the patient who needs to be placed in a nursing home should be given the opportunity to shop for a facility with attributes that match his or her needs, abilities, and personal preferences. Beverley (1976) offers a "shopping guide" and other tips on how to ease the trauma of the move into a nursing home or the move from one facility to another. No matter how disabled, confused, or apathetic a patient may be, he or she should be told about a forthcoming placement and be involved in the preparation process. He or she needs an opportunity to ventilate feelings and receive empathic understanding. Fears and apprehensions about a pending admission may be lessened if the elderly person can visit and tour the facility prior to confinement. During a preadmission visit, the individual can be introduced to staff and patients. The programs, services, and routines of daily life in the nursing home should also be carefully explained before the individual enters the home.

The family should be intensively involved in all of the preadmission and admission activities. A continuity of involvement in these phases of planning and preparation increases the chances that the family will remain involved on a regular and continuing basis after the patient's admission. Romney (1962) discusses the importance of and some procedures for extending family relationships into the nursing home. Involving family members in groups with other patients' relatives is an effective way to help them deal with their feelings about the patient's institutionalization. These group experiences help to motivate and reinforce family involvement for a continuing period of time.

Friends, neighbors, and other important social contacts should be involved in the preadmission planning period and admission adjustment period. All informal network interpersonal involvement helps to maintain the patient's social continuity and therefore minimizes the sense of personal loss.

It is imperative that the systems oriented assessment of the patient's functional needs and the patient care and psychosocial treatment plan be accomplished at the earliest possible time following admission. A delay in involving the patient in a highly individualized, goal-oriented, care environment could have serious debilitating consequences such as withdrawal, resistance, emotional isolation, confusion, disorientation, and depression.

## PROGRAMS TO ENHANCE PSYCHOSOCIAL FUNCTIONING

Nursing homes must make every possible attempt to provide a rich environment of psychosocial programs. This kind of environmental programming requires the involvement of all staff members, because the objective is to present a total environment that provides opportunities for the ongoing stimulation and reinforcement of the patient's active interest and involvement in daily living.

### Milieu Therapy

Milieu therapy involves the presentation of an active and stimulating daily environment in which both the physical and social structures are as noninstitutional in character as possible. The milieu as place and interpersonal system must approximate a real-life atmosphere similar to that of the family and community (see Gottesman, 1973; Steer & Boyer, 1975).

Recreational activities must be provided with enough variety to meet the personal interests of the residents. Recreation is fun: To be forced into a recreational activity in which one is not interested is contrary to the meaning of fun. If patients are unable to go to the special recreational areas, recreation must be delivered to them. Group recreational activities provide patients with the opportunity to socialize and develop friendships.

Recreational and socializing activities should not be confined to the physical setting of the nursing home. When a patient's health permits, he or she should be taken out into the community for recreational and social activities.

Some nursing homes have introduced pets into the facility in an attempt to make the environment as homelike as possible. Pets are also used to give residents an opportunity to assume some daily responsibility. Ongoing interaction with a pet can also provide the patient with a great deal of emotional satisfaction. A pet is a living thing to love and be close to and from which attention is received. For more detailed information on the use of pets in the care of the elderly, the reader is referred to the following sources: Levinson (1969; 1972), Kidd and Feldman (1981), Corson and Corson (1979), and Brickel (1979).

## Reality Orientation

Reality Orientation (R.O.), from an institutional perspective, is referred to as milieu therapy by Citren and Dixon (1977). They view it as a way to reorganize the physical and social structures of the institution in order to encourage and allow residents to behave in a more oriented fashion. The two components of an R.O. program are 24-hour reality orientation and R.O. groups. Drummond, Kirchoff and Searbrough (1978) tell us that around-the-clock R.O. programming consists of residents being informed by every contact person about the reality of time, place, and person. While providing all aspects of patient care, staff members inform patients about reality in a warm, informal, and respectful way. The staff person should introduce him- or herself by name, address the resident by name, point out the time of day, and explain the purpose of the contact.

This consistant verbal clarification of time, person, place, and purpose is augmented by the use of environmental props that provide cues for reality perception and oriented responses. Some commonly used props in the physical environment are signs, clocks, calenders, directional arrows, object labeling, newspapers, and pictures. R.O. bulletin boards post the name of the institution, name of community, calendar year and day, weather conditions and forecasts, and announcements of special events. These cues are spread throughout the institution, with each special area appropriately labeled such as day room, dining area, bathrooms, and recreational areas.

Reality Orientation classes (groups) are taught at two levels depending upon the group members' level of cognitive functioning. Classes are held five days a week for one half hour. Four to six members are included in each class. Membership should be heterogenous according to the individual's capacities to respond. This kind of grouping allows the more responsive and less confused to serve as role models for those who are the most severely disoriented. Using a variety of visual aids, as well as concrete items from the everyday world such as articles of clothing, food, and eating utensils, the instructor provides descriptions of reality, and the patients learn to identify and remember real items and their uses.

Group members learn each other's names, the time of day, the month, and the years. They discuss the weather and what they had to eat at their last meal. They identify concrete objects and play easy word-letter games. These kinds of procedures are used with classes composed of the moderately and severely disoriented. Advanced R.O. classes are held for those who are mildly confused and in some instances "graduates" from the basic-level classes. Schwenk (1979) points out that advanced classes use activities similar to those used in the basic classes; however, the members are expected to perform more quickly and more accurately. The advanced groups also use math, history, and geography content up to a sixth-grade level.

Patients are terminated from R.O. class when they are no longer confused in their daily functioning. The group worker must be careful not to set goals that either under- or overstimulate the members. Positive reinforcement should be used throughout the R. O. class experiences to reward each and every increment of learning. Praise, food, and hugging are strong reinforcers.

## GROUP WORK WITH NURSING HOME RESIDENTS

Much has been written about group work with the institutionalized elderly. The reader is referred to Irene Burnside's book (1978) on group processes and techniques with the elderly. Burnside recommends the wide use of small groups with homogeneous membership. The relationship between worker and members is a very important aspect of every group. All groups, regardless of their specific or special purpose, have in common the fostering of social interaction and meaningful social involvement. The worker must move at a slow pace, set limited and realistic group goals, and pay attention to individual member needs as well as to group needs. The worker must also be very active and take a great deal of responsibility for group movement.

Remotivation therapy is a group treatment approach used to stimulate individuals who have lost interest in the present and the future (see Dennis, 1978). Group members must have some ability to interact with others. Patients who are severely disoriented and regressed are not suitable for remotivation groups. They should be treated in reality orientation groups. In essence, the remotivation group is one step above the advanced-level reality orientation class. Garber (1965) points out that remotivation helps patients recognize themselves as individuals with unique characteristics that distinguish them from others.

A remotivation group should consist of a maximum of 15 members. Robinson's manual of remotivation techniques points out that group meetings should be held once or twice a week for 12 sessions, and that each meeting should cover five steps: (1) introductions and getting acquainted, (2) bridging reality by having individuals read an article aloud, (3) sharing the real world by developing a topic through the use of questions, visual aids, and props, (4) discussion among patients about work in relation to themselves, and (5) patients expressing pleasure about the group meeting and making plans for the next session. Each session focuses on a different discussion topic. Some sample topics are vacations, gardening, pets, transportation, and holidays. Remotivation group therapy offers the patient an opportunity to perceive reality about the past and present, share personal things with others, practice rational social role behaviors, and gain a more objective self-image.

Ebersole (1978) describes the use of reminiscing groups. He believes that any resident who engages in reminiscing behavior is suitable for inclusion in a reminiscence group. Group reminiscing helps to promote socialization skills and the development of friendships. Reminiscing groups are also recreational. Group discussion through reminiscing stimulates memory. As each member relates a meaningful past experience, others are stimulated to think about similar or different aspects of their past.

A reminiscing group should ideally include five to nine members and membership should be voluntary. The group should meet at the same time of day and at the same place at least once a week. This structure will give the members a sense of trust and something to anticipate and count on. The subject content for reminiscing can be selected by the group leader and/or group members. A frequently used discussion theme is memories of what was going on in one's life at the time of a well-known historical event; for instance, the stock market crash of 1929, the beginning of World War II, the crash of the Hindenburg, and so on.

Each group session may focus on a discussion of a different stage of the life cycle. Music, picture albums, posters, old newspapers, magazines, and other props can be used to facilitate remembering. Both pleasant and unpleasant things are recalled. Unpleasant memories can cause depressive feelings; therefore, the worker must be ready to deal with a member's distress.

Music therapy groups and art therapy groups are used in nursing homes to promote socialization, meaningful participation, and recreation (see Moore, 1978; Wolcott, 1978). Shapiro (1969) points out that music therapy provides patients with a pleasant experience that facilitates the expression of feelings and makes patients less defensive and negative about their environment.

Group psychotherapy is used with patients who are seriously impaired. Linsk, Howe and Pinkston (1975) describe the use of behavior techniques in group work with patients who have self-care deficiencies and cognitive impairment. Task-related questions are directed at group members after material is read to them. This study demonstrated that not only did the asking of many task-related questions increase participation, but the patients' verbalizations were more appropriate.

Saul and Saul (1974) describe group psychotherapy with patients who are angry, depressed, asocial, and disoriented. Group discussion focuses on the patients' current feelings and concerns about their daily environment. Patients are encouraged to talk about anything that is on their mind. The worker tries to show the patients how they can gain some control over life in the nursing home. These authors reported considerable improvement in the functioning of numerous group members after six months of therapy.

Mueller and Atlas (1972) describe a behavioral management group approach with socially regressed patients. Simple remotivation games such as name guessing are played, and members talk about the local (nursing home) community. Each time a patient participates verbally he or she is rewarded with sweets or cigarettes. After six weeks of therapy tokens replace the concrete reinforcers. The tokens can be used to purchase items at the gift shop. Hoyer, Kafer, Simpson, and Hoyer (1974) report the successful use of operant procedures in group treatment of nonverbal patients. Tokens are also used for reinforcement.

A self-government group or resident's council gives nursing home patients an opportunity to express their wishes, opinions, and complaints about their lifestyle and the care they are receiving. Miller and Solomon (1979) feel that a resident's council is a vital necessity in long-term facilities where older people live out their lives. A council is made up of patient representatives. When a council is established, it must be given the opportunity to effect some change. Thus it must have the support of administration and program personnel.

A council should meet on a regular basis, and between meetings members should be given the opportunity to talk with all of the interested patients they represent so they can bring the concerns of as many patients as possible to the council meetings. Periodically, membership on the council should be changed so as many capable and interested patients as possible can eventually have a part to play in the council's self-governing activities.

After organizing a patient's council group and making a direct effort to get its group process development underway, the social worker should refrain from too much group intervention. The aim is to help the group be as self-directed and independent as possible. The worker must be sensitive to the fact that the patients who exert group leadership may need individual attention to help them perform effective and democratic group leadership.

Administrative and program supervisory personnel should attend council meetings, so they can directly hear the patients' recommendations for changes in policies, programs, and services. It is understandable that patients cannot bring about major changes in the facility, but it is feasible for changes to be realized in numerous aspects of daily practices that are important to the patients. For instance, patients *can* have some influence on meal service, the scheduling of various program activities, visitation schedules, issues of privacy, issues regarding personal belongings, and how they spend much of their daily time.

The social worker may have to spend a considerable amount of time motivating and encouraging patients to feel comfortable in positions of leadership and representation since it is customary for nursing home patients to feel helpless and powerless. The social worker must be willing and prepared at any given time to advocate for the patients' council when promises made by administration have not been honored. The worker must also look out for the passive, timid, and somewhat frail council members who may be ignored or overwhelmed by the more aggressive and mentally capable members.

Naomi Feil created validation-fantasy therapy in the early 1960s as a group or individual treatment technique for working with the severely disoriented and confused elderly. She was discouraged by her repeated failures to help disoriented nursing home patients with the use of reality orientation treatment. Feil feels strongly that the goals of reality orientation are unrealistic and that the approach is misused and abused. Reality orientation does not focus on the feelings being experienced by the patient. It primarily involves forcing the worker's reality onto the disoriented person. Feil believes that R.O. can hurt patients because it makes them feel more alone, and consequently they withdraw further (see Feil, 1982).

Feil believes that the confused patient's fantasy is a type of inner reality. A patient's personal fantasies can be thought of as coping mechanisms that help the individual interpret and interact with external, objective reality. Feil further believes that the therapist does not have the right to try to deny the patient's inner reality (fantasy): Fantasy is almost the only coping mechanism that many confused patients possess.

The essence of validation-fantasy therapy (which Feil also calls "tuning-in therapy") is to help patients get in touch with their inner world and to help them express their feelings about fantasies and inner realities. This process, according to Fein, validates the confused person. Wetzler and Feil stress that validation-fantasy therapy involves "validating the right of the severely disoriented aged person to fantasize, to use private language, and to restore integrity through reliving the past, when present life holds no meaning" (1979, p. 1).

The validation therapist provides a link between past associations and present reality. The worker helps to make some sense (give some meaning to) out of the patient's confused thoughts, verbalizations, and behaviors. This process can help some confused patients become more aware of external reality. A film entitled *Looking for Yesterday* (Davis & Feil, 1979) contrasts reality orientation and validation therapy and demonstrates how validation therapy is used in groups.

The sharp difference between the two approaches is highlighted by the following example from the *Looking for Yesterday* film and manual.

> As an R.O. therapist, the worker tells a patient who is crying, "I want to go home," that she, the patient, is at home now, and that her new home is the nursing care facility. Another woman who cries that both of her parents have died is told by the R.O. therapist that her parents died a long time ago. Then the therapist asks the woman if she doesn't want to think about the nice, pretty day outside and the fact that it is springtime. In both of these instances the worker ignores the patient's feelings and makes no attempt to communicate with the patient's inner reality.
>
> Another lady in the film addresses numerous women, including the therapist, by the name of "Fay." She continuously puts things into, and takes them out of her purse. Operating as a validation therapist, the worker attends to the patient's feelings, tunes-in on her inner world of fantasy, and consequently learns that there is a logical relationship between the patient's free associations from the past and the current reality. In this case the therapist learns that the patient had worked as a bookkeeper for many years with another competent bookkeeper named "Fay" and that today the patient calls someone Fay if she respects that person. This patient's purse represents the filing cabinet that she had used so often in her daily work many years ago.

A set of detailed guidelines for validation therapy with groups is provided in the Wetzler and Feil (1979) manual, which includes instructions for how to compose a group, set a meeting agenda, and conduct group discussions.

Ms. Feil rejects reality orientation with the assertion that its effectiveness has not been proven by any research findings, while validation (fantasy) therapy has had positive results with confused patients. The authors wish to point out that sufficient research has not been done on either approach to support claims of effectiveness or ineffectiveness. In the authors' opinion both approaches may have merit and should be applied on a differential basis depending on patient needs, problem dimensions, and treatment goals. There is no apparent reason why both approaches could not be used simultaneously with the same patient population.

The foregoing discussion has barely touched the surface of the rich literature on group work with the elderly. For readings in addition to those cited above see Mayadas and Hink (1974), Morrison (1973), Euster (1971), Lesser, Lazamus, Frankel, and Hauasy (1981), Maizler and Solomon (1976), and Manaster (1967).

## INDIVIDUAL SOCIAL WORK TREATMENT

Individual psychosocial treatment may be strongly indicated as early as the point of preadmission planning and as late as the patient's final days of life. Group treatment should not be considered a routine substitute for one-to-one treatment. Individual therapy with nursing home patients can be as eclectic in perspective as it is with patients at the secondary level of social work practice in the community. Although chronically, and in most cases permanently, impaired nursing home patients can experience new presenting psychosocial problems at any given time, many such problems can be resolved with intensive, individual psychosocial treatment.

Cartensen and Fremouw (1981) contend that individual behavioral treatment is especially appropriate for understaffed nursing homes because it is relatively brief in duration and the treatment principles can be easily taught to nursing personnel. These authors describe the successful treatment of paranoid behavior in a 68-year-old wheelchair patient. This patient is hard of hearing but has good lipreading ability and good verbal skills. She is helpful around the ward (she assists in feeding other patients), but she refuses to acknowledge her helpfulness. The basic concern is the woman's fairly consistent belief that an aide from a nursing home where she used to live is going to poison her. The staff is fearful that the patient will stop taking her heart medicine.

The treatment consists of 2 staff training sessions and 14 individual treatment sessions. The staff is trained to ignore the patient's verbalizations of her fear of being poisoned and to reassure her that someone is going to talk with her about her fears. When the patient is not expressing paranoid ideation, the staff gives her a lot of positive reinforcement. The individual sessions focus on listening respectfully to the patient's expressions of fear, assuring her that she is safe, giving her corrective feedback, and having her keep a record and make a graph of her helpful activities on the ward. The patient is frequently praised for her good behaviors.

This course of treatment was successful in extinguishing the patient's obsession about being poisoned. She was no longer afraid to take her medication, and her emotional state in general greatly improved. She was able to acknowledge her helpfulness on the ward.

Haley (1983) points out that almost all behavioral treatment efforts with the elderly have utilized the operant approach. He describes the successful use of a self-management behavioral approach with an agitated elderly patient and discusses the differences between self-management and operant treatment. The patient treated by Haley is a 71-year-old, female nursing home resident of six years who has a history of numerous paranoid schizophrenic breakdowns. The staff sees the patient as paranoid, agitated, and threatening to leave the nursing home. She is disruptive because of her frequent angry outbursts and her accusations against other patients and staff members. The patient insists that her complaints are legitimate. The staff's assessment is shared with the patient by telling her that she tends to upset herself by her way of thinking—that others have no right to behave as they do. The patient relabels her problem as "tactlessness" and admits that she has a "sharp tongue."

Treatment is conducted in eight one-hour sessions. The patient is taught more effective behavioral responses through the use of role-play exercises and discussions of the value of making tactful, assertive responses. During the role-play sessions, the therapist plays the part of the patient and models appropriate responses. In later role-play sessions the patient practices repeating the modeled responses and begins to develop her own responses. She also develops a list of specific alternative self-statements to be used in coping with encounters that usually agitate her. Throughout the treatment period the patient is given heavy positive reinforcement in the form of staff praise for all appropriate behavioral responses.

The authors urge the reader to consult the full text of Haley's article because it provides excellent instructions on how to conduct cognitive-behavioral management with the institutionalized elderly. The authors believe that Haley's technique has great promise for effective use with many different kinds of cognitive and behavioral self-control problems among the elderly.

Ross's discussion of how two years of intensive individual casework helped to support a paranoid patient provides a sharp contrast to the above treatment procedures for the management of a disruptive patient with paranoid ideation. The patient treated by Mrs. Ross was a resident of the ambulatory floor of a large geriatric center. He was 88 years old and diagnosed as a borderline psychotic with severe oral, narcissistic problems manifested by projection and paranoid ideation. He was a constant source of irritation to other residents and to the staff. Treatment involved weekly half-hour interviews. The treatment goal was to enable the patient to tolerate others and in turn to enable others to tolerate him. The caseworker points out that "the following measures were taken in an attempt to establish a trusting relationship: (1) maintaining constancy through a specific weekly appointment time; (2) having the therapist maintain a listening, nondisputive attitude; and (3) having the therapist take the position of a protective authority" (1973, p. 109).

The primary assumption of the treatment was that if the patient knew he had to discipline himself to meet regularly with one person who understood and could help him, he would be more accepting of the limitations imposed upon him by the institution. The caseworker utilized many of the sustaining procedures of the psychosocial treatment approach. The worker assumed the role of advocate by expediting feasible environmental changes that reduced annoying pressure on the patient; for example, a private room was secured for the patient, and nursing staff refrained from criticizing him for not visiting his seriously ill wife, who was housed in the same facility.

Treatment goals were realized for this patient to the extent that he could tolerate the restrictions associated with institutional life. He could get along much better with other patients and members of the staff on a daily basis. He was much less paranoid and resorted to little if any projection. He no longer constituted a management problem, and he felt much less distressed about his confinement.

Ronch and Maizler (1977) discuss their successful experience with the use of insight-oriented, dynamically-based, individual psychotherapy with long-term care patients between the ages of 69 and 96 at the Miami Jewish Home and Hospital. They stress the use of reminiscing to help an emotionally distressed patient with the life review process. They believe that many patients suffer from dominating superegos, and that psychotherapy that facilitates the expression of repressed feelings about unresolved past conflicts helps the patient replace the strict superego defenses with more realistic and adaptive ones.

These authors strongly endorse the use of insight-oriented psychotherapy with the disturbed elderly, and they discuss how some of the traditional treatment techniques can be modified to fit the characteristics of older clients. They particularly stress the effective use of a simple touch and a warm smile to enhance the therapeutic relationship with an elderly client.

Wetzel discusses the application of a person-environment incongruence depression model in the treatment of the institutionalized depressed elderly. "The model posits that depression is a joint function of a person's predisposition to independence or dependence and significant environments that are incongruent with that person's accordant needs" (1980, p. 235). Wetzel discusses this theory's implications for micro- and macrointerventions within the nursing home. The microinterventions (therapy) focus on individual patient growth and development toward more independent, autonomous functioning. Patients are taught how to be less easily influenced by the dependency promoting behaviors of nursing home personnel. A crucial goal is to improve the depressed person's level of self-esteem.

Assertiveness training and reminiscing sessions may both be effective in promoting an improved self-concept for the patient. Helping the patient master some daily living tasks can significantly enhance self-esteem. The caseworker must select tasks that are perceived by the patient as worthwhile. To assure success each task must be broken down into increments. As the patient makes progress toward task mastery, steady and consistent positive reinforcement is offered by the therapist. The treatment techniques for guiding patient task mastery are outlined in the Reid and Epstein (1972) task-centered casework approach.

The foregoing discussion of one-to-one treatment with nursing home clients is just a brief sampling of the literature. It is not intended to reflect the wide range of treatment approaches and interventive procedures that can be used in individual therapy in the institutional setting.

## Case Illustration

**Presenting Problem.**   A part-time caseworker was assigned to the case of Mrs. A., a 75-year-old widow who had been a resident for the last five years in a small, privately owned nursing home. The patient was referred for counseling because plans had to be made for her relocation. Mrs. A. could no longer afford the high cost of care in the private nursing home. The administrator was willing to keep Mrs. A. for another six months at a much lower rate.

**Mrs. A.'s History.**   Mrs. A. was widowed at age 60. She and her husband had been childless and had enjoyed a comfortable lifestyle. Mrs. A. had always been a heavy social drinker but did not become a problem drinker until after the death of her husband, at which time she used alcohol to help herself cope with the grieving process. Within one year following Mr. A.'s death, Mrs. A. developed a serious dependency on alcohol. She had secluded herself in her apartment, where her lifestyle consisted of drinking and watching television. She lived in a fantasy world of TV soap operas.

Her husband had left a sizable trust fund for Mrs. A.'s care, which was managed by an attorney whom Mr. A. had appointed as Mrs. A.'s financial guardian. For three years Mrs. A. lived quite comfortably and could afford to purchase regular housekeeping services and have all needed merchandise, food, and supplies delivered to her home. During the 10-year period between the time of her husband's death and her institutionalization Mrs. A.'s physical and mental health gradually declined. During this period she had received no medical examinations or health care. The only interpersonal contacts she had had were with her housekeeper, delivery people, and guardian. The guardian had visited her approximately every 6 months during the 10-year period of her seclusion. With each visit he had informed her of the necessity of cutting back on her living expenses due to a gradual depletion of her income.

By the time she was institutionalized Mrs. A. was receiving only enough money each month to pay for rent, utilities, food, and "booze." She had lost the services of the housekeeper and was spending most of her food allowance on liquor. Because her physical health was deteriorated, her mental health in serious question, and her living environment hazardous, the attorney moved to have Mrs. A. declared incompetent (unable to care for herself), and she was admitted to a nursing home. Having no relatives, no friends, and being in a weakened physical condition and confused state of mind, Mrs. A. was unable to protest or defend herself against the unwanted transition.

Upon admission to the nursing home, arrangements were made for Mrs. A. to have a very comfortable style of care. It was anticipated that there would be sufficient income to pay for Mrs. A.'s care at this level for an indefinite period of time. It had taken about six months of intensive nursing care and medical attention to restore Mrs. A. to a relatively good degree of health. She had been successfully detoxified, her weight problem had been brought under control, and her diabetic condition was being controlled with insulin injections.

Within a year after her admission Mrs. A. was quite comfortable in a rather large private room that appeared more like a living room than a bedroom. She settled into a daily routine and lifestyle that included many hours of television, particularly the soap operas, and she was content unless attempts were made to get her to leave her room, which she refused to do. She got very little exercise, walking only to and from the bathroom with the aid of a walker. There was no organic pathology to explain the ambulation problem: Lack of exercise and poor motivation seemed to be the causes. All attempts to get Mrs. A. to eat in the dining room, sit in the day room, and participate in recreational activities had been unsuccessful. She had never received any community visitors. When approached in her room by staff or volunteer workers, Mrs. A. was always friendly and conversational. She talked enthusiastically about the soap operas.

When given an opportunity Mrs. A. would talk about her firm belief that her guardian had stolen all of her money and forced her into the nursing home. She also contended that her valuable antique furniture and expensive art items had been stolen by her guardian.

The nursing home staff generally believed that Mrs. A. was paranoid in these accusations. She was also considered to be confused and disoriented because she regularly mixed up her life with the lives of soap opera characters. When staff members talked with her on a casual and friendly basis, Mrs. A. always told them in great detail about her interactions with the soap opera characters. When special efforts were made to bring Mrs. A. into contact with reality, she was able to acknowledge that she was a resident in a nursing home. In essence Mrs. A. was completely content with her fantasy world.

**Diagnostic Impressions.**

1. Mrs. A. is in relatively good physical health. Diabetes is controlled successfully with one daily insulin injection. It is believed that Mrs. A. can easily learn to self-administer the insulin, but to date the nurse has been giving the injections.
2. Mrs. A.'s confusion and disorientation to time, person, and place seems to be associated with two long-standing environmental conditions: a lack of meaningful and stimulating interpersonal interaction outside of her room, and a constant daily exposure to and preoccupation with 10 hours of television fantasy.
3. Mrs. A.'s paranoid ideation is limited to the situation of the financial guardianship. In all other respects Mrs. A. seems to be a trusting person and welcomes social interaction—if it takes place in her room.
4. Mrs. A. doesn't have many skills required for coping with the minimal demands of daily living because all of her routine needs have been met by others for many years.
5. Because of her long-standing social isolation and her restriction to a narrow environment, Mrs. A. is quite anxious about a pending change to a new daily-living arrangement.
6. Mrs. A. does not appear to be depressed. She seems to be quite happy with her simple life and small living space.
7. Mrs. A.'s income has dwindled to a level low enough to make her eligible for supplemental social security income and the accompanying medicaid provisions. Medicaid payments, combined with the rest of her income, would not be enough to pay for Mrs. A.'s continued confinement in the present setting.
8. Mrs. A.'s income is sufficient to finance a living arrangement in a small boarding home, a personal care home, the ambulatory ward of a public nursing home, a foster care home, or an apartment that is shared with another elderly individual.
9. Even if Mrs. A. could afford to live in the community by herself, she would not be ready in six months to assume full responsibility for self-care. The caseworker believes that six months of intensive counseling (if successful) will be needed to ready Mrs. A. for daily adaptation to a semiprotective and supervised arrangement outside of an institution. A matter of concern is that she might resort to drinking once she is back in the community, where she will not be supervised as closely as she has been for the five years she has lived in the nursing home.

**Treatment Plan.**

1. Establish a trusting relationship with Mrs. A.
2. Inform Mrs. A. about the reality of her limited financial situation and the fact that she must relocate within six months.
3. Make a counseling contract with Mrs. A. that will utilize a problem-solving model regarding relocation. This approach will give Mrs. A. an opportunity to choose and decide from a variety of feasible and affordable alternative living arrangements. This process includes the following steps.
   *a.* Identify and describe all alternatives.
   *b.* Discuss pros and cons of each alternative.

    *c.* Select one alternative.
    *d.* Identify all necessary tasks to be undertaken by the worker and the client to prepare for and implement the actual move.
4. Functional goals.
    *a.* Physical functioning. Walk and exercise more frequently to improve ambulation. Learn to self-administer insulin injections.
    *b.* Social functioning. Socialize with other residents in the day room and recreation rooms. Take all meals in the patient's dining room.
    *c.* Psychological functioning. Expand perception of reality. Differentiate between TV fantasy and objective reality of daily living. Minimize paranoid ideation and preoccupation with TV fantasy, particularly when conversing with others.

**Session One.** The worker advised Mrs. A. that she wanted to talk with her about her financial situation and the necessity of an eventual move to a different living arrangement. Mrs. A. responded with a detailed accusation and story about how the attorney and the bank had stolen her money and possessions. Periodically, she injected some mysterious content from a soap opera into this account. The worker listened empathically, neither challenging nor confirming any aspect of Mrs. A.'s story. The worker focused on conveying her recognition and understanding of Mrs. A.'s distress.

**Session Two.** The caseworker deliberately engaged in a casual conversation with Mrs. A. about the current developments in one particular soap opera about which the worker was knowledgeable. On the few ocassions when Mrs. A. spoke irrationally about her own involvement in the TV story, the worker carefully and sharply confronted Mrs. A. with the difference between the TV story and Mrs. A.'s real-life situation. The worker told Mrs. A. how much she enjoyed talking about the program, but explained that she had to spend the remainder of their meeting talking about Mrs. A.'s situation.

    Mrs. A. attempted to dominate the session with ventilations about the attorney and the bank. The worker listened to Mrs. A.'s story for about 10 minutes and then asked Mrs. A. if she would give the worker 10 minutes of her concentration to hear some very important things.

    The worker offered Mrs. A. the following counseling contract:

1. The worker would meet with Mrs. A. in her room every Monday afternoon immediately following Mrs. A.'s favorite "soap." Mrs. A. could spend half of their time relating the TV story to the worker. The remainder of the Monday visit would be devoted to talking about Mrs. A.'s problem and working out a solution.
2. They would get together for one hour every Thursday at which time they would watch a soap opera and talk about Mrs. A.'s future plans.
3. The worker told Mrs. A. that in a few weeks they could take some short walks out of Mrs. A.'s room and eventually watch some TV in one of the day rooms.
4. She carefully itemized for Mrs. A. the subjects they would be talking about over the next few months.

**Three Month Casework Summary.**  By the end of three months of counseling (24 sessions) Mrs. A. had decided that she would prefer to live in a personal care home. She had made this choice because she understood she would be able to have her own room and because there would only be a small number of people living in such an arrangement. She also understood that in the personal care home she would have to eat her meals in the dining room and watch television in the day room. Mrs. A. was quite nervous about the latter provisions but knew that she had to comply with them. She also knew that she would have to exercise regularly so she could maintain good ambulation in the personal care home. She felt comfortable about giving herself insulin injections because the nurse had already started to teach her, and she was beginning to get the "hang of it".

During this phase of treatment the worker had been successful in getting Mrs. A. to gradually spend more and more time away from her room. The first experience involved standing for a few minutes in the hall outside of Mrs. A.'s room. During each session thereafter Mrs. A., accompanied by the worker, ventured a greater distance for a longer period of time away from her room.

On each of these in vivo desensitization outings the worker helped Mrs. A. to relax (be free of anxiety) by talking with her about the soap operas (Mrs. A.'s favorite topic of conversation). Mrs. A. had made such good progress in this area that one half hour of the 23d session had been held in the public television room in the presence of other patients, and one half hour of the 24th session had been held in the caseworker's office.

Mrs. A. no longer made any irrational references to her involvement in the lives of the soap opera characters. She was willingly doing her daily exercises and proudly reporting her progress to the worker. Mrs. A. no longer brought up the subject of the financial guardian.

During the 24th session two important decisions were made: (1) one session each week for the remainder of Mrs. A.'s stay in the nursing home would be held in the caseworker's office. These sessions would be devoted to discussing many important subjects related to Mrs. A.'s preparations for moving to the personal care home, and (2) Mrs. A. would spend at least one hour each week in public areas of the nursing homes such as the day room, TV room, recreation room, halls, and garden. She would also, each week, eat more of her meals in the patients' dining room.

**Final Casework Summary.**   Mrs. A. progressed much more rapidly than had been originally anticipated. For the first two sessions, the caseworker had escorted Mrs. A. to and from the office. Thereafter, Mrs. A. came and went on her own. For three weeks the worker had escorted Mrs. A. to different areas of the nursing home, showed her around, introduced her to numerous patients, and spent some brief time socializing with her. Thereafter, Mrs. A. managed these outings on her own. During the last month of her stay in the nursing home Mrs. A. could hardly ever be found in her room.

The weekly counseling sessions were very productive. Mrs. A. was able to talk about her long-standing social isolation, her past drinking problem, and her unresolved grieving for her late husband. Mrs. A. visited her new living arrangement and was enthusiastic about leaving the nursing home; however, she knew she would miss the caseworker, the nurses, and the patients she had recently befriended. At the time of her transfer to the personal care home, Mrs. A. was functioning at a very good level. She was fully ambulatory, free of confusion, totally oriented to reality, free of paranoid ideation, comfortably inclined to social interaction, and expressing new interest in life.

This case illustration demonstrates the dramatic improvement in human functioning that can be realized in cases of severe psychosocial impairment where the problem is not caused by organic pathology. Careful examination of the treatment strategy employed in this case should reveal that a range of procedures from a number of different treatment approaches were used by the clinical social worker.

### Discussion Questions

1. Identify the number of different treatment approaches which were applied in this case. Discuss the extent to which this caseworker engaged in eclectic intervention.
2. Speculate about the kinds of future interventions which might be applied to assure the best possible level of psychosocial functioning for this client in her new community based living arrangement.
3. Discuss future treatment speculations in terms of the concept of preventive intervention. What are the client's most vulnerable areas? What community services and counseling procedures might be used to minimize vulnerability?

## SUMMARY

A small percentage of the elderly are confined to mental hospitals. About half of these patients grew old in the hospital, while the rest experienced psychiatric illness for the first time late in life because they could not cope emotionally with being old. Some long-term patients can be restored to a level of psychosocial functioning that permits them to live in the community with minimal daily assistance. Individual and group psychosocial treatment can benefit many of those who became ill for the first time in old age. A number of patients are so extensively impaired in psychosocial functioning that they will never be able to leave the institution. In these instances the clinical social worker must advocate for permanent patients' rights to a "good quality of life" within the institution.

About 5 percent of the elderly reside in nursing homes, and a large majority of this functionally impaired population will never be well enough to return to the community. Ideally, clinical social work intervention should begin with the patient and the family at the time they are making arrangements for nursing home admission. Early social work intervention with the family increases the likelihood that the family will continue their involvement with the patient. The patient who is carefully prepared for admission makes a better overall adjustment to the nursing home.

The clinical social worker plays a significant role in the development of a comprehensive treatment plan for each patient both at the time of admission and through the ongoing review of patient progress. The social worker provides psychosocial treatment on an individual and a group basis. For the patient who cannot be restored to a level of functioning that would permit a return to community living, the goal of psychosocial treatment is to promote the best possible level of patient physical/psychological/social functioning within the institutional environment.

The social worker utilizes a wide range of group approaches within the nursing home. Reality orientation and remotivation groups help to modify patient confusion. Validation-group therapy provides a warm and empathic treatment relationship to severely disturbed and depressed patients.

The clinical social worker often provides in-service training to other nursing home personnel and volunteer workers. As a staff consultant and educator, the clinical social worker promotes total staff involvement in the development and implementation of therapeutic milieu programs. The federal "Bill of Rights" for nursing home patients and the existence of numerous governmental regulatory standards for nursing home care provide the social worker with the necessary sanctions to advocate for the humane treatment and care of all nursing home patients.

# Chapter 8

# Barriers to intervention at the primary, secondary, and tertiary levels of intervention: Implications for social work practice

## INTRODUCTION

Throughout the text the authors have identified and discussed a variety of strategies useful for working directly with or on behalf of older people at the primary, secondary, and tertiary levels of intervention. While we present the material in a straightforward and hopefully insightful manner, we recognize that certain existing barriers may interfere with successful implementation of many suggested strategies for intervention at these levels.

Our use of the term *barriers* is not intended to mean conditions that are immovable and fixed. Although barriers limit and obstruct, they *can* be surmounted. However, social workers using the approaches espoused in this text need to be aware of the boundaries and obstructions associated with the various preventive strategies and must find meaningful ways of overcoming them.

Barriers should challenge us to develop the most effective or optimal modes of intervention possible. For example, in this era of cost cutting and limited federal funding of social programs, how do we find ways to maximize our effectiveness? What methodologies, practices, and policies are required to help older individuals reach certain desired goals? What kinds of resources (both financial and human) are necessary to devise, carry out, and evaluate those activities that will promote and facilitate optimal functioning? Emphasis on a preventive focus—while challenging and exciting—frequently raises more questions than it answers.

Social workers need information about the purposes of preventive interventions. They need to know what each type of intervention is designed to do. They need to know how to implement the various preventive interventive procedures, when to implement them, and with what types of older people. Social workers also need to know when not to use certain preventive strategies, as well as what hazards or risks are associated with their use.

Social workers genuinely want to help people. Since they work with a variety of individuals of all ages, they must have a broad base of knowledge in order to emerge with a wide range of methodologies and practices that are effective at the various levels of preventive intervention.

Because of the growing numbers of older people in our population, it is almost a certainty that at some time in their professional career practitioners will count a variety of the elderly among their clientele. Included among these will be elderly populations with special concerns. Such populations include the frail elderly (those aged 75 and older), elderly women, elderly minority groups, persons of diverse racial and ethnic backgrounds, and the elderly poor. Although these populations are not necessarily mutually exclusive, they do generate special concerns because their members experience discrimination and prejudice from society, because they are poor and without adequate resources to maintain themselves, or both. It is incumbent upon social workers to be aware of these elderly populations, especially since they have such limited and unequal access to power and to certain opportunities in society (see Crandall, 1980).

In Chapter 1 the authors discuss the phenomenon of change experienced as loss and how older people adapt to change and loss. It is now a widely known and accepted fact that losses are prevalent in old age and highly characteristic of the aging process: This fact cannot be ignored. Thus when the worker sets out to assess the client's situation for the purpose of predicting and guiding treatment (intervention), attention must be directed to and data gathered about the extent to which any problems are associated with loss. For instance, retirement brings loss of work, status, association with co-workers, income, and a way of structuring one's time. How, therefore, can the retiree adjust to or compensate for these losses and their consequences?

Intervention on the primary level would focus on those activities that prepare people early in their work life to avoid some of the losses associated with retirement. With the help of primary intervention people can begin to anticipate how they will deal with such role losses as the work role, family role, social roles, and so forth. To ignore or minimize the stark realities of loss and aging increases the danger of overlooking that which might be prevented, that which might be restored, and that which might obviate further deterioration. Successful intervention at all levels is governed by the social worker's knowledge and skill and also by the motivation and capacities of the older individual.

Over the years the major professions have debated the issue of prevention versus treatment and care. Always facing limited resources, the professions have tried to come to grips with what the priorities of their functions should be. The question that is often raised is whether more effort should be placed on preventing problems from occurring in the first place than on (and at the expense of) treating those who are already experiencing problematic situations. It is difficult to argue against intervention where there is evidence that a problem exists.

In this vein many believe that "little can be done in the area of prevention until the cause of a problem is known" (Wittman, 1977, p. 1052). If social gerontologists waited to understand fully the biological, psychological, and social processes and complexities of older life, many needs would go unmet and the problems of aging and the aged would be exacerbated. Thus attempts must be made to prevent problems on the basis of our imperfect knowledge by concentrating our efforts on some of the known explanatory or influential variables (see Wittman, 1977).

Although the goals of preventive social work are rooted in the origin of the profession, social work has historically intervened only after problematic and disabling conditions have developed. Social work practice methodologies reflect this orientation. This focus exists despite the fact that social workers can maximize their effectiveness with those older persons who are highly motivated and can assume responsibility for their own growth and development.

Over the past several years, however, this focus has been changing as more practitioners advocate the use of preventive strategies as a mainstay of the psychosocial well-being of individuals, families, and community. It is to everyone's advantage that efforts be focused on discouraging or forestalling the development of some predicted or unfavorable event, rather than on intervening after the fact. This would seem to be the preferred approach, and it would certainly seem to be less costly. Perhaps the best example of the preventive focus as an important aspect of community mental health services is found in the Community Mental Health Centers Act of 1963, which is discussed in the next section of this chapter.

## COMMUNITY MENTAL HEALTH CENTERS ACT

The Community Mental Health Centers Act (P.L. 88–164) was established in 1963. The act authorized federal funds for construction of public and other voluntary, nonprofit community mental health centers. As defined in the initial legislation the term *community mental health center* meant the following:

> a facility providing services for the prevention or diagnosis of mental illness, or care and treatment of mentally ill patients, or rehabilitation of such persons, which services are provided principally for persons residing in a particular community or communities in or near which facility is situated.

The original act mandated the provision of consultation and educational services. This regulation was made in an effort to provide primary prevention to the community through indirect services to its residents. Mental health consultation helped the staff members of the various community agencies and other professional personnel to support the healthy functioning of their clients. Educational services promoted mental health by teaching the public about the kinds of attitudes and behaviors that helped people cope with normal problems and promoted their emotional well-being.

The act provided for the establishment of a nationwide network of outpatient clinics, each serving the residents of a specific geographic region. These regions are frequently referred to as catchment areas. Everyone who needed outpatient care was to be offered treatment, and residents were allowed to obtain help at their local clinic regardless of their ability to pay. In addition, the centers pledged to make services available to minority groups—including the elderly—in the same proportion as their numbers in the catchment area in which the clinic was located or the area the clinic was mandated to serve (See Sherwood & Mor, 1980).

The mental health centers put in place under this act enhanced the concept of community participation in shaping the priorities, needs, and planning for residents of that community. Despite this progress in the area of mental health, critics have raised questions regarding the extent to which older people are benefiting or have benefited from primary preventive services provided by mental health centers, especially since efforts geared to the elderly have been minimal.

Another question raised by critics relates to the extent to which these centers are actually carrying out their commitment. At least 11 percent of the total population in the United States is made up of people 65 and over. Were the centers fulfilling their commitment, they would be giving at least 11 percent of their services to the elderly—their actual percentage in the population. As it now stands only 4 to 5 percent of community mental health center patients are over 65 years of age (see Butler & Lewis, 1982).

Nevertheless, it must be pointed out that the inclusion of consultation and education services in the range of mandated activities for community mental health centers receiving federal funds was very helpful to mental health professionals who were able to reach a wider range of people through these services.

## BARRIERS TO PREVENTION AT ALL LEVELS OF INTERVENTION

Professional practice with and on behalf of the elderly at the primary, secondary, and tertiary levels of intervention is sometimes fraught with numerous barriers which may limit its effectiveness and expansion if we do not guard against them.

This chapter first identifies and discusses existing barriers in the areas of knowledge development, education and training, government policy, and the extent to which these restrictions affect the quality of clinical social work practice with the elderly. The remainder of the chapter addresses specific barriers at each of the three levels of intervention.

### Knowledge on Aging

Neither this text nor any other single volume could begin to summarize the knowledge base regarding that which is known about aging; that is, aging as a process, aging as a biopsychosocial phenomenon, and aging as a social condition in our society. Nevertheless, there is a real need for more and better knowledge about the aging process and the circumstances of the aged.

There is also a need for a variety of programs whereby knowledge about aging can be more generally and effectively shared with those who are providing services to the elderly or affect their well-being in other ways. Apropos of this, a major task for the profession is to find the most effective ways to make information about the processes of aging available to more people when and where they need it.

The delegates to the 1981 White House Conference on Aging declared their support of three broad sets of initiatives in the field of education. They are as follows: (1) to expand educational opportunities for the elderly, (2) to require and enrich training programs for personnel serving the elderly, and (3) to mount an educational program for the general public to combat the harmful effects of negative stereotypes about aging and the aged (see Johnson, 1982).

The delegates also proposed educational services ranging from enhancement to survival programs. Many of the recommendations pointed to the importance of education as the means by which the elderly continue to grow intellectually, to achieve satisfaction, to learn new skills, to learn about caring for themselves and others, and to contribute to the growth and development of our youth. What was clear about the 1981 White House Conference on Aging as compared with the conferences held in 1951, 1961, and 1971 was the emphasis on preventive services as distinct from remedial or amelioration services (see Johnson, 1982).

## Knowledge about Preventive Social Work

According to Wittman preventive social work is "an organized and systematic effort to apply knowledge about social health and pathology in such a manner as to enhance and preserve the social and mental health of individuals, families, and communities" (1962, pp. 136–137). This definition suggests that activities that are useful and effective in averting or discouraging the development of specific social problems (or in controlling the growth of such problems after they have presented beginning symptoms) must be applied (see Beck, 1959). Thus knowledge about human behavior and social pathology, appropriately applied, will eventually prevent or control the onset of problems or stressful situations for older individuals, their families, and the communities in which they live. The basic aim in preventive social work is to help individuals to maintain or achieve optimal levels of functioning or to prevent continually and more serious breakdown in social functioning.

Our concept of prevention, taken from the public health model, has been used throughout this text as a framework for organizing and identifying activities at the primary, secondary, and tertiary levels of intervention that are useful in working with the elderly.

Primary prevention involves an attempt to counteract harmful circumstances before they have a chance to develop. This conceptualization of primary prevention has led to an exploration of ways in which social workers and other helping professionals can intervene to reduce stressful situations. Several creative and productive preventive efforts have been developed by those working directly with or on behalf of the elderly. Such preventive efforts include, but are not limited to, the following:

1. Developing knowledge of resources and teaching older people how to establish linkages with agencies.
2. Using group approaches with family members who are experiencing problems caring for older relatives by providing them with information about adult development, the aging process, and available community resources.
3. Conducting short-term training for physicians and other health services personnel.
4. Offering seminars through places of employment for workers in the community who have regular contact with the elderly such as personnel in supportive services, as well as to the more general community workers such as mailmen, launderers, grocers, bankers, bus drivers, and so on (see Silverstein, 1984).
5. Counseling spouses and other relatives of those suffering incapacity (that is, stroke victims, heart bypass patients) to minimize stresses and losses in the well partner.
6. Arranging driver's education and defensive driving courses to upgrade the elderly's driving skills and to prevent loss of mobility.
7. Organizing and staffing hospice and widow-to-widow programs for the well-being of the survivor.
8. Arranging for and encouraging health screening and health education in settings used by the aged.
9. Conducting preventive outreach from agencies with programs for the elderly, so older people become acquainted with a worker in whom they can confide.
10. Developing telephone reassurance programs and systems to inform emergency personnel where older people's vital medical histories are located in case of an emergency.
11. Holding evening and weekend workshops for middle-aged children who are caretakers of elderly parents to strengthen their supportive role as caretakers and to reduce the incidence of institutionalization.
12. Providing information on safety to avoid victimization of the elderly.

Many of the interventive strategies identified above are discussed more thoroughly in Chapter 4. The authors believe that all of these strategies are designed to impart strength to older people and to strengthen the supportive role of others in the community, thus reducing the need for institutionalization.

## Secondary and Tertiary Prevention

Both secondary and tertiary preventive intervention are discussed at length in earlier chapters. Suffice it to say that "at the secondary and tertiary levels of prevention, prompt, adequate, and effective services must become available to all people at the point of initial crisis or felt need" (Wittman, 1977, p. 1053). This is not always easy because there are barriers to prevention at every level. Nevertheless, social work and all the other helping professions must gear their services to the highest possible level—preventive intervention. In this connection Geismar points out that "prevention is viewed as the most humane and advanced level of service because it is concerned with helping before" (1969, p. 11) the occurrence of pathology or malfunctioning.

There is no question that prevention—at whatever level—is important if the various professions are to make inroads into the ravages that aging often brings.

## Reagan Administration Philosophy

The philosophy of the Reagan administration with regard to public funds for social services is that government is the root cause of social and economic problems rather than the cure for them. As a result, the Reagan administration has greatly reduced federal funding in human services programs and has encouraged community funding of local programs; however, the latter have not materialized. In addition, the impact of inflation, decreased funding for the maintenance of existing programs, and increased services to special needs populations—the elderly, abused children, battered women, minorities, the handicapped—have seriously threatened the survivability of local programs.

During these times of federal cutbacks in social services programs, there is a need for innovative programs that will keep pace with inflation. But in times of dwindling resources how can social work be expected to do more with less?

Turem and Born (1983) identified four novel strategies for addressing cutbacks in services. Central to our concerns is the strategy that calls for the development of self-help and nonservice approaches by building client support groups. Preventive strategies such as these have the capacity to reach greater numbers of older people. Access to knowledge that affects the quality of life for older persons can, if utilized, result in improvements in people's levels of living and their comforts.

If the quality of life is to be improved for older people at the societal level, there must be a greater commitment of funds and resources from both the public and private sectors. In addition, there must be the development and implementation of the kind of "social policy that permits freedom from fear among those who, on becoming old, are without personal resources for maintenance of their economic and physical health" (Feldman & Feldman, 1974, p. 159).

## BARRIERS TO PREVENTION AT THE PRIMARY LEVEL

### Emphasis on Cure Rather than on Prevention

Generally speaking, preventive intervention has not been emphasized as a major strategy in the lives of the elderly. This is particularly true in the area of health care. Health care in the United States is aimed at cure, not prevention. This is exemplified by our health insurance plans. Health insurance generally covers crises requiring diagnosis and treatment, but not preventive measures such as physical examinations. Nursing homes, hospitals, and physicians are reimbursed for sick care, not for prevention or rehabilitation.

The preventive approach would stress ways in which health can best be maintained in older people. For example, preventive health care would emphasize health education, and health education would enable individuals to become knowledgeable about "how their body functions and to teach them how to look for pathological signs" (Crandall, 1980, p. 167).

### Staffing Patterns of Multipurpose Senior Centers

Multipurpose Senior Centers are cited in this text for two basic reasons: (1) the variety of social, educational, and recreational programs they provide to the community-based elderly, and (2) their preventive focus. Most participants in center activities can be described, relatively speaking, as well-elderly. Therefore, the programs and services available at these centers have broad implications for the well-elderly, their families, and the communities in which they live. Yet the staffing patterns at the multipurpose senior centers leave something to be desired. Few centers have well-trained social workers who are knowledgeable about social group work processes or are expert in providing consultation and educational services to older individuals, their families, and their communities. Since the group approach is an essential method of intervention in multipurpose senior centers, it is imperative that the expertise of social workers be relied upon, as this has long been an activity in which social workers have excelled.

One of the authors (Beaver) had an opportunity to conduct a group (on a voluntary basis) of older men and women who had lost a spouse within a period of two years. The group was conducted at Vintage, a multipurpose senior center in Pittsburgh, Pennsylvania, and consisted of a total of 14 men and women (4 men and 10 women) ranging in age from 60 to 76. All of the participants were completely ambulatory and were regular visitors to the center. Since they had been involved in many other group activities at the center, participating in another group was not novel to them. Even though the group met for a brief period of time, it was able to coalesce, and the majority of the group members were able to share their experiences of widowhood as well as their feelings about losing a mate. The group members expressed positive feelings about the group experience and the insights they gained from hearing other members talk about how they were coping with their loss.

## Attitudes of Mental Health Professionals

Butler & Lewis (1982) provide an interesting discussion of the attitudes of mental health professionals toward older people. Mental health professionals (psychiatrists, psychologists, and so on) frequently perceive older people as not being open to improvement via the available therapeutic techniques. Many therapists believe they have nothing useful to offer older people. This belief is based on the assumption that older people cannot change their behavior, or that their problems are all the result of untreatable organic brain diseases.

Unfortunately, many older people have bought into this negative view: Often they look at themselves and do not like what they see. This is why information about healthy old age is essential, not only for mental health professionals, but for older people themselves. Lack of knowledge about the normal processes of aging can be buttressed by educational thrusts that are designed to impart knowledge and skills to people at varying age levels.

Life-cycle education is sorely needed. Butler points out that this type of education is one in which "different psychological, personal, familial, occupational, and other tasks related to specific stages of life are taught" (1975, p. 389) Butler (1975) goes on to stress the importance of understanding and preparing for the transitions that take place throughout the life cycle such as marriage, parenthood, retirement, and widowhood. With respect to life-cycle education, the authors have already discussed the importance of preretirement programs (that is, programs aimed at preparation for retirement). It may well be that those who are less knowledgeable about aging are more likely to have negative attitudes toward it and to believe old age will be problematic for them (see Palmore, 1980).

## Primary Prevention at the Community Level

One of the obvious trends, particularly in the health sciences, is toward making people aware that they are responsible for their own well-being and toward giving them the knowledge they need to achieve it. The key issue here is how information such as this should be made available on the community level.

Communities are not often geared toward prevention. Consequently, it is sometimes difficult to introduce a preventive service at the community level. Older people may feel that they are "getting along all right" and may perceive a new service as a threat to their independence. Therefore, such services must be accompanied by community education so they can be perceived as worthwhile rather than threatening. Saul points out the following:

> The presence of a service on the community scene extends an older person's horizons, and is a message to him that when he decides he needs or wants it, it will be available. The availability of preventive services, therefore, augments a person's capacity to control his life and helps support his independence. (1974, p. 143)

Social workers and other helping professionals must assume more responsible and creative roles in their efforts to effect change in the lives of the well-elderly at the community level. This means community level educational efforts must place greater emphasis on the strengths of older people, their resilience, and their ability to cope with the vicissitudes of life. This kind of orientation infuses people with hope and empowers them to maximize their use of the available services.

We need to cite more examples in the literature of people who have coped with trying and embittering situations and still have positive feelings about their lives. The strength of black families provides us with one such example. Black people have experienced the flagrant wrongs of institutional racism, of being devalued by a status-oriented society, and of growing up in situations where opportunities for achieving the same goals as those of the dominant group are at best slim. And yet, when we examine the attitudes of older black people toward life or their sense of well-being, we find that their outlook is anything but negative. Doubtless the ego strength of this group derives in large part from the uniquely supportive black family structure. A great deal can be learned from older black people about "how to do more with less" and of how to develop successful coping and survival strategies throughout life.

Another example is that of various ethnic groups who came to this country with visions and hopes of improving their circumstances and were met instead with resentment and hostility from the small group of wealthy people who held an inordinate proportion of the society's wealth and power. Nevertheless, these groups of people held to their vision by assuring their children that they could and would overcome societal obstacles and achieve their goals.

Community educational programs must begin to portray the aging process in a light that shows that it can be accompanied by enhanced life satisfactions, ongoing personal growth, and "graduation to new forms of independence and self-reliance after successful termination of an established pace of economic, psychological, and social achievement" (Feldman & Feldman, 1974, p. 159).

In essence, community educational programs can be a great asset in providing successful agers with information about themselves, explaining the etiology of the physical changes inherent in the process of aging, and by pointing out the adaptations they might make in their mode of living. Such information should help older people to better organize their daily routine, to watch out for pitfalls in their daily lives, to avoid unnecessary mishaps and accidents, and to be more aware of and knowledgeable about what to do when infirmity begins to take hold.

## EDUCATIONAL FORMATS AND PREVENTION

A number of educational formats that lend themselves to preventive intervention were not discussed in the text because of time and space constraints. Among these are such observational methods as role playing, modeling, and videotaped demonstrations. Shaw and Thoresen (1974) found that videotaped modeling of people undergoing dental procedures that used relaxation techniques enabled more dental phobics to successfully complete dental treatment than did desensitization. When youngsters facing surgery were shown films of their peers coping, their fear arousal was reduced both before and after surgical procedures. This technique also prevented the rise in home adjustment problems that was found for unprepared controls. Although the Shaw and Thoresen (1974) research was focused on children, the approach used in this study lends itself to preventive practices with the elderly.

The use of mass media formats needs to be explored more extensively. The potential of the mass media remains scarcely tapped. Mass media procedures have been used at the University of Southern California on a communitywide basis to inform not only the elderly, but the public in general on how personal habits such as poor diet, smoking, overeating, and lack of exercise affect their health (see Maccoby & Farquhar, 1975). However, "personal guidance in conjunction with mass media achieves more extensive and rapid changes than the mass media alone" (Rosenthal & Bandura, 1978, p. 648).

The authors believe that the missing piece in primary prevention has been that of individualizing or giving personal guidance, and we view this as a viable role for casework. Most of the preventive thrust to date has been on providing general information. However, each person needs to know what works best for him or her. For instance, the same diet, exercise, or preventive social service program cannot be prescribed for every older person. Each of these activities needs to be personalized and shaped to meet the needs of the individual.

## BARRIERS TO CLINICAL SOCIAL WORK INTERVENTION AT THE SECONDARY LEVEL

Many of the psychosocial problems experienced by the elderly can be resolved by psychosocial treatment provided by clinical social workers. Numerous barriers to the provision of psychosocial treatment are encountered at various societal levels. These barriers limit the quantity and quality of clinical practice with the elderly. They are erected by public policy, social attitudes, agency procedures, practitioners, and clients.

## Societal Barriers

Federal policies on aging, health, and social welfare do not allow for sufficient funds to provide adequate psychosocial treatment services for those elderly who are troubled by acute problems of psychosocial functioning. There are no publically funded agencies that specialize in geriatric psychosocial treatment at the secondary level. Although some funds from medicare/medicaid and Title XX of the Social Security Act are used to provide social services for the elderly, they are not adequate for psychosocial treatment conducted by social workers. While the Older Americans Act provides considerable funding for a variety of community-based, social service programs, little of this funding is allocated for psychosocial treatment provided by professionally trained social workers.

Senior centers, congregate meal programs, and senior lounges use most of these funds to provide recreational programs, information and referral services, transportation services, and educational services. Some of these programs and agencies may provide a nominal amount of individual supportive counseling, but budgetary limitations prohibit the provision of a professional level of psychosocial treatment. This is unfortunate because these neighborhood-based agencies are readily accessible to a large number of older people who are in need of psychosocial treatment. The elderly are known to be reluctant to seek out psychosocial therapy, but they might be more willing to request help if it were readily available at their neighborhood senior centers.

The elderly are unlikely to request treatment from mental health centers because of the long-standing social stigma associated with mental and psychiatric facilities. The elderly constitute only 2 percent of the patients served by community mental health centers (see Lowy, 1979). Mental health centers in general do not make a special effort to reach out to those elderly in need of psychosocial therapy. Unless special grant monies are available for geriatric mental health programs, most outpatient psychiatric facilities do not employ geriatric specialists.

Those elderly clients who do find their way to mental health centers are usually treated by therapists who have only a limited knowledge and understanding of the psychosocial nature of aging, and these therapists frequently mistake acute psychological symptoms as signs of chronic illness. Many counselors are quick to conclude that cognitive disturbance in the elderly means chronic, irreversible impairment. They label their patients as senile and do not consider the application of intensive change-oriented therapeutic procedures. At best they provide sustaining supportive therapy.

Consider, for example, the case of Mrs. Miller (Chapter 5). If the caseworker had concluded that the client's severe impairment was due to "senility," no exerted attempt would have been made to change her behavior. Instead, Mrs. Miller would have been viewed as a chronically impaired person who required daily assistance from others in order to avoid nursing home placement. In the case of Mr. B. (presented at the end of Chapter 5), the strong suicidal intention and state of depression might have been sufficient reasons to institutionalize the client.

The tendency on the part of some caseworkers to presume chronic impairment in those elderly with psychological symptoms was vividly experienced in 1973 by coauthor Miller. Dr. Miller served as a field instructor for a unit of six MSW students who were in field placement at an urban community mental health center. The students received 80 case referrals from the social service department of the city public housing authority. All 80 clients were over the age of 65, had been long-term public housing residents, and all were described by the housing authority caseworkers as chronically mentally impaired. They were labeled senile or psychotic and considered unfit to remain in their independent living situations. It was presumed by the referring agency that the mental-health student caseworker would make nursing home or mental hospital placements for these "incurable" elderly clients. Clinical social work intervention with each client was initiated using the psychosocial systems approach. Eight months later all but 1 of the 80 clients were still living in their apartments.

Psychosocial treatment in this situation employed a variety of eclectic procedures. All clients realized a considerable improvement in their daily psychosocial functioning. Only a few of these clients needed ongoing assistance from concrete, home-delivered social services such as meals, homemaking, chores, and friendly visiting. With a few exceptions these clients were, by this text's definition, considered to be secondary- rather than tertiary-level cases. The one client who was placed in a nursing home was suffering from severe medical problems but was free of mental impairment.

When mental hospitals are faced with a shortage of professionally trained caseworkers, policy dictates that intensive therapeutic attention be given to younger patients, who are assumed to have much more recovery potential than the elderly. More often than not the elderly patients receive only humane, custodial treatment. Many acute cases of functional mental illness such as severe aging neurosis and episodic psychological depression are inaccurately diagnosed by hospital personnel as cases of chronic brain syndrome.

A large number of medical hospital patients are elderly. An acute episode of illness or injury usually has some serious effect on an individual's emotional and social functioning, and psychosocial treatment is indicated (see Chapter 5). Psychosocial treatment is known to enhance the patient's recovery from illness and/or help to prevent the onset of chronic functional impairment. Most hospitals have a well-established social service department staffed by professional medical caseworkers.

Although psychosocial treatment is readily available, hospital policy often blocks or frustrates its practice. In many hospitals policy does not permit the involvement of casework service unless it is prescribed by the patient's physician. This is often true even when a patient or relative asks to see a caseworker. Some physicians don't request psychosocial treatment because they simply don't value what social work has to offer, some fail to recognize the psychosocial aspects of the patient's illness, and others are not aware of the casework services that are available. Because medical casework is not a free service in most hospitals, some doctors do not prescribe it if it is not covered in the patient's health insurance plan. Since medicaid provides social service reimbursement, poor patients usually receive casework attention. More often than not doctors accept social service involvement for what are referred to as their "charity cases."

Hospital policy may also stand in the way of offering psychosocial crisis intervention. As pointed out in Chapter 3, effective crisis intervention depends upon the timing and intensity of contact. In some hospitals caseworkers are not available to intervene at the onset of many crises because they only work from 9 to 5, and the hospital does not provide casework service on an "on call" basis, 24 hours a day, seven days a week. Hospital policy may also hamper the provision of effective crisis intervention because caseworkers are not permitted to devote the extensive amount of time to one case that the crisis model demands.

When psychosocial casework service is extended to all elderly medical patients upon admission, many cases of chronic impairment can be prevented. The patient's social support system is very important to the patient's recovery and convalescence. Thus hospital policy should facilitate family involvement during the course of the patient's hospital treatment. To assure continuity of psychosocial care, the hospital caseworker should be permitted to provide postdischarge treatment during the period of time required to arrange for the smooth transfer of casework follow-up responsibilities to a community-based agency. When a hospital offers home health care services to a patient upon discharge, policy should allow for the hospital-based caseworker to continue on the case as a member of the home care team. As pointed out in Chapter 6, the most effective provision of home health care services is accomplished with the social worker as a service case manager.

When the hospital does not provide its own postdischarge, outpatient, follow-up, social work service, policy should place a high priority on executing skillful referrals to community agencies. The hospital caseworker needs to be given sufficient time to prepare the patient and the community-based caseworker for the continuation of care after discharge.

The bulk of clinical social work practice at the secondary level of intervention is provided by general, community-based social service agencies. These private, public, and sectarian agencies are often well staffed with professionally trained clinical social workers who offer individual, family, and group psychosocial treatment. Although these agencies have no age restriction for service eligibility, they tend to serve very few elderly clients unless they have special aging service contracts to provide geriatric counseling.

Rarely do these agencies make special efforts to reach out to those elderly in need of psychosocial treatment. For instance, they do not establish formal liaison relationships with medical hospitals, mental health centers, and community-based aging programs for the purpose of promoting referrals. And these agencies in turn tend not to initiate referrals on a routine basis to the general social service agencies. The elderly themselves tend not to seek out the agency on their own.

It is generally observed that the majority of adults in our society are not quick to seek out psychosocial treatment (psychotherapy/counseling) when experiencing psychosocial problems. This reluctance to seek professional help is even more prevalent among the elderly than it is among younger adults. Although part of this resistance is explained by the traditionally held values of self-reliance, independence, and privacy, the authors believe that the formal systems of care are partially at fault. Sufficient efforts are not made to inform the general aging population of the range of available counseling services, and access to these services is not facilitated.

Professional social work leaders and those public officials who promote the expansion of social care for the elderly must make a more exerted effort to upgrade job status and salary scales for clinical social workers in the field of aging at the secondary level of intervention. Each year more graduates with baccalaureate and master's degrees in social work are entering the field of aging. Many of these new practitioners received geriatric education along with their general training in clinical social work, and many are well prepared and highly motivated to work with the elderly at the secondary level of intervention.

### Administrative Barriers to Practice

Most agencies that profess to provide psychosocial treatment for elderly clients usually do not employ enough trained clinical practitioners to do so. In most settings caseloads are too large to allow for the provision of intensive psychosocial treatment. Although administrators are often aware of the discrepancy between the defined intended treatment and the actual treatment provided, they do not make deliberate efforts to resolve the discrepancy. When additional staff cannot be hired, administrators need to find ways to make the most efficient use of existing casework personnel without minimizing the quality of care. It is surprising that more agencies that try to provide psychosocial treatment but are faced with staff shortages do not implement a structured, short-term (brief) treatment program. The effectiveness of brief treatment is well known, as is its cost efficiency (see Reid and Shyne, 1969). Brief treatment consumes less staff time than the traditional, open-ended, extended approach to psychosocial treatment, and most treatment approaches and procedures discussed in Chapter 3 can be incorporated into brief treatment contracts.

Some agencies do not permit home interviewing, yet it is well known that in many cases contacts in the client's home are essential to effective treatment. Some agencies are bound to tradition and continue to offer only individual counseling services, despite the overwhelming evidence that many problems are most effectively treated through family therapy and/or small group treatment.

Some agencies do not sanction or endorse the use of certain treatment approaches and procedures in spite of the fact that their clinical caseworkers have been trained in an eclectic perspective. Krill (1968) speaks to the tendency in some settings to embrace one particular therapeutic approach in a dogmatic fashion. Although an eclectic orientation to clinical social work practice is a definite contemporary trend, there are still pockets of resistance to eclecticism (see Gelfand, 1972).

The authors have observed a considerable hesitancy on the part of some geriatric caseworkers to consider the application of behavioral and cognitive procedures with elderly clients, because their supervisors and administrators do not strongly endorse the use of these approaches.

Most clinical social work authorities today view the roles of advocacy and brokerage as central and essential components of the clinical social work function. Experts such as Zastrow (1981), Germain and Gitterman (1980), and Fischer (1978) devote considerable attention to the importance of these practice roles. In numerous places throughout this text the use of advocacy and brokerage are illustrated in conjunction with clinical psychosocial treatment (see especially Chapter 5).

Many agencies do not provide caseworkers with the mechanisms, structures, time, and sanctions required to engage in case advocacy and to serve as brokers for their clients. Administrators and supervisors may pay lip service to the belief that effective psychosocial treatment often requires direct casework intervention with numerous individuals and groups within the larger social environment, but they fail to facilitate this kind of intervention.

Agency administrators frequently do not encourage or provide mechanisms that enable their clinical workers to systematically supply them with case information that identifies and documents serious gaps in agency resources and discrepancies in agency practices. Many agencies do not provide adequate funds to purchase continuing education for their clinical workers. With the rapid expansion of practice knowledge, continuing education is essential to the updating of practice skills. An agency with a small number of master's level, trained, clinical staff should use these workers regularly to provide in-service training to those practitioners with less formal training.

## Implications for Clinical Practitioners

What can the typical clinical social work practitioner do in his or her place of employment to effect policy modification that may improve the quality of psychosocial treatment to the agency's elderly clientele?

The caseworker must not be afraid to advocate for clients within his or her agency. While taking care to avoid an adversary stance, the caseworker needs to provide the administration with written documentation of all gaps and shortcomings in services to clients. Workers should convey the belief and attitude that the administrative personnel share their concerns. Case-workers can act under the assumption that all members of the agency are united on issues that concern the well-being of their clients. In effect, the caseworker is saying to the administrator, "I am supporting you in your efforts with our funding sources to secure the resources we need to improve service."

When a worker has an idea that a change in practice or procedure will be more effective or efficient, he or she should propose a definite plan for procedural change to the administration. Groups of workers who share the same concerns about agency problems can organize problem-solving commit-tees and volunteer their services in helping administration to solve policy problems.

As a professional person, the clinical caseworker must take responsibility for keeping abreast of the advances in the field. Pertinent periodicals should be read on a regular basis, and new practice procedures that are based on empirical research should be given priority. Treatment procedures that have been demonstrated to be effective in cases similar to those encountered by the worker should be incorporated into the caseworker's practice.

Clinical workers must challenge the administration's attempt to discourage or disallow the use of particular treatment procedures when the procedures in question are within the worker's ability, are accepted by the profession, have been demonstrated to be effective, are within the bounds of ethical practice, and are indicated for use by the case assessment. The challenge is made by simply going ahead and implementing the indicated treatment activities. The message this sends to the administration is that "I am doing what I have been professionally trained to do."

Clinical social workers must be their own watchdogs to avoid falling into the trap of therapeutic dogmatism—using the same treatment strategy for all cases. They must also avoid the extreme opposite tendency—trying something new with each new case.

Many of the frustrations experienced by clinical social workers in the field of aging are similar to the ones experienced by caseworkers in many other fields of practice. Through organized, active participation in profes-sional membership associations such as the National Association of Social Workers, clinical social workers can work together to break down the barri-ers that hinder the provision of psychosocial treatment to the elderly.

## BARRIERS TO CLINICAL SOCIAL WORK INTERVENTION AT THE TERTIARY LEVEL

This text equates the field of long-term care with the tertiary level of intervention with the elderly. The elderly at this level of care are functionally impaired to the extent that they need daily assistance from others in the community or confinement to an institution. The psychosocial aspects of physical and cognitive impairment in the elderly are considerable in magnitude. The roles and functions of clinical social work with the impaired elderly were identified and discussed in Chapters 6 and 7. The following discussion identifies some of the barriers that affect the quantity and quality of clinical social work intervention with the impaired elderly who live in the community and with those who are confined to institutions. The practice barriers at this level are similar to those identified in the preceding discussion of intervention at the secondary level.

### Societal Barriers

The importance of clinical social work to the long-term care of the community-based and institutionalized elderly is widely acknowledged; however, inadequate funding drastically restricts its practice. Although the medicare, medicaid, and Title XX sections of the Social Security Act finance a variety of social services for the impaired elderly, there is insufficient funding to meet the need for service case management and psychosocial treatment, the two most valuable components of clinical social work practice in long-term care. The Older Americans Act, one of the major federal funding sources for social services for the community-based elderly, allocates only a small portion of its resources to long-term care programs.

Because of funding constraints, those agencies responsible for the bulk of service provision to the home-bound functionally impaired are unable to employ a sufficient number of clinical social workers to adequately execute the important function of service case management. Caseworkers are burdened with large caseloads and cannot devote sufficient time to needs assessment, service monitoring, and psychosocial counseling. Adequate funding is not available to meet the existing need for psychosocial counseling in home health care programs. Clinical social work practice is also scarce in most day-care facilities.

Adequate levels of clinical social work intervention are not made available to the institutionalized elderly. Mental hospitals usually cannot afford or choose not to provide professional clinical social work intervention for their long-term, chronically impaired, elderly patients except in those cases where relocation to another long-term care facility is indicated. Little clinical treatment is devoted to promoting the best possible "quality of life" for those who are considered to be lifetime residents.

Most of the institutionalized elderly are in nursing homes. Most private, sectarian, and small public nursing homes suffer a great shortage of clinical social workers. These facilities provide only the minimal amount of professional social work service required to qualify them for medicare and medicaid reimbursements.

Garner and Mercer (1980) cite the tremendous lack of professionally trained social workers in nursing care facilities throughout the country. Their study of nursing homes in the state of Arkansas reveals that few homes employ social workers beyond the reimbursement requirement, and that the efforts of these workers have little if any impact on the psychosocial care of patients. A study of the beliefs and attitudes of nursing home administrators in the state of Florida reveals that almost all administrators view the psychosocial needs of patients to be secondary to their physical care needs (see Pearman and Searles, 1976). The authors believe that the conditions in Arkansas and Florida are representative of the nursing home industry throughout the nation.

It is generally observed by many social work consultants that the meager amount of psychosocial intervention provided by understaffed nursing homes consists of recreational programming and supportive group discussions. These programs are usually conducted by employees who are referred to as "recreational specialists" or "activity specialists." Although dedicated and hard working, these employees usually have had little if any formal geriatric or clinical social work training.

Large public nursing homes, particularly those in metropolitan areas and those affiliated with institutions of higher education and research, have clinical social work staffing levels well beyond the minimal requirements. Nevertheless, they do not have a sufficient number of professional social work geriatric specialists to provide the desired level of psychosocial treatment. Most professional and public leaders who are familiar with the current conditions of long-term care in nursing homes recognize the overwhelming need to increase the level of clinical social work practice in nursing homes and the need to elevate the professional standards of practice.

Geriatric social work is projected by various observers to be the largest growth area in social work over the next few decades. It is also projected that the need for geriatric social work in long-term care will drastically increase in the years ahead. When one takes into consideration two well-known and solid facts about the current status of long-term care for the elderly, it remains to be seen just how much professional geriatric social work practice will take place in long-term care over the next few decades: (1) current private and public funding, although massive, practically ignores the psychosocial needs of the impaired elderly, and (2) there are no current proposals on the policy drawing boards that suggest a solution to this problem in the near future.

The reader is referred to two fairly recent publications that address the central issues of long-term care today and for the future: (1) Eustis et al. (1984), and (2) Crystal, (1982). The first book is rich in facts about long-term care needs, the state of current practice, and makes future projections.

The second book documents the observation that the gap between the best-off and the worst-off, the poor, the sick, and the functionally impaired is widening, and that benefits in this country favor the well-elderly at the expense of those in need of long-term care.

### Administrative Barriers

In some community-based, long-term care agencies and nursing homes, the barriers to clinical practice are not due solely to inadequate staffing levels. Some administrative policies and procedures thwart the caseworker's use of treatment interventions that he or she believes are necessary for effective patient care, are within his or her ability, and for which sufficient time is available. For instance, some agencies that rely heavily on the service case management function prohibit (through policy) case managers from providing direct counseling to clients and their informal caretakers. Or in some nursing homes a policy may exist that does not allow clinical social workers to form certain kinds of patient treatment groups, or to encourage the family's active participation in a patient's treatment and care programs. Some nursing home administrators are known to place a low priority on casework interventions that attempt to improve a patient's level of independent functioning unless there is good reason to predict that the patient can be relocated to a community living arrangement.

Observers believe that many nursing home administrators who are faced with limited funds for psychosocial treatment could nevertheless offer more than they do. For instance, greater use could be made of well-trained volunteers and paraprofessionals who could be supervised by clinical social workers. Administrators might also fill some service gaps through staff exchange arrangements with other long-term care agencies. For example, a trained group worker in one nursing home might work one day a week in another nursing home that does not have a skilled group worker on its staff, and in exchange for this service, the other nursing home might receive an equal amount of time from a physical therapist.

Administrators could also attempt to provide more psychosocial services to their clients by urging general social service agencies that provide low-cost counseling to pick up some of their cases. For example, there is no reason why counselors from family agencies and mental health centers could not provide individual psychosocial therapy to some nursing home patients. Any agency that conducts home interviewing could conduct "nursing home" interviewing without violating its policies.

In pursuit of more funding for psychosocial services, nursing home directors need to engage in patient advocacy. They should work together with their social work employees to organize advocacy strategies. They must provide the time and means necessary for agency employees to collect accurate case data that clearly document the need for more psychosocial care resources.

Those who administer understaffed community based agencies and nursing homes must be alert to the potential for employee "burnout." Directors and supervisors must seek ways to prevent burnout in work-burdened caseworkers. For example, a lot of the routine paperwork usually required of social workers might very well be done by well-trained clerical personnel. In-service training programs and off-site continuing education opportunities should be provided as often as possible so social work personnel can keep pace with the updating of practice skills. Even though caseworkers may not be in a position to use the updated skills and newly learned procedures in their current positions, their morale can be greatly boosted by these opportunities for professional development. Administrators should use their most skilled clinical social workers as trainers and staff developers for employees who have less professional education.

Administrators and directors of long-term care agencies and nursing homes have many common problems regarding inadequate levels of qualified social work personnel. These administrators should band together and form action coalitions to solicit assistance from all segments of the private and public systems of care for the elderly. Major targets of this unified advocacy for resources should be the senior centers, which usually have multiple funding sources but tend not to serve to any appreciable extent the psychosocial needs of the functionally impaired elderly. Pressure should also be put on the Area Agency on Aging (AAA) to secure more funding for social work intervention in long-term care. As the officially designated local agency for service coordination, resource allocations, resource development, and long-range service planning for the elderly in general, the AAA must find a way to generate more funding for qualified clinical social work practice in the field of long-term care.

## Implications for Clinical Practitioners

What can clinical social workers do to modify policy and agency procedures that hinder psychosocial intervention with the functionally impaired elderly? When the client's psychosocial needs are not being adequately met, caseworkers must consistently inform their superiors about the existing problems, provide them with accurate data that document the problems, provide their analyses of the problems, and offer their ideas and assistance in seeking solutions. When the barriers to practice are rooted in the agency's policies and procedures, caseworkers must avoid an adversary position with administration, but they must take a strong stand for reform. Germain and Gitterman provide an excellent set of guidelines to assist employees in their attempts to modify agency policy. They call this set of guidelines "The Process of Influencing Employing Organizations" (1980, pp. 303–339). This process stresses ways of avoiding unproductive conflict and threats to employment security while simultaneously gaining the administration's cooperation and partnership in bringing about policy modification.

In nursing homes social workers need not be afraid to advocate for many of the patients' rights since numerous rights to care are now guaranteed by federal and state regulations (see Chapter 7).

Often the clinical social worker in long-term care settings is faced with value conflicts and ethical dilemmas. These difficulties can seriously hamper the caseworker's job performance and, if not resolved, they can produce morale problems. Moody (1983) offers an extensive discussion of the complex nature of ethical dilemmas in long-term care practice with individuals, families, and groups regarding issues rooted in social welfare policy and those dilemmas that arise among professional colleagues. He stresses the importance of analyzing each dilemma in terms of five questions. (1) Is the issue an ethical dilemma or a practical problem? (2) What is the source of the problem? (3) How is the issue framed by the profession's value perspective? (4) What is the appropriate level for social action? and (5) How can ethical theories help clarify the dilemma and its range of possible solutions?

Dilemmas in long-term care often arise around a patient's right to self-determination. For example, a severely mentally impaired, sickly, elderly client who is in immediate need of protection refuses to accept institutionalization or any other form of protective care. Some workers create a moral dilemma for themselves when they choose to falsify case information because they believe that doing so is the only way a client can be declared eligible for a desperately needed service.

Clinical social workers who perceive themselves as overburdened and frustrated in their efforts to serve clients must guard against their own burnout potential. They must avoid falling into a practice rut, which usually results in noncreative and mechanical work performance. Burnout can often produce workers who become theoretically dogmatic and ignore the individualization of clients.

Those workers who are enthusiastic about their jobs—in spite of the many frustrations they encounter—must be cautious in how they use the practice knowledge available to them. They should keep in mind that no treatment technique or procedure has inherent value in and of itself. The right and best interventions are those that fit the case dimensions, and those which, upon application, show some evidence of early results. Workers should be aware of the fact that many experts make strong assertions about the universal application of their approaches when in fact empirical data are not available to support their claims. For instance, Feil's charges against the efficacy of reality orientation procedures have not been firmly substantiated nor has her claim about the superiority of fantasy therapy (see Chapter 7). The worker must keep an open mind by acknowledging the possibility that in one case reality orientation may be extremely helpful, while in another fantasy therapy may produce excellent results.

Although we cannot be absolutely sure from one case to the next what technique will work best, with whom, or under what circumstances, we do know that much research has been done in recent years that demonstrates the effectiveness of certain procedures. Clinical social workers in the field of long-term care are encouraged to look toward all sources of psychosocial practice knowledge for interventive procedures that might be useful in their work with the elderly.

The barriers to practice addressed in this chapter are the kinds that have traditionally frustrated professional practitioners in the various fields of human service. Medicine, psychiatry, social work, nursing, and other human problem-solving professions with a broad mission have always had to work within constraints that emanate from a variety of social sources. It has been customary for professional educators in all human service professions to identify for their students those constraints and barriers pervasive in the practice arenas. Those being trained for professional practice are taught how to recognize, analyze, and deal with the common and inevitable barriers they will face throughout their careers.

Because barriers of one kind or another will always exist, they present an ever-present challenge to professional practitioners to strengthen their ideologies, their knowledge base and practice skills, and to continuously reexamine and evaluate the effectiveness and efficiency of their practice.

The barriers identified in this chapter are addressed to social work practice with and on behalf of the elderly, but barriers of the same order and magnitude exist in fields of practice with all age groups and problem categories.

It is wishful and irrational thinking to believe that the day will come when few if any barriers will exist, and it is equally irrational to accept their existence with a defeatest attitude and an immobile stance. With the probable exception of insufficient resources to meet the needs of clients and fund professional practice, many of the barriers facing practitioners 5 years from now, 10 years from now, and later will be somewhat different from those faced today. The future will be different, but there will be barriers that constrain and frustrate practice. The effective practitioners of the future will continue to tackle the ever-present challenges—as do their competent colleagues of the present.

## SUMMARY

Prevention has always been a concern of social work, but historically most of social work's efforts have focused on treatment and rehabilitation. Nevertheless, over the past few years all of social work practice has been addressing itself in one form or another to the issue of prevention.

The public health model, which differentiates conceptually among primary, secondary, and tertiary prevention, has helped social work to incorporate and refine prevention as a viable interventive strategy. Primary prevention is viewed as the most humane and advanced level of interventive clinical social work.

The authors strongly believe that if prevention is to play a major role in social work, it must be built into community or system-oriented programs as a way of avoiding problems. In this way all levels of prevention or preventive intervention can be made available.

The roles discussed in this text, particularly those that emphasize primary intervention, are discussed less frequently in the social work literature than those aimed at secondary or tertiary prevention. Historically, the clinical role of social casework has been the principle focus of attention—often to the exclusion of other roles.

A number of societal, professional, and individual barriers to primary prevention were identified in the first part of the chapter. The early 1980s witnessed less federal government involvement in social programs, and less government involvement has meant a shift of responsibility toward the local and corporate arenas. Social workers must understand and assess what the federal cutbacks mean and respond to them in an informed and planful way.

Older people who have aged successfully and are able to manage their lives and affairs effectively should no doubt find educational and consultative activities especially viable. Educational services that are designed to reach more people can, if well planned, be carried out more efficiently, at lower costs, and more effectively than services designed for only a limited number of people.

Barriers to clinical social work practice at the secondary and tertiary levels of intervention are erected by society, agencies, practitioners, and clients. Sufficient funding is not available to provide an adequate level of psychosocial treatment for those elderly who have acute problems and for those who are functionally impaired.

Mental hospitals often provide only custodial care to their acutely ill elderly patients. Mental health centers underserve the acutely ill who reside in the community. Medical casework service is readily available in most acute care hospitals, but frequently its full benefits are not extended to elderly patients. The effective use of crisis intervention is often restricted by hospital policy. Psychosocial treatment is not made available to many patients who are in need of postdischarge, home-health care.

General social service agencies which provide a range of professional counseling services do not reach out to the elderly who have acute problems in psychosocial functioning. Senior centers are utilized by many of the elderly, but these centers offer little if any clinical social work treatment.

Those agencies that provide psychosocial treatment to the elderly are usually understaffed; consequently, clinical social workers are burdened with large caseloads. Effective practice in some agencies is restricted because policy does not sanction the social work roles of advocacy and brokerage.

Clinical social workers are encouraged to actively influence policy reform in their agencies. They must provide administration with accurate documentation of the problems caused by ineffective policies. Agency administrators and their clinical practitioners should work together in pursuit of an adequate funding level for psychosocial treatment.

There is a tremendous shortage of clinical workers in the field of long-term care. Service care management is a vital social work function for protective service and other community-based agencies that provide care for the functionally impaired elderly. Due to large caseloads and rigid administrative policies, many case managers are not able to conduct thorough needs assessments, provide adequate coordination of services, or offer counseling to their clients.

Funding is not available for the provision of an adequate level of clinical social work practice in most nursing homes. Those social workers who are employed in nursing homes are frequently burdened with large caseloads and an overload of routine paperwork.

The future of clinical social work practice in long-term care may be promising, since geriatric social work is projected by numerous authorities to be the largest growth area in social work over the next few decades.

# References

Aldrich, C. K. & E. Mendkoff. "Relocation of the Aged and Disabled: A Mortality Study." *Journal of the American Geriatrics Society* 11 (1963), pp. 185–94.

Anderson, C. H. & J. R. Gibson. *Toward a New Psychology.* Homewood, Ill.: The Dorsey Press, 1978.

Anderson, F. "Preventive Medicine in Old Age." In *Textbook of Geriatric Medicine and Gerontology,* ed. J. C. Brockelhurst, M.D. London: Churchill Livingstone, 1978.

Anderson, O. "The Social Strategy of Disease Control: The Case of Senile Dementia." *Behavioral Aspects of Senile Dementia,* Bethesda, Md.: National Institutes of Health, 1978.

Andres, R. "Relation of Physiologic Changes in Aging to Medical Change of Disease in the Aged." *Mayo Clinic Proceedings* 42 (1967), pp. 411–14.

Andrews, F. M. & S. B. Withey. *Social Indicators of Well-Being.* New York: Plenum Press, 1976.

Ash, P. "Pre-Retirement Counseling." *The Gerontologist,* 6 (1966), pp. 97–99.

Atchley, R. C. "Retirement and Leisure Participation: Continuity or Crisis?" *Gerontologist,* 2 (1971), pp. 13–17.

————. *The Social Forces in Later Life.* Belmont, Calif.: Wadsworth, 1971.

————. *The Social Forces in Later Life.* 2d ed., Belmont, Calif.: Wadsworth, 1977.

————. *The Social Forces in Later Life.* 3d ed. Belmont, Calif.: Wadsworth, 1980.

————. *The Sociology of Retirement.* Cambridge, Mass.: Schenkman, 1976.

Augilera, D. C. & J. M. Messick. *Crisis Intervention: Theory and Methodology.* St. Louis: C. V. Mosby, 1974.

Axlerod, T. "Innovative Roles for Social Workers in Home Care Programs." *Health and Social Work* 3 (1978), pp. 48–66.

Azarnoff, R. S. & J. S. Seliger. *Delivering Human Services.* Englewood Cliffs, N.J.: Prentice-Hall, 1982.

AARP Educational and Service Programs. 1909 K Street, N. W., Washington, D.C.

Baer, B. L. "Developing a New Curriculum for Social Work Education." In *The Pursuit of Competence in Social Work*. eds. F. Clark & M. Arkava. San Francisco: Jossey-Bass, 1979.

Baer, B. L. & R. Federico. *Educating the Baccalaureate Social Worker*. Cambridge, Mass.: Ballinger Publishing, 1978.

Bandura, A. "Psychotherapy Based Upon Modeling Principles." In *Handbook of Psychotherapy and Behavior Change,* eds. A. E. Bergin & S. Garfield. New York: John Wiley & Sons, 1971.

Barrow, G. M. & P. A. Smith. *Aging, The Individual and Society*. 2d ed. St. Paul, Minn.: West Publishing Company, 1983.

Bartlett, H. M. *The Common Base of Social Work Practice*. New York: National Association of Social Workers, 1970.

Baum, M. & R. Baum. *Growing Old*. Englewood Cliffs, N.J.: Prentice-Hall, 1980.

Bayne, J. R. D. "Management of Confusion in Elderly Persons." *CMA Journal,* 118 (1978), pp. 138–41.

Beattie, W. M. "Aging and the Social Services." In *Handbook of Aging and the Social Sciences*. eds. R. H. Binstock & E. Shanas. New York: Van Nostrand Reinhold, 1976.

Beaulieu, E. M. & J. Karpinski. "Group Treatment of Elderly with Ill Spouses." *Social Casework,* 62 (1981), p. 557.

Beaver, M. L. *Human Service Practice with the Elderly*. Englewood Cliffs, N.J.: Prentice-Hall, 1983.

Beck, A. T. *Cognitive Theory and the Emotional Disorders*. New York: International University Press, 1976.

Beck, B. "Prevention and Treatment." Mimeographed. New York: National Association of Social Workers, 1959.

Belsky, J. K. *The Psychology of Aging: Theory, Research and Practice*. Monterey, Calif.: Brooks/Cole Publishing, 1984.

Berkman, B. G. "Early Social Service Case Finding for Hospitalized Patients." *Social Casework,* 53 (1972), pp. 256–65.

Berkman, B. G. & H. Rehr. "Social Needs of the Hospitalized Elderly." *Social Work,* 52 (1972), pp. 80–8.

Beverley, V. "Helping Your Patient Choose and Adjust to a Nursing Home." *Geriatrics,* (1976), pp. 115–26.

Bierman, E. L. & W. R. Hazzard. "Old Age, Including Death and Dying." In *The Biologic Ages of Man*. eds. D. W. Smith & E. L. Bierman. Philadelphia: Saunders, 1973.

Birren, J. & J. Moore, eds. *Sexuality and Aging: A Selected Bibliography*. Los Angeles: University of Southern California Press, 1975.

Blenkner, M. "Environmental Change and the Aging Individual." *Gerontologist,* 7 (1967), pp. 101–5.

Bloom, M. *Primary Prevention—The Possible Science.* Englewood Cliffs, N.J.: Prentice-Hall, 1981.

Blum, J. E., J. L. Fosshage & L. F. Jarvik. "Intellectual Changes and Sex Differences in Octogenarians." *Developmental Psychology* 7 (1972), pp. 178–87.

Botwinick, J. "Intellectual Abilities." In *Handbook of the Psychology of Aging,* eds. J. E. Birren & K. W. Schaie. New York: Van Nostrand Reinhold, 1977.

Bourestrom, N. "Social Roles in Nursing Homes." Paper presented to the Human Aging Conference, University of Minnesota, Minneapolis, April, 1976.

Bradford, L. P. & M. I. Bradford. *Retirement.* Chicago: Nelson-Hall, 1979.

Brickel, C. M. "The Therapeutic Role of Cat Mascots with a Hospital Based Geriatric Population: A Staff Survey." *Gerontologist,* 19 (1979), pp. 368–71.

Brill, N. *Working with People—The Helping Process.* Philadelphia: Lippincott, 1973.

Brody, E. M. "Aging." In *Encyclopedia of Social Work.* 17th ed. Washington, D. C.: National Association of Social Workers, 1977.

_____. *Long-Term Care of Older People.* New York: Human Sciences Press, 1977.

_____. "Aged Parents and Aging Children." In *Aging Parents,* ed. P. Ragan. Los Angeles: University of Southern California Press, 1979.

Brody, E. M. & S. Brody. "Decade of Decision for the Elderly." *Social Work,* 19 (1974), p. 544.

Bromley, D. B. *The Psychology of Human Aging.* 2d ed. Baltimore: Penguin Books, 1974.

Burnside, I. M. "Group Work with the Mentally Impaired Elderly." In *Working with the Elderly: Group Processes and Techniques,* I. M. Burnside, ed. North Scituate, Mass.: Duxbury Press, 1978.

_____. "Mental Health in the Aged." In *Aging: Prospects and Issues.* Ethel Percy Andrus Gerontology Center, 1973.

_____ ed. *Working with the Elderly: Group Processes and Techniques.* North Scituate, Mass.: Duxbury Press, 1978.

Butler, R. "Easing the Problems of Aging." *Exxon USA.* 22, no. 1, (1983), pp. 12–16.

_____. "The Life Review: An Interpretation of Reminiscence in the Aged." *Psychiatry,* 26 (1963), pp. 65–75.

_____. *Why Survive? Being Old in America.* New York: Harper & Row, 1975.

Butler, R. & M. I. Lewis. *Aging and Mental Health.* 2d ed. St. Louis: C. V. Mosby, 1977.

_____. *Aging and Mental Health.* 3d ed. St. Louis: C. V. Mosby, 1982.

_____. *Sex After Sixty.* New York: McGraw-Hill, 1975.

Caplan, Gerald. *Principles of Preventive Psychiatry.* New York: Basic Books, 1964.

Carkhuff, R. *Helping and Human Relations* vol. 1. New York: Holt, Rinehart & Winston, 1969.

————. *Helping and Human Relations* vol. 2. New York: Holt, Rinehart & Winston, 1969.

————. *The Art of Problem Solving.* Amherst, Mass.: Human Resource Development Press, 1973.

————. *The Development of Human Resources.* New York: Holt, Rinehart & Winston, 1971.

Carkhuff, R. & R. Berenson. *Beyond Counseling and Therapy.* 2d ed. New York: Holt, Rinehart & Winston, 1977.

Carr, A. C. "Bereavement as a Relative Experience." In *Bereavement: Its Psychosocial Aspects,* eds. B. Schoenberg, I. Gerber, A. Wiener, A. H. Kutscher, D. Peretz, & A. C. Carr. New York: Columbia University Press, 1975.

Carstensen, L. L. & W. J. Fremouw. "The Demonstration of a Behavioral Intervention for Late Life Paranoia." *Gerontologist,* 21 (1981), pp. 329–33.

Christenson, C. & J. Gagnon. "Sexual Behavior of Older Women." *Journal of Gerontology,* 20 (1965), pp. 351–56.

Citrin, R. S. & D. N. Dixon. "Reality Orientation: A Milieu Therapy Used in an Institution for the Aged." *Gerontologist,* 17 (1977), pp. 39–43.

Clark, M. & B. Anderson. *Culture and Aging.* Springfield, Ill.: Thomas, 1967.

Cohen, E. S. "An Overview of Long-Term Care Facilities." In *A Social Work Guide for Long-Term Care Facilities.* ed. E. M. Brody. Rockville, Md.: National Institute of Mental Health, 1975.

Cohen, G. "Prospects for Mental Health and Aging." In *Handbook of Mental Health and Aging,* eds. J. Birren and R. Sloane. Englewood Cliffs, N.J.: Prentice-Hall, 1980.

Cohen, P. M. "A Group Approach for Working with Families of the Elderly." *Gerontologist,* 23 (1983), pp. 248–50.

Colville, W. J., T. W. Costello & F. L. Rouke. *Abnormal Psychology.* New York: Barnes and Noble, 1968.

Comfort, A. "Age Prejudice in America." *Social Policy,* 7 (1976), pp. 3–9.

Coni, N., W. Davison & S. Webster. *Lecture Notes on Geriatrics.* Oxford, England: Blackwell Scientific Publications, 1980.

Cook, A. S. "A Model for Working with the Elderly in Institutions." *Social Casework,* 62 (1981), pp. 421–25.

Cook, F., W. Skogan, T. Cook & G. Antunes. "Criminal Victimization of the Elderly: The Economic and Physical Consequences." *Gerontologist,* 18 (1978), pp. 338–49.

Coopersmith, S. *The Antecedents of Self Esteem.* San Francisco: W. H. Freeman, 1967.

Cornican, E. "Task Centered Model for Work with the Aged." *Sociology Casework*, 58 (1977), pp. 490–93.

Corson, S. A. & E. Corson. "Pets as Mediators of Therapy in Custodial Institutions for the Aged." *Current Psychiatric Therapies*, 18 (1979), pp. 195–205.

Craighead, W. E., M. J. Mahoney & A. R. Kazdin. *Behavior Modification: Principles, Issues and Applications.* Boston: Houghton Mifflin, 1976.

Craik, F. I. M. "Age Differences in Human Memory." In *Handbook of the Psychology of Aging,* eds. J. E. Birren & K. W. Schaie. New York: Van Nostrand Reinhold, 1977.

Crandall, R. C. *Gerontology—A Behavioral Science Approach.* Reading, Mass.: Addison-Wesley Publishing, 1980.

Crystal, S. *America's Old Age Crisis.* New York: Basic Books, 1982.

Cureton, T. K., Jr. "Exercise." *The World Book Encyclopedia.* Vol. 6 Chicago: World Book-Childcraft International, Inc., 1981.

*Current Population Reports, Special Studies: Demographic Aspects of Aging and the Older Population in the United States.* Series P-23, No. 59. Washington, D. C.: U. S. Government Printing Office, 1976.

Davis, R. & E. Feil. *Looking for Yesterday.* Cleveland: Edward Feil Productions, 1979.

Decker, D. L. *Social Gerontology.* Boston: Little, Brown, 1980.

Dennis, H. "Remotivation Therapy Groups." In *Working with the Elderly: Group Processes and Techniques,* ed. I. M. Burnside. North Scituate, Mass.: Duxbury Press, 1978.

Dibner, A. S. "The Psychology of Normal Aging." In *Understanding Aging: A Multidisciplinary Approach,* ed. M. G. Spencer and C. J. Dorr. New York: Appleton-Century-Crofts, 1975.

Donahue, W., ed. *Senate Special Committee on Aging. Adequacy Hearings.* Washington, D. C., 1975.

Drummond, L., L. Kirchoff & D. Scarbrough. "A Practical Guide to Reality Orientation: A Treatment Approach for Confusion and Disorientation." *Gerontologist,* 18 (1978), pp. 568–73.

Duckworth, G. L. & A. Rosenblatt. "Helping the Elderly Alcoholic." *Social Casework,* 57 (1976), 296–302.

Ebersole, P. P. "Establishing Reminiscing Groups." In *Working with the Elderly— Group Processes and Techniques.* ed. I. M. Burnside. North Scituate, Mass.: Duxbury Press, 1978.

Ebersole, P. P. & P. Hess. *Toward Healthy Aging.* St. Louis: C. V. Mosby Co., 1981.

Eggert, G., C. Granger, R. Morris, & S. Pendleton. "Caring for the Patient with Long-Term Disability." *Journal of the American Geriatrics Society,* 32 (1977), pp. 102–14.

Eisdorfer, C. "The WAIS Performance of the Aged: A Retest Evaluation." *Journal of Gerontology,* 18 (1963), pp. 169–72.

Eisdorfer, C. & D. Cohen. "Diagnostic Criteria for Primary Neuronal Degeneration of the Alzheimer's Type." *Journal of Family Practice,* 11 (1980), pp. 553–57.

_____. "The Cognitively Impaired Elderly: Differential Diagnosis." In *The Clinical Psychology of Aging.* eds. M. Storandt, I. Siegler & M. Elias. New York: Plenum Press, 1978.

Eisdorfer, C., D. Cohen & C. Preston. *Behavioral and Psychological Theories for the Older Patient with Cognitive Impairment.* Seattle: University of Washington Press, 1981.

Elkind, D. "Erik Erikson's Eight Ages of Man." In *Readings in Adult Psychology: Contemporary Perspectives.* eds. L. R. Allman & D. T. Jaffe. New York: Harper & Row, 1977.

Ellenbogen, B. L. "Health Status of the Rural Aged." In *Older Rural Americans: A Sociological Perspective.* ed. E. Youmans Lexington: University of Kentucky Press, 1967.

Ellis, A. "Rational-Emotive Therapy." In *Current Psychotherapies,* ed. R. Corsini Itasca, Ill.: F. E. Peacock, 1973.

_____. *Reason and Emotion in Psychotherapy.* New York: Lyle Stuart, 1962.

Ellis, A. & R. Harper. *A New Guide to Rational Living.* North Hollywood, Calif.: Wilshire Book Company, 1976.

Engen, T. "Taste and Smell." In *Handbook of the Psychology of Aging.* eds. J. E. Birren & K. N. Schaie. New York: Van Nostrand Reinhold, 1977.

English, N. "Long-Term Care in the Community." In *Older Persons and Service Providers.* ed. G. Sorenson New York: Human Sciences Press, 1981.

Erikson, E. H. *Childhood and Society.* 2d ed. New York: Norton, 1963.

Ernst, M. & H. Shore. *Sensitizing People to the Processes of Aging: The In-Service Educator's Guide.* 2d ed. Denton, Tex.: North State Texas University, 1976.

Euster, G. L. A. "A System of Groups in Institutions for the Aged." *Social Casework,* 52 (1971), pp. 523–29.

Eustis, N., J. Greenberg & S. Patten. *Long-Term Care for Older Persons: A Policy Perspective.* Monterey, Calif.: Brooks/Cole Publishing Co., 1984.

Evans, R. I. *Dialogue with Erik Erikson.* New York: Harper & Row, 1967.

Federal Council on Aging. *Report on National Policy for the Frail Elderly.* Washington, D.C.: U. S. Department of Health Education and Welfare, 1976.

Federal Council on Aging. *The Need for Long Term Care.* U. S. Department of Health and Human Services, Washington, D.C., 1981.

Federico, R. *The Social Welfare Institution.* Lexington, Mass.: D.C. Heath and Co., 1973.

Feil, N. *Validation: The Feil Method.* Cleveland: Edward Feil Productions, 1982.

Feldman, A. G. & F. L. Feldman. "Community Strategies and the Aged." In *Professional Obligations and Approaches to the Aged*. eds. A. N. Schwarts & I. N. Mensh Springfield, Ill.: Thomas, 1974.

Feldman, F. L. & F. H. Scherz. *Family Social Welfare*. New York: Atherton Press, 1967.

Ferrari, N. A. *Institutional and Attitude Change in an Aged Population: A Field Study in Dissonance Theory*. Cleveland: Western Reserve University, 1962.

Fischer, J. *Effective Casework Practice*. New York: McGraw-Hill, 1978.

Fischer, J. & H. L. Gochros. *Planned Behavior Change: Behavior Modification in Social Work*. New York: The Free Press, 1975.

Fischman, J. "The Mystery of Alzheimer's." *Psychology Today*, 1 (1984), p. 27.

Flannery, R. B., Jr. "Behavior Modification of Geriatric Grief: A Transactional Perspective." *International Journal of Aging and Human Development*, 5 (1974), pp. 197–203.

Frazier, E. & C. Lincoln. *The Negro Church in America: The Black Church Since Frazier*. New York: Schocken Books, Inc., 1974.

Freedman, N. "Depression in a Family Practice Elderly Population." *Journal of the American Geriatric Society*, 30 (1982), pp. 372–77.

Friedlander, W. A. & R. Z. Apte. *Introduction to Social Welfare*. 5th ed. Englewood Cliffs. N. J.: Prentice-Hall, 1980.

Garber, R. S. "A Psychiatrist's View of Remotivation." *Mental Hospitals*, 16 (1965), pp. 219–21.

Garner, J. & S. Mercer. "Social Work Practice in Long-Term Care Facilities: Implications of the Current Model." *Journal of Gerontological Social Work*, 3 (1980), pp. 71–77.

Geismar, L. L. *Preventive Intervention in Social Work*. Metuchen, N. J.: The Scarecrow Press, Inc., 1969.

Gelfand, B. "Emerging Trends in Social Treatment." *Social Casework*, 53 (1972), pp. 156–62.

Gelfand, D. E. & J. K. Olsen. *The Aging Network: Programs and Services*. New York: Springer, 1980.

George, L. K. & L. B. Bearon. *Quality of Life in Older Persons*. New York: Human Sciences Press, 1980.

Germain, C. B. ed. *Social Work Practice: People and Environments*. New York: Columbia University Press, 1979.

Germain, C. B. "Introduction: Ecology and Social Work." In *Social Work Practice: People and Environments*. ed. C. B. Germain. New York: Columbia University Press, 1979.

Germain, C. B. & A. Gitterman. *The Life Model of Social Work Practice*. New York: Columbia University Press, 1980.

Getzel, G. & J. Mellor. "Introduction: Overview of Gerontological Social Work in Long-Term Care." *Journal of Gerontological Social Work*, 5 (1982), pp. 1–4.

Gilbert, J. G. *Understanding Old Age.* New York: The Ronald Press Company, 1952.

Gilbert, N., H. Miller & H. Specht. *An Introduction to Social Work Practice.* Englewood Cliffs, N.J.: Prentice-Hall, 1980.

Glamser, F. O. "The Impact of Preretirement Programs on the Retirement Experience." *Journal of Gerontology*, 36 (1981), 244–50.

Glasser, W. *Reality Therapy: A New Approach to Psychotherapy.* New York: Harper & Row, 1965.

Gochros, H. & J. Gochros, eds. *The Sexually Oppressed.* New York: Association Press, 1977.

Golan, N. "Crisis Theory." In *Social Work Treatment.* ed. F. Turner London: Free Press, 1974.

_____. "Crisis Theory." In *Social Work Treatment—Interlocking Theoretical Approaches.* ed. F. Turner New York: The Free Press, 1979.

Goldberg, S. R. & F. Deutsch. *Life-Span Individual and Family Development.* Monterey, Calif.: Brooks/Cole, 1977.

Gomberg, E. "Drinking and Problem Drinking Among the Elderly." *Alcohol, Drugs, and Aging.* University of Michigan: Institute of Gerontology, 1976.

Gottesman, L. E. "Milieu Treatment of the Aged in Institutions." *Gerontologist*, 13 (1973), pp. 23–26.

_____. *Report to Respondents: Nursing Home Project.* Philadelphia: Philadelphia Geriatric Center, 1971.

_____. "Resocialization of the Geriatric Mental Patient." *American Journal of Public Health*, 55 (1965), pp. 1964–970.

_____. "The Response of Long Hospitalized Aged Psychiatric Patients to Milieu Treatment." *Gerontologist*, 7 (1967), pp. 47–48.

Gottesman, L. E. & E. Hutchinson. "Characteristics of the Institutionalized Elderly." In *A Social Work Guide for Long-Term Care Facilities.* ed. E. M. Brody. Rockville, Md.: National Institute of Mental Health, 1975.

Gramlich, E. P. "Recognition and Management of Grief in Elderly Patients." *Geriatrics*, 23 (1969), pp. 87–91.

Grintzig, L. "Selected Characteristics of Residents in Long-Term Care Institutions." Mimeographed. *Long-Term Care Monograph*, No. 5. Washington, D.C.: George Washington University, 1970.

Haber, D. "Promoting Mutual Help Groups Among Older Persons." *Gerontologist*, 33 (1983), pp. 251–53.

Halbfinger, J. D. "The Aged in Institutions." Unpublished doctoral dissertation, Case Western Reserve, 1976.

Haley, W. E. "Behavioral Self-Management: Application to a Case of Agitation in an Elderly Chronic Psychiatric Patient." *Clinical Gerontologist,* 1 (1983), pp. 45–51.

Harbert, A. S. & L. H. Ginsberg. *Human Services for Older Adults: Concepts and Skills.* Belmont, Calif.: Wadsworth, 1979.

Harris, L. and Associates. *The Myth and Reality of Aging in America.* Washington, D.C.: National Council on Aging, 1975.

Hartford, M. E. & R. Parsons. "Groups with Relatives of Dependent Other Adults." *Gerontologist,* 22 (1982), pp. 394–98.

Hausman, C. P. "Short-Term Counseling Groups for People with Elderly Parents." *Gerontologist,* 19 (1979), pp. 102–7.

Havighurst, R. J. *Developmental Tasks and Education.* 3d ed. New York: McKay, 1972.

————. "Personality and Patterns of Aging." *Gerontologist,* 8 (1968), pp. 20–23.

————. "Successful Aging." *Gerontologist,* 1 (1961), pp. 1–13.

Havighurst, R. J., J. M. A. Munnichs, B. L. Neugarten & H. Thomas. eds. *Adjustment to Retirement.* Assen, Netherlands: Van Gorcum, 1969.

Hendricks, J., & C. D. Hendricks. *Aging in Mass Society.* Cambridge, Mass.: Winthrop Publishers, Inc., 1981.

Hennessy, M. J. "Music and Music Therapy Groups." In *Working with the Elderly— Group Processes and Techniques.* ed. I. M. Burnside. North Scituate, Mass.: Duxbury Press, 1978.

Heston, L. L., A. R. Mastri, V. E. Anderson & J. White. "Dementia of the Alzheimer Type." *Archives of General Psychiatry,* 138 (1981), pp. 1085–98.

Hing, E. "Characteristics of Nursing Home Residents." *Vital and Health Statistics.* Series 13, No. 51. Rockville, Md.: National Center for Health Statistics, 1981.

Holcomb, W. L. "Spiritual Crises Among the Aging." In *Understanding Aging: A Multidisciplinary Approach.* eds. M. G. Spencer & C. J. Dorr. New York: Appleton-Century-Crofts, 1975.

Hollis, F. *Casework: A Psychosocial Therapy.* New York: Random House, 1964.

————. *Casework: A Psychosocial Therapy.* 2d ed. New York: Random House, 1972.

————. "The Psychosocial Approach to the Practice of Casework." In *Theories of Social Casework.* eds. R. W. Roberts & R. H. Nee. Chicago: The University of Chicago Press, 1970.

Horn, J. L. & R. B. Cattell. "Refinement and Test of the Theory of Fluid and Crystallized Intelligence." *Journal of Educational Psychology,* 57 (1966), pp. 253–70.

Hoyer, W., R. Kafer, S. Simpson & F. Hoyer. "Reinstatement of Verbal Behaviors in Elderly Mental Patients Using Operant Procedures." *Gerontologist,* 14 (1974), pp. 149–52.

Hurlock, E. B. *Developmental Psychology.* New York: McGraw-Hill, 1968.

Huttman, E. D. *Introduction to Social Policy.* New York: McGraw-Hill, 1981.

Huyck, M. H. *Growing Older.* Englewood Cliffs, N. J.: Prentice-Hall, 1974.

Institute of Medicine. *The Elderly and Functional Dependency.* Washington, D.C.: National Academy of Science, 1977.

Jacobson, E. *You Must Relax: A Practical Method of Reducing the Strains of Modern Life.* New York: McGraw-Hill, 1934.

Jarvik, L. F., F. J. Kallman & A. Falek. "Intellectual Changes in Aged Twins." *Journal of Gerontology,* 17 (1962), pp. 289–94.

Johnson, H. R. "Education." *Gerontologist,* 22 (1982), pp. 125–26.

Jorgensen, L. A. & R. Kane. "Social Work in the Nursing Home." *Social Work in Health Care,* 1 (1976), pp. 471–82.

Kahana, E. "The Humane Treatment of Old People in Institutions." *Gerontologist,* 13 (1973), pp. 282–89.

Kahana, E. & R. M. Coe. "Alternatives in Long-Term Care." In *Long-Term Care: A Handbook for Researchers, Planners and Providers.* ed. S. Sherwood. New York: Spectrum Publications, Inc., 1975.

Kalish, R. A. *Late Adulthood: Perspectives on Human Development.* Monterey, Calif.: Brooks/Cole, 1975.

————. *Late Adulthood: Perspectives on Human Development.* 2d ed. Monterey, Calif.: Brooks/Cole, 1982.

Kamerman, S. B., R. Dolgoff, G. Getzel & J. Nelsen. "Knowledge for Practice: Social Science in Social Work." In *Shaping the New Social Work.* ed. A. J. Kahn. New York: Columbia University Press, 1973.

Kanfer, F. H. & J. S. Phillips. *Learning Foundations of Behavior Therapy.* New York: John Wiley & Sons, 1970.

Kaplan, J. *A Social Program for Older People.* Minneapolis: University of Minnesota Press, 1953.

Kark, S. L. *Epidemiology of Community Medicine.* New York: Appleton-Century-Crofts, 1974.

Kart, C. S. *The Realities of Aging.* Boston: Allyn & Bacon, 1981.

Kastenbaum, R. *Growing Old.* New York: Harper & Row, 1979.

Katona, G., J. N. Morgan & R. E. Barfield. "Family Patterns and Morale in Retirement." In *Social Aspects of Aging.* eds. I. H. Simpson and J. E. McKinney. Durham, N. C.: Duke University Press, 1969.

Keller, J. F. & G. A. Hughston. *Counseling the Elderly.* New York: Harper & Row, 1981.

Kelley, J. "The Aging Male Homosexual." In *The Sexually Oppressed.* eds. H. L. & J. S. Gochros. New York: Association Press, 1977.

Kennedy, C. E. *Human Development: The Adult Years and Aging.* New York: Macmillan, 1978.

Kidd, A. H. & B. M. Feldman. "Pet Ownership and Self-Perceptions of Older People." *Psychological Reports,* 48 (1981), pp. 867–75.

Killian, E. C. "Effect of Geriatric Transfers on Mortality Rates." *Social Work,* 15 (1970), pp. 19–26.

Kimmel, D. C. *Adulthood and Aging.* New York: John Wiley & Sons, 1974.

Kirschner, C. "The Aging Family in Crisis: A Problem in Living." *Social Casework,* 57 (1979), pp. 209–16.

Kitchell, M. "Screening for Depression in Hospitalized Geriatric Medical Patients." *Journal of American Geriatric Society,* 30 (1982), pp. 174–77.

Knopf, O., M.D. *Successful Aging.* Boston, Mass.: G. K. Hall and Co., 1977.

Knowles, M. S. "Adult Education." In *Encyclopedia of Social Work.* 17th ed. Washington, D.C.: National Association of Social Workers, 1977.

Kolb, L. C. *Modern Clinical Psychiatry.* Philadelphia: W. B. Saunders, 1977.

Kosberg, J. I. "The Nursing Home: A Social Work Paradox." *Social Work,* 18 (1973), pp. 104–10.

Kosberg, J. I. ed. *Preventive Intervention in Social Work.* Washington, D.C.: National Association of Social Workers, 1979.

Kral, V. A. "Neurosis of the Aged: A Neglected Area." *Clinical Gerontologist,* 1 (1983), pp. 29–36.

Krill, D. "Determining Client Modefiability." *Social Casework,* 49 (1968), pp. 602–11.

Krout, J. A. "Correlates of Service Utilization Among the Rural Elderly." *Gerontologist,* 23 (1983), pp. 500–504.

Landry, F. "Exercise." In *Academic American Encyclopedia.* Princeton, N.J.: Arete Publishing Company, Inc., 1980.

Leavell, H. R. & E. G. Clark. *Preventive Medicine for the Doctor in His Community.* New York: McGraw-Hill, 1958.

————. *Textbook of Preventive Medicine.* New York: McGraw-Hill, 1953.

Leitenberg, H., ed. *Handbook of Behavior Modification and Behavior Therapy.* Englewood Cliffs, N.J.: Prentice-Hall, 1976.

Lemon, B. W., V. L. Bengtson & J. A. Peterson. "An Exploration of the Activity Theory of Aging: Activity Types and Life Satisfaction Among In-Movers to a Retirement Community." In *Aging in America.* eds. C. S. Kart & B. B. Manard. New York: Alfred Publishing Co., 1976.

Lesser, J., L. W. Lazarus, R. Frankel & S. Hauasy. "Reminiscence Group Therapy with Psychotic Geriatric Inpatients." *Gerontologist,* 21 (1981), pp. 291–96.

Lester, D. *The Elderly Victim of Crime.* Springfield Ill.: Charles C Thomas, 1981.

Levinson, B. *Pets and Human Development.* Springfield, Ill.: Charles C Thomas, 1972.

Levinson, B. M. "Pets and Old Age." *Mental Hygiene,* 53 (1969), pp. 364–68.

Lewis, M. I. & R. N. Butler. "Life Review Therapy." *Geriatrics,* 29 (1974), pp. 165–73.

Lieberman, M. A. "Psychological Correlates of Impending Death: Some Preliminary Observations." *Journal of Gerontology,* 20 (1965), pp. 181–90.

Liebowitz, B. "Impact of Intra-Institutional Relocation." *Gerontologist,* 14 (1974), pp. 293–94.

Lindemann, E. "Symptomatology and Management of Acute Grief." *American Journal of Psychiatry,* 101 (1944), pp. 141–48.

Linsk, M., M. Howe & E. M. Pinkston. "Behavioral Group Work in a Home for the Aged." *Social Work,* 20 (1975), pp. 454–63.

Linstrom, R. C. "Social Services in Institutions." *Gerontologist,* 15 (1975), p. 98.

Lipner, J. & E. Sherman. "Hip Fractures in the Elderly: A Psychodynamic Approach." *Social Casework,* 56 (1975), pp. 97–103.

Loether, H. J. *Problems of Aging.* 2d ed. Encino, Calif.: Dickenson, 1975.

Loewenberg, F. M. *Fundamentals of Social Intervention.* New York: Columbia University Press, 1977.

Long, I. "Human Sexuality and Aging." *Social Casework,* 57 (1976), pp. 237–44.

Lopata, H. Z. *Widowhood in an American City.* Cambridge, Mass.: Harvard University Press, 1970.

Lowenthal, M. F., G. G. Brissette, J. A. Buehler, R. C. Pierce, B. C. Robinson & M. L. Iner. *Aging and Mental Disorder in San Francisco.* San Francisco: Jossey-Bass, 1967.

Lowenthal, M. F. & B. Robinson. "Social Networks and Isolation." In *Handbook of Aging and the Social Sciences.* eds. R. H. Binstock & E. Shanas. New York: Van Nostrand Reinhold, 1976.

Lowy, L. *Social Work with the Aging.* New York: Harper & Row, 1979.

Maccoby, N. & J. N. Farquhar. "Communication for Health: Unselling Heart Disease." *Journal of Communication,* 25 (1975), pp. 114–26.

MacMillan, D. "Features of Senile Breakdown." *Geriatrics,* 24 (1969), pp. 109–18.

Maizler, J. & J. Solomon. "Therapeutic Group Process with the Institutional Elderly." *Journal of the American Geriatrics Society,* 24 (1976), pp. 542–46.

Manaster, A. "The Family Group Therapy Program at Park View Home for the Aged." *Journal of American Geriatric Society,* 15 (1967), pp. 302–6.

Manney, J. *Aging in American Society.* University of Michigan (Wayne State): Institute of Gerontology, 1975.

Marble, B. B. & M. I. Patterson. "Nutrition and Aging." In *Understanding Aging: A Multidisciplinary Approach.* eds. M. G. Spencer and C. J. Dorr. New York: Appleton-Century-Crofts, 1975.

Maslow, A. H. *Motivation and Personality.* New York: Harper & Row, 1954.

Mayadas, N. S. & D. L. Hink. "Group Work with the Aging: An Issue for Social Work Education." *Gerontologist,* 14 (1974), pp. 449–45.

McMahan, A. & P. Rhudick. "Reminiscing Adaptational Significance in the Aged." *Archives of General Psychiatry,* 10 (1964), pp. 292–98.

Medley, M. L. "Marital Adjustment in the Post-Retirement Years." *Family Coordinator,* 26 (1977), pp. 5–12.

Memmler, R. L. & D. L. Wood. *The Human Body in Health and Disease.* 4th ed. Philadelphia: J. B. Lippincott Company, 1977.

Mercer, S. & R. Kane. "Helplessness and Hopelessness in the Institutionalized Aged." *Health and Social Work,* 4 (1979), pp. 90–16.

Messinger, W. "Residents' Legal Status and Rights in Nursing Homes." In *Older Persons and Service Providers.* ed. G. Sarensen. New York: Human Sciences Press, 1981.

Meyer, C., ed. *Preventive Intervention in Social Work.* Washington, D.C.: National Association of Social Workers, 1974.

Miller, D. & M. A. Lieberman. "The Relationship of Affect State and Adaptive Capacity to Reactions to Stress." *Journal of Gerontology,* 20 (1965), pp. 181–90.

Miller, I. & R. Solomon. "The Development of Group Services for the Elderly." In *Social Work Practice: People and Environments.* ed. C. Germain. New York: Columbia University Press, 1979.

Miller, M. *Suicide After Sixty: The Final Alternative.* New York: Springer, 1979.

Miller, N. & G. Cohen, eds. *Clinical Aspects of Alzheimer's Disease and Senile Dementia.* New York: Raven Press, 1981.

Miller, S. J. "The Social Dilemma of the Aging Leisure Participant." In *Older People and Their Social World.* eds. A. M. Rose and W. A. Peterson Philadelphia: F. A. Davis, 1965.

Mishara, B. & R. Kastenbaum. *Alcohol and Old Age.* New York: Grune and Stratton, 1980.

———. "Self-Injuries Behavior and Environmental Change in the Institutionalized Elderly." *International Journal of Aging and Human Development,* 4 (1973), pp. 133–45.

Montgomery, J. E. "Living Arrangements and Housing of the Rural Aged in a Central Pennsylvania Community." Proceedings of a research conference on housing, *Patterns of Living and Housing of Middle-Aged and Older People,* Washington, D.C., March 1965.

Moody, H. "Ethical Dilemmas in Long-Term Care." *Gerontological Social Work Practice in Long-Term Care,* 5 (1983), pp. 97–111.

Moore, C. E. "Using Music with Groups of Geriatric Patients." In *Working with the Elderly: Group Processes and Techniques.* ed. I. M. Burnside North Scituate, Mass.: Duxbury Press, 1978.

Morrison, J. "Group Therapy for High Utilizers of Clinic Facilities." In *Psychosocial Nursing Care of the Aged.* ed. I. M. Burnside. New York: McGraw-Hill, 1973.

Morrow, W. *Behavior Therapy Bibliography.* Columbia: University of Missouri Press, 1971.

Morycz, R. K. "Family Burden and Outpatients with Alzheimer's Disease." Unpublished Doctoral Dissertation, University of Pittsburgh, 1982.

Mueller, D. J. & L. Atlas. "Resocialization of Regressed Elderly Residents: A Behavioral Management Approach." *Journal of Gerontology,* 27 (1972), pp. 390–92.

Nader, R. *Introduction to Old Age: The Last Segregation.* New York: Grossman Publishers, 1971.

National Center for Health Statistics. U. S. Department of Health Education and Welfare. *The National Nursing Home Survey—1977 Survey for the United States.* Washington, D.C.: DHHS Publication, 1979.

Neugarten, B. L. "Successful Aging in 1970 and 1990." In *Successful Aging: A Conference Report.* ed. E. Pfeiffer. Durham, N.C.: Center for the Study of Aging and Human Development, 1974.

Newman, B. M. & P. R. Newman. *Development Through Life: A Psychosocial Approach.* Homewood, Ill.: The Dorsey Press, 1975.

Newman, S. "Impact of Intergenerational Programs on Children's Growth and on Old People's Life Satisfaction." Paper presented at a national symposium on Innovation in Gerontological Education, Washington, D.C. March 1982.

Oberleder, M. "Crisis Therapy in Mental Breakdown of the Aging." *Gerontologist,* 10 (1970), pp. 111–14.

Odell, L. M. & C. E. Odell, Sr. *You and the Senior Boom.* Hicksville, N.Y.: Exposition Press, 1980.

Ogren, E. H. & M. W. Linn. "Male Nursing Home Patients: Relocation and Mortality." *Journal of the American Geriatrics Society,* 19 (1971), pp. 229–39.

O'Leary, K. D. & G. T. Wilson. *Behavior Therapy: Application and Outcome.* Englewood Cliffs, N.J.: Prentice-Hall, 1975.

Orbach, H. L., C. Tibbetts & W. Donahue. *Trends in Early Retirement.* Ann Arbor: University of Michigan, Wayne State: Institute of Gerontology, 1969.

Palmore, E. "The Facts on Aging Quiz: A Review of Findings." *Gerontologist,* 20 (1980), pp. 669–72.

Parad, H. J. "Preventive Casework: Problems and Implications." In *Crisis Intervention: Selected Readings.* ed. H. J. Parad. New York: Family Service Association of America, 1965.

———. "Crisis Intervention." In *Encyclopedia of Social Work,* 16 (1971), pp. 196–202.

Patterson, R. D. "Grief and Depression in Old People." *Maryland State Medical Journal,* 18 (1969), pp. 133–37.

Patti, R. J. "Social Work Practice: Organizational Environment." In *Encyclopedia of Social Work.* Vol. 2. Washington, D.C.: National Association of Social Workers, Inc., 1977.

Patton, C. V. "The Older Volunteer: Social Role Continuity and Development." *Gerontologist,* 17 (1977), pp. 355–61.

Pearman, L. & Searles, J. "Unmet Social Service Needs in Skilled Nursing Facilities: Documentation for Action." *Social Work in Health Care,* 1 (1976), pp. 457–70.

Perlman, H. H. *Social Casework: A Problem Solving Process.* Chicago: University of Chicago Press, 1957.

Peterson, J. A. "Marital and Family Therapy Involving the Aged." *Gerontologist,* 13 (1973), pp. 27–30.

Pfeiffer, E. "Psychopathology and Social Pathology." In *Handbook of the Psychology of Aging.* eds. J. E. Birren and K. W. Schaie. New York: Van Nostrand Reinhold, 1977.

Pileseker, C. "Help for the Dying." *Social Work,* 20 (1975), pp. 190–94.

Pincus, A. "Reminiscence in Aging and Its Implications for Social Work Practice." *Social Work,* 15 (1970), pp. 47–53.

Pincus, A. & A. Minahan. *Social Work Practice: Model and Method.* Itasca, Ill.: F. E. Peacock, 1973.

Rabbitt, P. "Changes in Problem Solving Ability in Old Age." In *Handbook of the Psychology of Aging.* eds. J. E. Birren & K. W. Schaie. New York: Van Nostrand Reinhold, 1977.

Raimy, V. *Misunderstandings of the Self.* San Francisco: Jossey-Bass, 1975.

Rakowski, W. & T. Hickey. *Basic Concepts in Aging.* University Park, Penn.: The Gerontology Center, The Pennsylvania State University, 1976.

Rapoport, L. "Crisis Intervention as a Mode of Brief Treatment." In *Theories of Social Casework.* eds. R. W. Roberts and R. H. Nee. Chicago: The University of Chicago Press, 1970.

Rathbone-McCuan, E. & J. Trugardt. "The Older Alcoholic and the Family." Paper presented to the National Alcoholism Forum. St. Louis, Mo.: National Council on Alcoholism, 1978.

Rechtschaffen, A. "Psychotherapy with Geriatric Patients: A Review of the Literature." *Journal of Gerontology,* 14 (1969), pp. 73–84.

Reid, W. & L. Epstein. *Task-Centered Casework.* New York: Columbia University Press, 1972.

Reid, W. J. & A. Shyne. *Brief and Extended Casework.* New York: Columbia University Press, 1969.

Richmond, M. *The Long View.* New York: Russell Sage Foundation, 1930.

Riegel, K. F. "History of Psychological Gerontology." In *Handbook of the Psychology of Aging.* J. E. Birren & K. W. Schaie. New York: Van Nostrand Reinhold, 1977.

Rimm, D. C. & J. C. Masters. *Behavior Therapy: Techniques and Empirical Findings.* New York: Academic Press, 1974.

Robertson, D., R. Griffiths & L. Cosin. "A Community Based Continuing Care Program for the Elderly Disabled." *Journal of Gerontology,* 32 (1977), pp. 334–39.

Robinson, A. M. *A Manual for Use in Nursing Homes.* Philadelphia: American Psychiatric Association; and Smith, Kline, & French Laboratories' Remotivation Project, (n.d.)

Rogers, C. *Client-Centered Therapy.* Boston: Houghton Mifflin, 1951.

_____. *Counseling and Psychotherapy.* Boston: Houghton Mifflin, 1942.

_____. "The Necessary Conditions of Therapeutic Personality Changes." *Journal of Counseling Psychology,* 31 (1957), pp. 95–103.

Rogers, D. *The Adult Years—An Introduction to Aging.* Englewood Cliffs, N.J.: Prentice-Hall, 1979.

Romney, L. S. "Extension of Family Relationships into a Home for the Aged." *Social Work,* 7 (1962), pp. 31–34.

Ronch, J. & J. Maizler. "Individual Psychotherapy with the Aged." *American Journal of Orthopsychiatry,* 47 (1977), pp. 277–83.

Rose, C. L. & J. M. Magey. "Aging and Preference for Later Retirement." *Aging and Human Development,* 3 (1972), pp. 45–62.

Rosen, G. "The Evolution of Social Medicine." In *Sociology of Medicine.* ed. R. M. Coe. New York: McGraw-Hill, 1978.

Rosenthal, T. L. & A. Bandura. "Psychological Modeling: Theory and Practice." In *Handbook of Psychotherapy and Behavior Change.* eds. S. L. Garfield & A. E. Bergin. New York: John Wiley & Sons, 1978.

Rosin, A. J. & M. M. Glatt. "Alcohol in Excess in the Elderly." *Quarterly Journal of Studies of Alcohol,* 32 (1971), pp. 52–59.

Roskin, M. "Integration of Primary Prevention into Social Work Practice." *Social Work,* 25 (1980), pp. 192–97.

Ross, F. "Social Work Treatment of a Paranoid Personality in a Geriatric Institution." *Journal of Geriatric Psychiatry,* 6 (1973), pp. 204–35.

Ross, H. K. "The Neighborhood Family: Community Mental Health for the Elderly." *Gerontologist,* 23 (1983), pp. 243–47.

Rubin, I. *Sexual Life After Sixty.* London: Allen & Unvin, 1969.

_____. "The Sexless Older Years—A Socially Harmful Stereotype." In *Social Problems of the Aging.* eds. M. Seltzer, S. Corbett & R. Atchley. Belmont, Calif.: Wadsworth Publishing, 1978.

Safford, F. "A Program for Families of the Mentally Impaired Elderly." *Gerontologist,* 20 (1980), pp. 656–60.

Salzman, C. "Depression in the Elderly." *Journal of the American Geriatric Society,* 26 (1978), pp. 303–8.

Sanford, J. "Tolerance of Debility on Elderly Dependents by Supporters at Home: Its Significance for Hospital Practice." *British Medical Journal,* 3 (1975), pp. 471–73.

Saul, S. *Aging—An Album of People Growing Old.* New York: John Wiley & Sons, 1974.

Saul, S. & S. Saul. "Group Psychotherapy in a Proprietary Nursing Home." *Gerontologist,* 14 (1974), pp. 446–50.

Schaie, K. W. & J. Geiwitz. *Adult Development and Aging.* Boston: Little, Brown, 1982.

Scheibla, S. H. "Medicare is Sick." *Barrons,* January 16, 1984.

Schlossberg, N. K., L. E. Troll & Z. Leibowitz. *Perspectives in Counseling Adults: Issues and Skills.* Monterey, Calif.: Brooks/Cole, 1978.

Schmandt, J., V. Bach & B. Radin. "Information and Referral Services for the Elderly Welfare Recipients." *Gerontologist,* 19 (1979), pp. 21–27.

Schooler, K. A. "A Comparison of Rural and Non-Rural Elderly on Selected Variables." In *Rural Environments and Aging.* ed. R. Atchley. Washington, D.C.: The Gerontological Society, 1975.

Schwartz, A. N. "A Transactional View of the Aging Process." In *Professional Obligations and Approaches to the Aged.* eds. A. N. Schwartz & I. N. Mensh. Springfield, Ill.: Charles C Thomas, 1974.

Schwartz, A. N. & J. A. Peterson. *Introduction to Gerontology.* New York: Holt, Rinehart & Winston, 1979.

Schwenk, M. A. "Reality Orientation for the Aged: Does it Help?" *Geronotologist,* 19 (1979), pp. 373–77.

Shanas, E. *The Health of Older People.* Cambridge, Mass.: Cambridge University Press, 1962.

Shanas, E. & G. L. Maddox. "Aging, Health, and the Organization of Health Resources." In *Handbook of Aging and the Social Sciences.* eds. R. H. Binstock & E. Shanas. New York: Van Nostrand Reinhold, 1976.

Shanas, E., P. Townsend, D. Wedderburn, H. Friis, P. Milhoj & J. Stehouwer. "The Psychology of Health." In *Middle Age and Aging.* ed. B. L. Neugarten. Chicago: University of Chicago Press, 1968.

Shapiro, A. "A Pilot Program in Music Therapy with Residents of a Home for the Aged." *Gerontologist,* 9 (1969), pp. 128–33.

Shaw, D. W. & C. E. Thoresen. "Effects of Modeling and Desensitization in Reducing Dental Phobia." *Journal of Counseling Psychology,* 21 (1974), pp. 415–20.

Sherwood, S. & V. Mor. "Mental Health Institutions and the Elderly." In *Handbook of Mental Health and Aging.* eds. J. Birren & R. B. Sloan. Englewood Cliffs, N.J.: Prentice-Hall, 1980.

Silverstein, N. M. "Informing the Elderly About Public Services: The Relationship Between Sources of Knowledge and Service Utilization." *Gerontologist,* 24 (1984), pp. 37–40.

*Social and Economic Characteristics of the Older Population: 1978.* Special Studies, Series P-23, No. 85. Washington, D.C.: U. S. Department of Commerce, 1979.

Solomon, K. "The Depressed Patient: Social Antecedents of Psychopathologic Changes in the Elderly." *Journal of the American Geriatric Society,* 29 (1981), pp. 14–17.

Sorensen, G. "Long-Term Care in the Institution." In *Older Persons and Service Providers.* ed. G. Sorensen. New York: Human Sciences Press, 1981.

Steer, R. A. & W. P. Boyer. "Milieu Therapy with Psychiatric-Medically Infirm Patients." *Gerontologist,* 75 (1975), pp. 138–41.

Stenback, A. "Depression and Suicidal Behavior in Old Age." In *Handbook of Mental Health and Aging.* eds. J. E. Birren & R. B. Sloane. Englewood Cliffs, N.J.: Prentice-Hall, 1980.

Stoddard, S. *The Hospice Movement.* Briarcliff Manor, N.Y.: Stein and Day, 1978.

Talbee, L. R. "Reality Orientation: A Therapeutic Group Activity for Elderly Persons." In *Working with the Elderly—Group Processes and Techniques.* ed. I. M. Burnside. North Scituate, Mass.: Duxbury Press, 1978.

Teare, R. J. "A Task Analysis for Public Welfare Practice and Educational Implications." In *The Pursuit of Competence in Social Work.* eds. F. Clark & M. Arkava. San Francisco: Jossey-Bass, 1979.

Terry, R. D., & H. Wisniewski. "Structural Aspects of Aging of the Brain." In *Cognitive and Emotional Disturbance in the Elderly.* eds. C. Eisdorfer & R. O. Friedal. Chicago: Yearbook Medical Publishers, 1977.

Theodorson, G. A. & A. G. Theodorson. *A Modern Dictionary of Sociology.* New York: Thomas Y. Crowell, 1969.

Thomas, E. J. "Behavioral Modification and Casework." In *Theories of Social Casework.* eds. R. Roberts & R. Nee. Chicago: University of Chicago Press, 1970.

————. "The Socio-Behavioral Approach: Illustrations and Analysis." In *The Socio-Behavioral Approach and Application to Social Work.* ed. E. J. Thomas. New York: Council on Social Work Education, 1967.

Tift, J. "Mental Health and Aging." In *Older Persons and Service Providers.* ed. G. Sorensen. Human Sciences Press, 1981.

Tobin, S. S. & Lieberman, M. A. *Last Home for the Aged.* San Francisco: Jossey-Bass, 1976.

Truax, C. B. & R. Carkhuff. *Toward Effective Counseling and Psychotherapy.* Chicago: Aldins, 1967.

Turem, J. S. & C. E. Born. "Doing More with Less." *Social Work,* 28 (1983), pp. 206–10.

Turner, F. J. "Psychosocial Therapy." In *Social Work Treatment*. ed. F. Turner. London: Free Press, 1974.

———. *Social Work Treatment—Interlocking Theoretical Approaches*. New York: The Free Press, 1979.

United States Bureau of the Census. *Census of Population: 1970, Volume I, Characteristics of the Population, Part I, United States Summary, Section I*. Washington, D.C.: U.S. Government Printing Office, 1973.

United States Department of Health and Human Services. "Age Page." National Institute on Aging. Washington, D.C.: Public Health Service, 1983.

———. Health Care Financing Administration. "Conditions of Participation for Skilled Nursing and Intermediate Care Facilities." *Federal Register*, 1980.

Vladeck, B. C. *Unloving Care: The Nursing Home Tragedy*. New York: Basic Books, 1980.

Ward, R. A. *The Aging Experience*. New York: J. B. Lippincott, 1979.

Ward, R. A. *The Aging Experience*. (2d ed.). Philadelphia: J. B. Lippincott, 1984.

Wasow, M. & M. Loeb. "The Aged." In *The Sexually Oppressed*. eds. H. Gochros & J. Gochros. New York: Association Press, 1977.

Wasser, E. "Protective Practice in Serving the Mentally Impaired Aged." *Social Casework*, 52 (1971), pp. 510–22.

Watson, D. L. & R. G. Tharp. *Self-Directed Behavior*. Monterey, Calif.: Brooks/Cole Publishing, 1972.

*Webster's New World Dictionary*. New York: Van Nostrand Reinhold, 1966.

*Webster's New World Dictionary*. New York: World Publishing, 1970.

Wechsler, D. *The Measurement and Appraisal of Adult Intelligence*. 4th ed. Baltimore: Williams and Wilkins, 1958.

Weeks, J. W. *Aging: Concepts and Social Issues*. Belmont, Calif.: Wadsworth Publishing, 1984.

Weg, R. B. "Changing Physiology of Aging: Normal and Pathological." In *Aging—Scientific Perspectives and Social Issues*. eds. D. S. Woodruff & J. E. Birren. New York: Van Nostrand, 1975.

———. "The Physiology of Sexuality in Aging." In *Sexuality and Aging*. ed. R. Solnick. Los Angeles: University of Southern California Press, 1978.

Welford, A. T. *Aging and Human Skill*. Oxford: Oxford University Press, 1958.

———. "Motor Performance." In *Handbook of the Psychology of Aging*. eds. J. E. Birren & K. W. Schaie. New York: Van Nostrand Reinhold, 1977.

Wells, L. E. & G. Marwell. *Self-Esteem*. Beverly Hills, Calif.: Sage Publications, 1976.

Werner, H. *A Rational Approach to Social Casework*. New York: Association Press, 1965.

———. "Cognitive Theory." In *Social Work Treatment*. ed. F. Turner. New York: Free Press, 1974.

Wetzel, J. W. "Interventions with the Depressed Elderly in Institutions." *Social Casework,* 61 (1980), pp. 234–39.

Wetzler, M. A. & N. Feil. *Validation Therapy with Disoriented Aged Who Use Fantasy Manual.* Cleveland: Edward Feil Productions, 1979.

Whitbourne, S. K. & C. S. Weinstock. *Adult Development.* New York: Holt, Rinehart & Winston, 1979.

Whipple, D. V. *Dynamics of Development: Euthenic Pediatrics.* New York: McGraw-Hill, 1966.

White House Conference on Aging. *Toward a National Policy on Aging.* Vol. 1. Washington, D.C.: White House Conference on Aging, 1971.

Williamson, J. B., A. Munley & L. Evans. *Aging and Society: An Introduction to Social Gerontology.* New York: Holt, Rinehart & Winston, 1980.

Wittman, M. "Preventive Social Work." In *Encyclopedia of Social Work.* 17th ed. Washington, D.C.: National Association of Social Workers, 1977.

_____. *The Social Worker in Preventive Services.* New York: Columbia University Press, 1982, pp. 136–37.

Wolcott, A. B. "Art Therapy: An Experimental Group." In *Working with the Elderly: Group Process and Techniques.* ed. I. M. Burnside. North Scituate, Mass.: Duxbury Press, 1978.

Wolpe, J. *Psychotherapy by Reciprocal Inhibition.* Stanford, Calif.: Stanford University Press, 1958.

_____. *The Practice of Behavior Therapy.* 2d ed. New York: Pergamon Press, 1973.

Woodruff, D. S. & J. E. Birren. "Training for Professionals in the Field of Aging: Needs, Goals, Models, and Means." In *Professional Obligations and Approaches to the Aged.* eds. A. N. Schwartz & I. N. Mensh. Springfield, Ill.: Charles C Thomas Publisher, 1974.

World Health Organization. *World Health Organization Charter.* Geneva, Switzerland: World Health Organization, 1946, p. 1268.

Yawney, B. A. & D. L. Slover. "Relocation of the Elderly." *Social Work,* 18 (1973), pp. 86–95.

Youmans, E. G. "Age Group and Health Attitudes." *Gerontologist,* 14 (1974), pp. 249–51.

Young, E. F. *Dictionary of Social Welfare.* New York: Social Sciences Publishers, Inc., 1948.

Zarit, S. H. "Gerontology—Getting Better all the Time." In *Readings in Aging and Death: Contemporary Perspectives.* ed. S. H. Zarit. New York: Harper & Row Publishers, 1977.

Zastrow, C. *The Practice of Social Work.* Homewood, Ill.: The Dorsey Press, 1981.

Zimberg, S. "The Elderly Alcoholics." *Gerontologist,* 14 (1974), pp. 221–24.

# Author Index

# Subject Index

## A

Abnormal Grief, 156–57
Abuse to the elderly, 181
Accurate empathy, 85
Administration on aging, 176
Administrative barriers to practice
  at secondary level, 235–36
  at tertiary level, 240–41
Advocacy
  acts of, 146, 150, 154, 159
  for the frail elderly, 181
  for the home bound, 178
  for policy change, 236–37
  in long-term care field, 177
  in nursing homes, 198, 200–201, 211
  strategies for, 240–42
Aging
  impact of stresses, 6
  nature of, 5
  stresses of, 6
Alcoholism, 157–58
Alzheimer's disease
  consequences for caretakers, 184
  description of, 29
  effect of Alzheimer's disease on the family, 29
  extent of, 174
  feelings of family members, 30
  onset of, 174
  pre-senile dementia, 29
  progression of Alzheimer's disease, 29
  Sharon Lofton case example, 29–30
  stages of, 174–75
  symptoms of, 174–75
Area Agency on Aging, 241
Art therapy, 206
Assertiveness training, 90–91, 143, 153–54

## B

Baccalaureate level workers, 178, 197
  roles played by, 72
Barriers to prevention on all levels
  barriers to knowledge development, 224–25
  emphasis on educational services, 225
  initiatives to knowledge development, 225
Barriers to prevention at the primary level
  attitudes of mental health professionals, 229
  emphasis on cure rather than prevention, 228
  emphasis on life cycle education, 229
  emphasis on trained social workers with group work experience, 228–29
  need for more emphasis on prevention particularly in health care, 228
  staffing patterns of multipurpose senior centers, 228
Barriers to practice at the secondary level, 231–37
  administrative, 235–36
  implications for clinical practitioners, 237
  societal, 232–35
Barriers to practice at the tertiary level, 238–43
  administrative, 240–41
  implications for clinical practitioners, 241–43
  societal, 238–40
Behavior
  as learned tendencies, 86
  modeled, 87
  operant, 87
  respondent, 86
Behavioral approach, 85–91
  problem assessment, 86
  range of theory, 85–86

*This book has been set VideoComp in 10 point Ver-
milion, leaded 2 points, and 9 point Vermilion, leaded
3 points. Chapter numbers are 20 point Vermilion
and chapter titles are 24 point Vermilion Bold. The
size of the type page is 29 x 44½ picas.*